The original Ridotto, No. 1362 Calle
del Ridotto to Calle Vallaresso
(No. 1332).

⊗

Tombs

Frari —
Dandolo

① Figured in life presented to
Mary

Gilt → depositori of Mary

Then

② 

Foscari

③

**THE BLUE GUIDES**

**BLUE GUIDE**

# VENICE

ALTA MACADAM

*Maps and plans drawn by John Flower*

**A & C Black**
London

**W W Norton**
New York

Third edition 1986
Reprinted 1987

Published by A. & C. Black (Publishers) Limited
35 Bedford Row, London WC1R 4JH

© A. & C. Black (Publishers) Limited 1986

Published in the United States of America by
W. W. Norton & Company, Inc.
500 Fifth Avenue, New York, N.Y. 10110

Published simultaneously in Canada by
Penguin Books Canada Limited
2801 John Street, Markham, Ontario L3R 1B4

Printed in Great Britain by
Richard Clay Ltd, Bungay, Suffolk


ISBN 0-7136-2802-2
ISBN 0-393-30080-3        {U.S.A.}

# FOREWORD

In the twentieth year since the launching by Unesco of the international campaign for the preservation of Venice the publication of a new edition of *Blue Guide Venice* is particularly opportune. It is not always realised that the most welcome visitors to Venice are those who genuinely wish to know what the city has to offer. Amongst these, regular visitors will have noticed what a notable improvement has occurred over these past twenty years not only in the appearance of the city but also in the range of its cultural amenities. For Venice is not just an outsize museum: it is a real live city which has recovered from the effects of the great natural disaster of 1966. To all those individuals and organizations like the British fund, *Venice in Peril*, who have devoted time, energy and money to help in bringing about this change, the issue of a new edition of the *Blue Guide* will be very gratifying because it is a sign that international interest in the welfare of the city continues at a high level. No one can fail to perceive the extent to which the Superintendent of Fine Arts, Dr F. Valcanover, has transformed the whole technique of caring for painting and other works of art or how much active restoration of monuments sponsored by the Italian authorities is currently in progress. It is fair to add, however, that not only the stimulus to these activities but also some of the most distinguished achievements are attributable to the private organizations for Venice of which thirty or more have emerged since 1966.

Although it is to be hoped that users of this Guide will find time and opportunity to see as much of their work as possible, this is not the place to attempt a list of them. Most of them are mentioned in the text which follows. But two perhaps deserve special mention because, with the support and guidance of the Superintendencies, they constitute the joint work of several Committees and individuals—Italian, American, French, German, Swedish, Dutch and British—under the leadership of the Venice in Peril Fund. The first of these is the Basilica on the island of Torcello, where the main achievement has been the complete restoration of the mosaics including the huge Last Judgment on the West wall. Hidden from view for so long, they are now fully visible. The second is the Oratory of the Crociferi hospice, opposite the church of the Gesuiti. The outstanding characteristic of this relatively small building, very severely damaged by the 1966 flood, is that its walls and ceiling are covered by canvases by one single artist, Palma il Giovane. Apart from their historical significance, the new-found brilliance of these paintings causes the Oratory to glow as though it were a casket of jewels.

In wishing all success to the new edition of the *Blue Guide*, Venice in Peril gladly seize the opportunity to express to its publishers their gratitude for their faithful support of the Fund's activities over a number of years.

Ashley Clarke
Venice in Peril Fund
June 1985

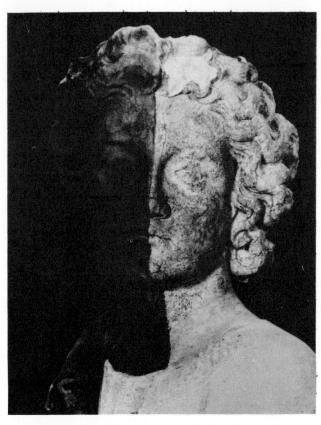

*The head of 'Prudence' during restoration (detail from the Porta della Carta)*

# PREFACE

This new edition of *Blue Guide Venice* went to press in 1985 just when a model was on exhibition of the definitive 'Progettone' to safeguard the city's future. After years of debate on the best method of controlling the high tides it has been decided that moveable barriers should be constructed at the three entrances to the lagoon, at the Lido, Malamocco, and Chioggia. The funds for this undertaking have been made available by the Italian government through the special law, passed in 1973, and renewed in 1984, and work is due to begin in September. The three entrances will be narrowed so that less water enters the lagoon, and moveable barriers will be used to control exceptionally high tides which, up to now, have flooded a quarter of the city on an average of twice a year. These barriers, 18 metres high, will rest flat on the sea bed when not in use. Part of the funds will be spent also on cleaning the polluted waters of the lagoon, as well as continuing research on its ecology and tidal systems. In 1985, too, routine dredging of the city's canals was started up again, a vital precaution which used to be carried out annually throughout the Republic and up until 1945.

Since 1980 the Venetian Carnival has become a colourful spectacle enjoyed by thousands of visitors. In the week before Lent the city is invaded by masqueraders, and concerts and plays are held. However, in 1985 the city had to be 'closed' when some 120,000 people came to Venice on a single day during Carnival week. The authorities will presumably therefore have to organize the festivities in the future in order to protect the city.

Since the last edition several fine new museums have been opened, including the Museum of Diocesan Art, the Cini Collection, and the Lace Museum on Burano. The Ca' d'Oro which had been closed for decades has finally been reopened and its collections beautifully rearranged after restoration. The splendid basilica of Santa Maria e Donato on Murano has also been reopened after painstaking restorations which have lasted for many years. The interiors of San Stae and the little Oratorio dei Crociferi can also now be visited. Restorations of works of art continue: the Golden Horses of San Marco, the Torcello cathedral mosaics, and Tintoretto's Paradise in Palazzo Ducale stand out as some of the most notable achievements in the past few years in this field. The debate has begun on how to make use of the vast area occupied by the Arsenal; this may soon be vacated by the armed forces which at present occupy it and keep it closed to the public.

The official tourist authorities in Venice, as in the rest of Italy, are undergoing reorganization and amalgamation, so that the old Ente Provinciale del Turismo and Azienda Autonoma will no longer exist in their present form. This should be a positive step in streamlining the information and assistance available for visitors. Also in 1985 the European system of using 'stars' to indicate the category of a hotel was introduced in Venice, and the confusing terms 'pensione' and 'locanda' were dropped. All hotels are now graded from 5-star luxury class down to 1-star, and prices vary accordingly, which simplifies the operation of choosing suitable accommodation.

In the preparation of this edition the author is indebted in the first instance to *Philip Rylands*, member of the executive committee of the Venice in Peril Fund and Administrator of the Peggy Guggenheim Collection in Venice. As in the past, he generously provided advice on numerous occasions, and made many useful corrections and additions to the guide. *Bruce Boucher* of University College, London, kindly read the text and made a number of suggestions for its improvement. As for the last edition, the author is extremely grateful to *Signora Dina Di Stefano* of the Azienda Autonoma del Turismo who cast her expert eye over the details of the practical information section.

*John Flower* has made minor corrections to his atlas and plans for this edition, as well as supplying five new ground plans of Museums, etc. His handsome plans and very detailed atlas of the whole city greatly enhance the guide.

Any suggestions for the improvement of the guide will always be welcomed.

**The Venice in Peril Fund.** Following the catastrophic flood of November 1966 a number of funds, both Italian and foreign, were set up to restore works of art and buildings of historic and artistic merit in the city. The British fund established then was responsible for the complete restoration of the Madonna dell'Orto; it was succeeded in 1971 by the Venice in Peril Fund whose recent work is outlined in Sir Ashley Clarke's Foreword to this book.

Donations to further this work can be sent to the Venice in Peril Fund, Kensington Palace Barracks, Kensington Church Street, London W8 4EP.

**Acknowledgements.** Thanks are due to the following for permission to reproduce illustrations:
Archivi Alinari (pages 89, 147, 195, 199)
Archivio Fotografico della Soprintendenza per i Beni Ambietali e Architettonici di Venezia (pages, 6, 70, 92, 177)
Christie's (pages 99, 111, 183)
Conway Library, Courtauld Institute of Art (pages 116, 125, 132, 172, 187, 190)
The Mansell Collection (pages 104-5, 119, 120, 137, 163, 193)

# CONTENTS

## MAPS AND PLANS

# VENETIAN ART AND ARCHITECTURE

## by PHILIP RYLANDS

**The Veneto-Byzantine Period**. In the 8th century AD some of the Venetian islands must already have been 'built-up' and populous. Yet no architecture of this time survives, excepting perhaps the foundations of the Baptistery of Torcello. The oldest building in the lagoon is the Basilica at Torcello, which was rebuilt around 1008. Its architectural affinities are Latin—that is to say, with Ravenna. The simple plan is typical of Early Christian churches such as S. Francesco in Ravenna: the nave and side-aisles terminate in side-chapels and a chancel framed by a triumphal arch. Several other early Venetian churches have the same plan: S. Eufemia on the Giudecca for example (rebuilt 11C), S. Zan Degolà (founded 1007 and subsequently rebuilt), S. Nicolò dei Mendicoli (rebuilt after 1105) or S. Donato, Murano (1125–40).

In 639, when the Basilica of Torcello was founded, the lagoon was under the jurisdiction of the Exarch of Ravenna, and hence a dependency of the Byzantine Empire. Venice maintained vital economic and cultural ties with Constantinople throughout its early history and this gave rise to an alternative and Greek tradition of church building: that of the central plan or Greek cross. Examples of this are S. Fosca (Torcello, early 11C) and S. Giacomo di Rialto (rebuilt early 17C on an 11C plan) but above all San Marco itself.

San Marco was conceived originally as a shrine for Apostolic relics, in particular those of St Mark whose corpse was stolen from Alexandria in 828/9 and who was henceforward to be the city's patron saint. It was for this reason that the first San Marco, of 830–6, was modelled on the church of the Apostles in Constantinople, which was a five-domed Greek cross; and this prototype was maintained when San Marco was rebuilt after 976, and again c 1063–94. Despite Romanesque or western features, such as the slightly lengthened nave and the relative 'openness' of the east end, the visual impact of San Marco, with its massive cube-like and domed spaces, is entirely Byzantine.

Initially the decoration of the church was very limited. It included the earliest mosaics to have survived in the building: the Apostles in niches around the central door (late 11C) and the four Saints around the main apse (early 12C). It seems likely that these were executed by Byzantine emigrés and this is confirmed by recent research at Torcello, where the Apostles in the apse, and the oldest parts of the Last Judgement are now thought to date from this period.

San Marco, the State church, was the focus of Venetian artistic life in the middle ages, and Venetian politics were more relevant to art than at any subsequent moment of the Republic's history. The completion of the third (and present) San Marco at the end of the 11C, modelled as we have seen on the church of the Apostles in Constantinople, occurred at a high point of friendly relations between Venice and Byzantium. When in 1105 doge Ordelafo Falier (1102–18) ordered the 'Pala d'oro' for San Marco from the palace workshops in Constantinople, it probably included enamel images of the Doge with the Emperor (Alexius Comnenus) and the Empress.

For the main part of the century little attention seems to have been given to the arts, perhaps due to the effort of commerce and of Empire building. In 1106 a fire in San Marco caused a setback and apart from the work of restoration, there seems to have been a lull in activity that continued up to the 1170s.

The dogeship of the immensely rich Sebastiano Ziani (1172–78) seems to have initiated a new spate of work. In an inspired piece of town planning Ziani acquired and razed the land in front of San Marco, and the Piazza took approximately its present dimension. In the same decade granite columns (known as Marco and Todaro) were set up in the Piazzetta San Marco and the bases decorated (probably by Lombard masons) with Venetian Trades, the most notable figure sculpture of the century. Work was begun again at San Marco with the decoration of the three principal cupolas (east, crossing and west) by a team of mosaicists some of whom must have been trained in Constantinople. In the same period (the last quarter of the 12C) the mosaics were continued at Torcello (the apsidal Virgin and Child and the reworking of parts of the Last Judgement).

With the capture of Constantinople in 1204 Venetian art and the decoration of San Marco underwent a tremendous upheaval. An immense quantity of booty was brought back from the East: works of art, such as the Tetrarchs, various sculptural reliefs, the famous Golden Horses, relics and reliquaries, and also building materials in the form of capitals, coloured marble columns, and carved slabs. A small number of these Byzantine trophies found their way to different parts of the city, such as the 'Virgin Orans' in S. Maria Mater Domini, or the unknown Emperor (late 12C) in the Campiello Angaran at S. Pantalon. But the major part of this windfall was settled on San Marco.

At this point it was decided to give the building its present investment of massed marble columns and encrusted reliefs. In 1209 doge Pietro Ziani (1205–29) ordered the enlargement of the 'Pala d'oro' to include enamels acquired from Constantinople, such as the seven uppermost panels, while an image of the Byzantine Emperor, former symbol of Venice's subjection, would have been eliminated. Work on the mosaics continued steadily in the first half of the century, with presumably an influx of Byzantine refugees to augment the Venetian workshops. This would account for the renewed Byzantine influence on certain mosaics of 1200–20, such as the Agony in the Garden over the south aisle, and the iconic panels of Christ and Saints on the lower side-aisle walls.

The first three cupolas of the narthex, with scenes from Genesis, were decorated at this time. The mosaics were copied from an early 5C manuscript of the type of the Cotton Bible, which exists in charred fragments (burnt 1731) in the British Museum. The use of Early Christian prototypes appears to have been a characteristic of Venetian art around 1230–70. It has been suggested that the cause of this so-called proto-Renaissance was the desire of the Venetian government to associate itself with the remote past, at a time when the Byzantine Empire was eclipsed and Venice was seeking to inherit its mantle. This archaic style was especially apparent in sculpture and includes the tomb of the Tiepolo doges (died 1249 and 1275) at SS. Giovanni e Paolo, and in particular the ciborium columns over the high altar of San Marco—works which some critics still believe belong to the 6C but which have been shown on iconographic grounds to be mid-13C.

At least two sculptural workshops were busy in San Marco in this period. One was led by the so-called **Heracles Master** who developed his style by copying Byzantine reliefs. His earliest work is probably the relief of Heracles and the Hydra (W facade of San Marco) which is an idiosyncratic copy of the late Antique relief on the same facade. The Heracles Master and his workshop were responsible for all the portal decorations on the outside of San Marco, excepting that of the central porch, and a series of reliefs on the N facade. The decoration of the Porta S. Alipio (c 1270) exemplifies the great elegance and surface complexity of the Heracles Master's later work.

In the same period, 1235–65, a team of Lombard-Emilian masons, the best of whom would have been trained under Benedetto Antelami of Parma, carved the archivolts of the central porch. The soffit of the middle arch, with the Months, and the soffit of the outer arch, with the Trades, are considered the finest sculpture of the century in Venice. They consist of small scenes of great naturalism and clarity, perfectly disciplined by the requirement of shallow relief.

In 1261 the Byzantines recaptured Constantinople, and when diplomatic and trade relations were re-established in the 1270s and '80s, a new wave of Byzantine influence overlaid the achievements of the Heracles Master and of the Central Porch workshop. This late-13C style is marked by a roundness of form and an emphasis on human sentiment typical of the Paleologan style—the style which inspired Cimabue and Duccio in Tuscany and which in Venice appears in a more imitatively Byzantine guise. In San Marco, the Virgin of the Rifle (S aisle pier) dates from this period.

Meanwhile the mosaics of the later 13C (1258–80) include the Rediscovery of St Mark's Relics in the south transept, and the completion of the narthex cycle. The latter make an interesting parallel to events in the field of sculpture. In the 1260s the mosaicists developed a heavier figure style that makes itself felt in the more dense compositions of the 2nd Joseph cupola (N wing), but in the 1270s the renewed Byzantine influence reverses this, resulting in the 5th and 6th cupolas (Joseph and Moses) at the end of the cycle, where livelier figure groups and a freer spatial sense reflect contemporary Byzantine art.

**The Venetian Palace**. It is now generally thought that Venice's oldest surviving domestic architecture dates from the 13C. This includes the Rialto palaces such as Palazzo Loredan, Ca' Farsetti, the Donà Palaces, and Palazzo Businello, as well as Ca' da Mosto and the Fondaco dei Turchi, which all share the Byzantine stilted arch. The original elevations of these palaces, with only two stories, long galleries and vestigial tower blocks at the ends, are based ultimately on the ancient Roman villa. Whether this is a revival, in the archaicizing spirit of the proto-Renaissance (c 1230–70), or a survival through Byzantium, has not been ascertained. But in either case, domestic architecture of the 13C reflects Venice's sympathies for Byzantine and Early Christian art.

Already palaces had developed the internal room structure that was to remain unchanged throughout the Republic's history, though constantly adapted to different sites in Venice's cramped city plan. This consisted of a space-economical cube (enclosed courtyards came later) with central axial rooms running the full depth of the building from the canal frontage. The ground floor is open at both ends and called the 'androne', while the corresponding room on the upper floor—the 'piano nobile' where the living quarters are—is called the 'salone' or 'portego'. Smaller rooms open more or less symmetrically off these axial rooms. This arrangement determined the typical appearance of the palace facade: an arch cluster in the centre corresponds to the 'androne' and 'salone', while windows at wider intervals light the lateral rooms.

The Venetian facade is characteristically 'open' compared to the fortified character of contemporary palaces in other Italian cities. This reflected not only the civic calm of Venice but also the need for windows in a building without a central courtyard. Given the consistency of palace elevations, the most distinctive indication of architectural change is the arch type over the loggia and windows (see diagram p000). By the 3rd quarter of the 13C, a point had broken upwards the pure curve of the Byzantine soffit (see for example Palazzo Bragadin-Favretto on the Grand Canal and Palazzo Falier at SS. Apostoli), evidence of Islamic influence; and before the end of the century the ogee arch was perfected.

**The Fourteenth Century**. The Byzantine style of the late 13C lingered on into the 1300s. For example the carved and painted altar-relief (dated 1310) of S. Donato, Murano, retains the character of a Byzantine icon. In 1300 the goldsmith **Bertuccio** signed the 2nd door from the left on the W facade of San Marco. The design is based on an ancient Roman type, and is therefore evidence of the duration of the imitative and archaic spirit of the Duecento. Bertuccio's doors to the right of the central porch include a row of female heads of a purely classical type. The quality of Venetian metal-work at this time is illustrated by the resetting of the 'Pala d'oro' in 1345, by **Gian Paolo Boninsegna**.

In general however the level of Venetian sculptural activity and the quality of Venetian sculpture were low, principally because little work remained at San Marco. The great masterpiece of this period, the tomb of San Simeone (S. Simeone Grande, c 1317–18), is not by a Venetian, but by **Marco Romano**.

Under doge Giovanni Soranzo (1312–28) the baptistery at San Marco was remodelled and three reliefs on the end wall (the Baptism of Christ, St Theodore and St George) date from this time. Though based on Byzantine prototypes, they show an interest in lively movement and realistic detail that looks forward to Gothic art. Work in the baptistery continued under doge Andrea Dandolo (1343–54) who was responsible for the mosaics, including the well-known figure of Salome by the entrance. With her hanging ermine sleeves, and her twisting stance, she indicates precisely the incipient Gothic mood.

One of the principal sculptural workshops of the time was led by **Andriolo de' Santi**, most of whose work is in Padua. However, the tomb of Duccio degli Uberti (died 1336) in the Frari has recently been attributed to him, and he seems to have been the inventor of a tomb design, with the sarcophagus and effigy placed on wall-brackets and sheltered by an arch, that became standard in Venice. Among the innumerable examples of this, the tombs of St Isidore (before 1355) at San Marco and of doge Michele Morosini (died 1382) at SS. Giovanni e Paolo are particularly rich, and have both been attributed to the circle of Andriolo. Andriolo had a son **Giovanni de' Santi** who carved the miraculous Virgin and Child at the Madonna dell'Orto.

The most important sculptural workshop in the mid-century was undoubtedly that of the Ducal Palace. In 1340 the Senate resolved to enlarge the Sala del Maggior Consiglio and it was this decision that gave the Palace its present appearance, for the extension was carried

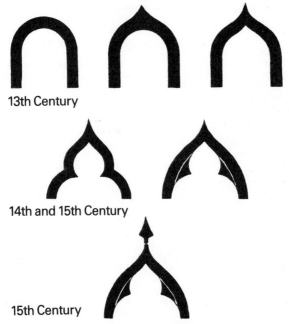

13th Century

14th and 15th Century

15th Century

*The orders of Venetian, Byzantine and Gothic arches, after John Ruskin*

out over the Molo and the Piazzetta (for six bays only, corresponding to the depth of the sala itself) by loggias in the form of regular Gothic arches on the ground floor, and a superbly decorative combination of ogee arches and quatrefoils on the upper floor. This gave the Ducal Palace its extraordinary illogic of massive walls above, and light arcades below. The distinctive quatrefoil appears earlier at San Marco, where several windows with Gothic tracery had been added between 1312–28. The first architect, and presumably the great inventor, was **Filippo Calendario** who was later to be executed for his part in the Falier Conspiracy (1355).

The work was well advanced by 1344 when one of the capitals was dated, and probably complete by 1365 when the decoration of the interior began. Some of the finest of the capitals and corner groups have been attributed to Calendario himself, who would have been both architect and sculptor. Certainly the author of the Drunkenness of Noah at the Ponte della Paglia corner also carved the Adam and Eve at the Piazzetta corner, and the capital of the Zodiac and Planets (below Adam and Eve). The latter may even have been the source of Calendario's name. The workshop must have been extensive, and the result was a flowering of virtuoso and Gothic naturalism that completely dispels the Byzantine influence in Venetian sculpture.

To the 14C belong Venice's largest churches, SS. Giovanni e Paolo was founded in 1246 but the present church was probably begun c 1333, while S. Maria Gloriosa dei Frari was begun in 1330. Their plans are traditional for the monastic orders (Dominican and Franciscan respectively), with a spacious Latin cross and rows of side-chapels off the transepts. The lack of verticality is typically Italian, and instead the visual impression is of immense space. The width of the nave at SS. Giovanni e Paolo is achieved by a characteristic Venetian resort: the columns support vaults not of masonry but of lath and plaster. The architects lacked confidence in the muddy foundations shared by most Venetian buildings, and one of the distinctive traits of Venetian Gothic churches is the wooden tie-beams spanning the aisles and arches.

The great brick basilicas of SS. Giovanni e Paolo and the Frari are paralleled by small churches of the same period or soon after. The interior of Santo Stefano (rebuilt 14C) is light and colourful, and its vault, designed on the principal of a ship's keel (*carena di nave*), is a reminder of Venice's maritime trade. The Madonna dell'Orto (rebuilt from the late-14C) is similar in visual effect, though the plan is more old-fashioned (comp. the Basilica at Torcello). Like SS. Giovanni e Paolo and the Frari, the facade is divided by pilaster strips, and pierced by a large round window. It was completed in the early 15C and was to inspire the churches of S. Maria della Carità and S. Gregorio.

More slowly than sculpture, painting in the 14th century gradually broke free of Byzantium. **Paolo Veneziano** was Venice's first great panel painter. His major work in Venice, the polyptych of the Coronation of the Virgin (1354–8) in the Accademia, is closely bound to the prototype of all such polyptychs, the 'Pala d'oro'. The Byzantine influence is still very strong and determines the narrative compositions, the facial types, the extensive use of gilding, and above all the enamel-like colour—often eccentric but always brilliant. Paolo's work is really the key link between the intense colour patches of Byzantine mosaics and enamels, and the tradition of Venetian Renaissance painting begun a century later by Giovanni Bellini. His other works in Venice include the lunette of Francesco Dandolo's tomb (died 1339) at the Frari, which is of unprecedented breadth and scale. Even the apparently 'modern' elements of Paolo's work, such as the tendency to imply solid form with organic light, are now thought to depend from the Paleologan renascence in Byzantium, and to be independent of Giotto's work in the Arena chapel, Padua (c 1306).

**Lorenzo Veneziano** (no relation) succeeded Paolo as the leading painter in Venice. Lorenzo developed the realistic and humanizing aspect to the point where it could be called Gothic. His colour is lighter, though no less luminous, and dark unmodelled 'shadows' are dismissed. Gold highlights become less pervasive and three-dimensional form, disposed in graceful curves, asserts itself. The Annunciation polyptych (Accademia, 1357) illustrates this, and the exchange between the Virgin and the Archangel assumes a new element of sweetness and humanity.

A significant pictorial event of the mid-century was the commission given to **Guariento** to paint the Coronation of the Virgin on the end wall of the Sala del Maggior Consiglio. Although only the ruin of this survives (see p000) some idea of its original appearance can be gained from a Coronation by Jacobello del Fiore in the Accademia (1438). Lorenzo Veneziano's style, which was continued by his followers **Stefano 'Plebanus' di S. Agnese** and **Nicolò di Pietro** was eventually to be swept into the International Gothic current in the early 15C.

**Architecture and Sculpture in the Fifteenth Century**. At the turn of the century, the leading sculptors in Venice were **Pierpaolo** and **Jacobello Dalle Masegne**, who together signed the rood-screen of San Marco, with its fourteen marble statues, in 1394. Their style is purely Gothic—attenuated figures with curvilinear draperies and a tendency to the S-shape in the stance. They were influenced by the work of **Nino Pisano** whose signature appears on the tomb of doge Marco Corner (SS. Giovanni e Paolo, post 1368).

The successors to the Dalle Masegne were **Giovanni Bon** and his son **Bartolomeo**. Giovanni Bon was active primarily as an architect, and in 1424 he was commissioned to build the Ca' d'Oro. This is Venice's most ornate Gothic palace—its distinctive feature being the complex tracery of the upper loggias which is an enrichment of that of the Ducal Palace. Such tracery, with well-integrated quartrefoils, clearly identifies Venice's late Gothic palaces, such as Palazzo Barbaro at S. Stefano, and Ca' Foscari.

Bartolomeo Bon was the principal mason-architect in Venice from about 1430 to his death soon after 1464. In 1423 it had been decided to extend the Piazzetta facade of the Ducal Palace towards San Marco, and in 1438 Bartolomeo and his father were commissioned to design the ceremonial gateway that links the two buildings: the Porta della Carta, perhaps the most important late Gothic monument in Venice. In the 1450s Bon's sculpture, such as the Charity over the portal of the Scuola di S. Marco, shows a marked classical influence, and this tendency is also reflected in his late architecture. The incomplete Ca' del Duca (begun 1457) has a rusticated ground story, while both the portáls of SS. Giovanni e Paolo and the Madonna dell' Orto (c 1460) have early Renaissance elements, and the Gothic 'crocket-capitals' struggle to become Corinthian.

On this evidence the land entrance to the Arsenal, designed as a Roman triumphal arch (c 1460), has also been attributed to Bon, although the name of **Antonio Gambello** is traditionally associated with it. Gambello clung to Gothic long after 1460, and his church of S. Zaccaria (begun 1458), if completed, would have been closer than any other to a north European church. His death in 1481, and Codussi's appointment in 1483, resulted in the present confusion of styles, but the Gothic ambulatory and radiating chapels, which are unique in Venice, survived the takeover.

The transition from Gothic to early Renaissance in Venetian sculpture was considerably blurred by the activity of Tuscan masons at San Marco and the Ducal Palace during the first half of the century. The first of these were **Nicolò Lamberti** who assisted from 1416 with the external decoration of the upper story of San Marco, and his son **Piero di Nicolò Lamberti**, who with a collaborator named **Giovanni di Martino da Fiesole** signed the tomb of doge Tommaso Mocenigo (1423) at SS. Giovanni e Paolo. These were essentially Gothic artists who had nevertheless witnessed the earliest activity of Donatello before their departure from Florence. **Nanni di Bartolo** had collaborated with Donatello around 1420 on the campanile prophets in Florence. He was probably the author of the Baptism of Christ lunette at the Frari (1437) which recalls Ghiberti's Baptism on the N doors of the Florentine baptistery. Several other 'Tuscan' sculptures of the period in Venice resemble the style of Ghiberti, who came here in 1424/5. These include the lunette of the Madonna and angels outside the Corner chapel at the Frari, and the Madonna and saints arch into Campo S. Zaccaria (both c 1430–40).

In the 1460s the transition from Gothic to early Renaissance became complete with the activity of **Antonio Rizzo** and **Pietro Lombardo**. Rizzo's earliest Venetian works are the little altars of St Paul and St James in San Marco, which imitate the design of Desiderio's tabernacle in S. Lorenzo, Florence; though the hard cutting and angular drapery are purely Lombard. Rizzo's major work is the tomb of doge Nicolò Tron (Frari, c 1473) which has a Lombard classicism quite unlike the Foscari tomb opposite. As 'proto' of the Ducal Palace from 1483–98 Rizzo's main contribution was the Giant's Staircase, which is over-ornate in the Lombard manner, and replete with reliefs of winged victories and military trophies *all' antica*.

Pietro Lombardo's earliest tombs, such as that of doge Pasquale Malipiero (SS. Giovanni e Paolo, 1467–70), are based on Bernardo Rossellino and Desiderio's works in S. Croce, Florence. Like his earliest architectural venture, the chancel of S. Giobbe (begun 1471), these rework Florentine motifs in a ponderous idiom of over-decorated entablatures and pilasters. The architectural frame of his sculptural masterpiece, the tomb of doge Pietro Mocenigo (SS. Giovanni e Paolo, 1476–81), is based on Rizzo's Tron tomb, and marks a lighter and more concentrated style—with the emphasis clearly given to the triumphal arch around the Doge and his coffin. The reliefs of Hercules, and the warriors in Roman armour, are completely in the Renaissance spirit. The slender figures, spiritual and abstracted in expression, with clinging drapery and angular limbs, become standard in the early Renaissance.

Pietro Lombardo's little church of S. Maria dei Miracoli (1481–9) is one of the most memorable in Venice. Here he forsakes the Tuscan contrast between grey stone and white plaster in favour of marble encrustation, like that of San Marco. This, combined with narrow round arches, Corinthian style capitals, and decorated friezes and pilasters, becomes the so-called Lombardesque style in Venice, and can be seen on Pietro's facade of the Scuola di S. Marco, and on Palazzo Dario (Grand Canal).

However, the finest architecture of the early Renaissance is owed to a more considerable talent: **Mauro Codussi**. In 1469 he was appointed 'proto' of the monastery of S. Michele in Isola, and designed Venice's first Renaissance church. He gave the facade a traditional Venetian silhouette (comp. S. Giovanni in Bragora) translated into classical pediments and pilasters, and incorporated decorative elements from Bon's last works (under whom he may have trained: comp. the portal of the Madonna dell'Orto and the Ca' del Duca in particular). The interior has a traditional plan but with the addition of pendentive domes over both chancel and side-chapels, in imitation of San Marco. Codussi's other architecture also shows this blend of ancient and modern and his work has been dubbed 'neo-Byzantine'. For example his little church of S. Giovanni Crisostomo, a Greek cross with extended apse and chapels, is identical in plan to one of Venice's oldest churches, S. Giacomo di Rialto. Codussi also designed palaces, including Palazzo Corner-Spinelli at S. Angelo, which has the first stone facade *alla Romana* in Venice (c 1490). This and his Palazzo Vendramin-Calergi (Grand Canal) share a distinctive two-light window with an oculus that was first employed by Alberti in Florence, and which reappears in buildings by Codussi's followers such as the Scuola di S. Rocco.

**Tullio Lombardo** (son of Pietro) first emerges in the 1480s executing carvings for S. Maria dei Miracoli (c 1485). With his younger brother

**Antonio** he carried out the most elaborate ensemble of statuary and reliefs of the Venetian early Renaissance: the tomb of doge Andrea Vendramin (SS. Giovanni e Paolo, c 1488–93). This, with the later tomb of doge Giovanni Mocenigo (finished c 1500) in the same church, represents a literal revival of classical art equivalent to Verrocchio's antiquarianism of the late 1460s in Florence. They heralded a phase, in the first decade of the 16C, of nostalgia for the culture of the ancient world. For example, Tullio's 'Double Portrait' in the Ca' d'Oro (c 1500) imitates ancient Roman funeral portraits. In 1505 **Alessandro Leopardi**, whose greatest achievement was the completion of Verrocchio's monument to Bartolomeo Colleoni, cast bases for the standards of the Venetian Republic in Piazza San Marco and decorated them with antique nereids and tritons.

**Painting in the Fifteenth Century**. In 1409 Gentile da Fabriano arrived in Venice to decorate the Sala del Maggior Consiglio with frescoes of Venetian history. This commission initiated the International Gothic phase of Venetian art, which lasted until the middle of the century. None of the frescoes, which were continued by Pisanello, has survived; but their influence can be felt in the work of a whole generation of painters, and they established a tradition of large history paintings as interior decor for the Venetian scuole, the Ducal Palace itself, and even certain churches, such as S. Zaccaria, whose upper walls are covered with late-17C histories.

The work of **Jacobello del Fiore**, such as the triptych of Justice with Archangels Michael and Gabriel (Accademia, 1421), combines the tendency of the late 14C with an International Gothic decorativeness of swirling curvilinear patterns and exaggerated swaying postures. The gold background is replaced by dark blue, and Jacobello used a typical feature of International Gothic: raised and gilded gesso work to highlight costume. The change that has taken place can be understood by comparing Jacobello's triptych with Nicolò di Pietro's Madonna Enthroned and Angels (1394) that hangs nearby.

Jacobello's follower **Michele Giambono** gave his figures a softness and delicacy (see for example the St James polyptych, Accademia) which is the equivalent of Stefan Lochner's work in the Cologne school. His surprisingly elaborate and lucid architecture in the Cappella dei Mascoli mosaic (San Marco) is perhaps a reflection of the lost Ducal palace frescoes.

Two other major artists were at work at this time. **Antonio Vivarini** was a follower of Jacobello and founded a family workshop at Murano that was to rival that of the Bellini. His pictures reflect the International Gothic style—with opulent and fashionable dress, palely modelled flesh, raised gesso work, and abundant flora. In the 1440s he collaborated with **Giovanni d'Alemagna** (see for example the S. Sabina polyptych at S. Zaccaria, 1443). Antonio moderated the linear agitation of Jacobello's work in favour of a more statuesque figure style—a tendency which may have been inspired by Masolino's putative visit to Venice on his return from Hungary in the 1430s. There seems little doubt that the forcefully modelled heads in Antonio's Madonna with the Latin Fathers (Accademia, 1446) reveal the impact of **Andrea del Castagno** (a Florentine follower of Masaccio and Donatello) who painted frescoes in S. Zaccaria in 1442. (New (8st).

In the single work of one of Antonio Vivarini's followers, the Madonna Enthroned (S. Francesco della Vigna, c 1465) by **Antonio da Negroponte**, we see pseudo-antique reliefs and Renaissance architecture wholly submerged in an exuberant and pantheistic Gothic style.

The second major figure of the early quattrocento was **Jacopo Bellini**. He was a pupil of Gentile da Fabriano and may even have followed him to Florence in the 1420s. Most of his work has perished, but two sketchbooks (Louvre and British Museum) testify to his fascination for drawing objects from nature and for studying landscape and perspective. A new human interest appears in his half-length Madonnas in the Accademia, and it was in this ambience of lively observation of the natural world that Gentile and Giovanni Bellini, Jacopo's sons, were trained.

**Giovanni Bellini** can be said to be Venice's first Renaissance painter and the man who more than any other prepared the way for the great flowering of the 16C. His early paintings, such as the Crucifixion in the Museo Correr (c 1460) are similar to his father's late work, but show an interest in the lyrical quality of light. This is evident even during the 1460s when Giovanni's style was overlaid by the sculptural manner of his brother-in-law Mantegna (see the St Vincent Ferrer polyptych in SS. Giovanni e Paolo). Donatello's work in Padua (1443–53), consisting of bronze statuary and reliefs in S. Antonio, was of major importance both as a source of motifs and as a spur to explore human emotion. In the 1470s Giovanni adopted the medium of oil painting, probably on the example of the Sicilian **Antonello da Messina** who came to Venice in 1475–6 and who had learnt the technique from a follower of Jan van Eyck. Oil paint considerably enhanced Giovanni's ability to multiply colour tones and to explore atmospheric effects (see the Frari triptych of 1488). His goal was to paint the idealised, but human and emotive presence of saints in religious images, and to this end he developed the trick of imagining painted architecture as an extension of the carved frame. In the S Zaccaria Madonna (1505) he softened and even concealed form with shadow but at the same time painted with dazzling and saturated colours. This altarpiece achieved a contemplative and luminous monumentality that drew Venetian painting abreast of events in central Italy for the first time.

**Gentile Bellini** was active chiefly as a history painter. In 1472 he undertook the decoration of the Sala del Maggior Consiglio. In 1479–81 he travelled to Constantinople to paint the Sultan's portrait, and in his absence Giovanni also began working in the Ducal Palace, and continued after Gentile's return. Their work was entirely destroyed by fire in 1577.

In the 1490s Gentile painted for the Scuola di S. Giovanni Evangelista the Procession in Piazza S. Marco (Accademia, 1496) a magnificent topography that records the old facade mosaics of San Marco before their replacement, as well as the appearance of the Piazza before its Renaissance transformation.

**Bartolomeo Vivarini** began his career collaborating with his elder brother Antonio. Like Giovanni Bellini he was deeply influenced by Mantegna in the 1460s. His best works date from the early 1470s, including the remarkable Misericordia triptych in S. Maria Formosa (1473) which has several Flemish traits. His figures later become mannered and repetitive and he never shrugged off the harsh and dry manner of the 1460s which had become archaic by the '80s.

**Architecture and Sculpture in the Sixteenth Century**. Architecture of the first three decades made little advance over the achievements of the previous century. The decorative Corinthian-style vocabulary remained the same, though used with greater energy and fantasy on such buildings as the Palazzo dei Camerlenghi (completed 1525) and the Cappella Emiliana at S. Michele in Isola (1529–32), both by **Guglielmo dei Grigi**. The Scuola di S. Rocco was begun in 1515 by **Bartolomeo Bon the younger** and continued by **Antonio Abbondi lo Scarpagnino** and **Giangiacomo dei Grigi** (son of Guglielmo). The finest building of the period was designed in the tradition of Codussi. Begun in 1500, S. Salvatore by **Giorgio Spavento** is a majestic sequence of domed Greek crosses, with additional domes over the side chapels. The view down the nave evokes the basilica of San Marco, but with the austere grey Istrian stone and white plaster in place of marble and mosaic.

There was relatively little sculptural activity in this period. Tullio Lombardo was kept busy with architecture (at S. Salvatore for example) and with sculptural commissions outside Venice. Antonio Lombardo left for Ferrara in 1506 and died in 1516. **Paolo Savin** completed his work in the Cappella Zen (San Marco, completed 1516) and may have designed the famous Moors that strike the hour on Codussi's 'Orologio'.

By the late 1520s, the achievements of the central Italian High Renaissance had begun to filter through, and the antiquarian phase of the opening of the century had passed. **Bartolomeo di Francesco da Bergamo** struggled to achieve a Michelangelesque contrapposto and breadth of form in his St John the Baptist at S. Michele in Isola (1530–4) while inside the Cappella Emiliana **Giovanni Antonio da Carona's** reliefs derive from Andrea Sansovino's Santa Casa at Loreto. These are minor masters, however, and in retrospect the arrival of **Jacopo Sansovino** in 1527, following the Sack of Rome, was a turning point in Venetian sculpture and architecture.

Sansovino had not initially intended to settle in Venice, but on the death of Bartolomeo Bon the younger in 1529 he was appointed 'proto' of San Marco. He did perhaps more than any other, with the exception of Longhena, to change the face of the city. Three churches by him have survived: S. Francesco della Vigna (begun 1534), S. Martino di Castello (begun 1540) and S. Giuliano (begun 1553), and he is the probable author of the choir of S. Fantin (begun 1548), perhaps the most impressive pendentive dome in Venice. His Palazzo Dolfin (Grand Canal, begun 1538) shows a correct treatment of the classical orders unprecedented in Venice, and Palazzo Corner della Ca' Grande at S. Maurizio (begun after 1545), inspired by Bramante's 'House of Raphael', comes closer to the Roman High Renaissance than any other Venetian building. His most conspicuous contribution can be seen in the area of San Marco. Here his remarkable ability to express function through design explains the unreconcilable conflict between the muscular and fortress-like Mint (Zecca) and the refined and elegant Library on the W side of the Piazzetta.

When Sansovino arrived in Venice he was already 41 years old, and a successful career in Rome and Florence lay behind him. He was trained as a sculptor by Andrea Sansovino and adopted a Raphaelesque style of graceful beauty and easy contrapposto; a style he was to perpetuate in Venice through his own work and that of his pupils up to the end of the century. The Loggetta bronzes (1545) epitomise this tradition, and contain numerous references to

Sansovino's youth in Rome. Yet they also represent the precise classical equivalent of the Bon workshop statuary that faces them on the Porta della Carta. Here too we see a decorative and colouristic treatment of architecture, and an interplay of pattern between the statues (ranged vertically on the Porta della Carta instead of horizontally) across the architectural barriers. Inside San Marco Sansovino was charged with the refurbishing of the choir, and here again his work combines characteristics of both Venice and central Italy. For example the Sacristy door (commissioned 1546) is in the tradition of Ghiberti and uses motifs from Raphael and Donatello, but there is also an element of mannerism (see the Resurrected Christ and the soldiers) appropriate to Venice in the 1540s. With such works Sansovino endowed the city with some of the finest sculpture of the Italian cinquecento.

Sansovino had several pupils and assistants, including **Danese Cattaneo**, who followed him to Venice. Cattaneo designed the lateral figures on the tomb of doge Leonardo Loredan (SS. Giovanni e Paolo, completed 1572). **Alessandro Vittoria** joined Sansovino's workshop in 1543. His taste for Michelangelesque torsions in such figures as the St Sebastian (c 1600) at S. Salvatore, or the St Jerome (1576) at the Frari, ran counter to that of Sansovino, though he produced highly elegant figures such as the St John the Baptist at S. Zaccaria (c 1550) while still under Sansovino's influence. Cattaneo's pupil, **Girolamo Campagna** was a prolific sculptor who perpetuated Sansovino's most graceful manner. His finest achievement was his interpretation of Vassilacchi's design for the main altar of S. Giorgio Maggiore (1593–4). This has a strenuous vitality that anticipates the Baroque.

Apart from Sansovino, two other leading Italian architects were active in Venice in the third quarter of the century. **Michele Sanmicheli** designed Palazzo Corner at S. Polo (c 1545), and the overpowering Palazzo Grimani (Grand Canal, begun after 1556), with its water entrance designed as a Roman triumphal arch, and its Corinthian order on all three stories.

The work of **Palladio** was to be more influential, and the major part of his ecclesiastical architecture is to be seen here. He designed the facade of S. Francesco della Vigna (c 1565), the Refectory (1560–62) and church of S. Giorgio Maggiore (begun 1566) and the church of the Redentore (begun 1576). All his church facades consist of interlocking Corinthian temple fronts, but that of the Redentore is the most successful solution, with the clear subordination of all elements to the central portico. Inside, every trace of Lombardesque relief carving and marble encrustation is gone, and his architecture, with its use of the giant order of columns, has an imperial grandeur. Palladio's grouping of large airy spaces in sequence was inspired by his study of ancient Roman baths (from which the typically Palladian lunette—the 'thermal' window—is derived), and his massing of impressive geometric forms evokes the Pantheon.

Sansovino's successors included **Vincenzo Scamozzi**, who spent much of his career completing buildings by others. His chief contribution to Venice was the completion of Sansovino's Library, and the design of the Procuratie Nuove (S side of the Piazza). **Gian Antonio Rusconi** assisted in the renovation of the Ducal Palace after fires in 1574 and 1577, as did **Antonio da Ponte** who is conspicuous as the architect of the Rialto Bridge (1588–91). He designed this with great tact as an extension of Sansovino's Fabbriche Nuove. His also are the Prisons (1589) which were completed by **Antonio Contino**, the architect of the Bridge of Sighs (c 1600).

**Painting in the Sixteenth Century**. Giovanni Bellini's fame has tended to overshadow other painters working around the turn of the century. **Cima da Conegliano** anticipated Bellini in setting his paintings in luminous Veneto landscapes (see for example the St John the Baptist and four Saints in the Madonna dell'Orto, c 1492). His magisterial Baptism of Christ in S. Giovanni in Bragora was the model for a later version by Giovanni Bellini in Vicenza. **Alvise Vivarini** (son of Antonio) trained under his uncle Bartolomeo. He was contracted in 1494 to work beside the Bellinis in the Sala del Maggior Consiglio. His later work, such as the Risen Christ in S. Giovanni in Bragora (1498) shows a precocious development of lively movement and gesture. Alvise's pupils included **Jacopo de' Barbari**, author of an aerial view of Venice of 1500, **Marco Basaiti**, who completed Alvise's last work, the Milanese chapel altarpiece in the Frari, and, possibly, **Lorenzo Lotto**, an eccentric genius who spent the best part of his career in the Marches and Bergamo. A few of his works can be seen here and in particular the Apotheosis of St Nicholas (the Carmini, 1527).

**Vittore Carpaccio** can be counted among the followers of Gentile Bellini. He devoted most of his career to narrative cycles for the scuole, such as those of S. Giorgio degli Schiavoni and S. Ursula (the latter now in the Accademia). These large works are imagined with great human charm and with an absorbing quantity of detail recording the topography, architecture, costume, furniture and manners of the period. He was also the author of what seems to be Venice's earliest genre painting: the 'Two Women' in the Museo Correr.

In the late 15C and early 16C Giovanni Bellini ran a large workshop of apprentices and journeymen that included **Francesco Bissolo, Andrea Previtali, Nicolò Rondinelli** and **Rocco Marconi**. They more or less perpetuated the Bellinesque manner, but with three pupils of Giovanni Bellini—Giorgione, Sebastiano, and Titian—Venetian painting entered a new phase.

**Giorgione** was an artist of legendary greatness few of whose works have survived. For example his decoration of the canal facade of the Fondaco dei Tedeschi with figures in the classical style exists in a single spectral fragment (Ca' d'Oro). The 'Tempesta' in the Accademia rivals contemporary German painting in its skilful description of a landscape in a certain state of the weather. The elusive meaning and poetic mood of this picture have done much to increase his fame. Giorgione's great importance rests perhaps on the practice of painting *alla prima*, without drawings, which did much to influence what became the characteristically Venetian free handling of paint.

**Sebastiano del Piombo** was among the first to adopt this new freedom. A remarkable development in his figure style took place during the execution of the organ shutters at S. Bartolomeo, where he switched from a Bellinesque idiom (St Louis and St Sinibald) to an athletic and Roman figure style (St Sebastian and St Bartholomew).

In 1511 Sebastiano left Venice permanently for Rome, and this, combined with Giorgione's premature death from the plague in 1510, and Lotto's continued absence, left **Titian** the most talented young painter in Venice. Unlike Giorgione, Titian's fame rests solidly on an immense output of portraits, mythologies and religious paintings. He established his reputation with a sequence of early altarpieces including the Assumption (1516–18) and the Pésaro Madonna

(1519–26), both in the Frari, and the Death of St Peter Martyr (1530, destroyed 1867) of which a copy exists in SS. Giovanni e Paolo. Though he spent most of his career in Venice, the majority of his work was done for patrons abroad: the Marquises and Dukes of northern Italy, Cardinals and Popes, the Hapsburg courts, Charles V and Philip II themselves. Nevertheless Venice has retained a handful of altarpieces in addition to those mentioned above, as well as one of his largest paintings, the Presentation of the Virgin in the Accademia (1534–38) and one of his last, the Pietà (Accademia, 1576, completed by Palma Giovane) which, with its dimmed colour, glimmering light, and painterly rendering of form, is a noble example of his late style.

Titian's greatness lay in his combination of a sensitivity to light and colour inherited from Giovanni Bellini, with the figure style and language of gesture learned from central Italian and ancient Roman art. In the 1540s Mannerism made a brief appearance in his work, partly through contact with Giulio Romano, whose *di sotto in su* ceilings at the Palazzo del Té, Mantua, were the inspiration for Titian's Old Testament canvases, with tumbling figures, in the sacristy of S. Maria della Salute. In general however, Titian prolonged the Italian Renaissance long after it had been transformed elsewhere.

Titian had one conspicuous rival during the first part of his career: the itinerant Friulan **Pordenone**. After visiting Rome, Pordenone developed an idiosyncratic figure style which gave rise to such masterpieces as the S. Lorenzo Giustinian and Saints (Accademia, commissioned 1532) and the Annunciation (S Maria degli Angeli, Murano, 1537), a commission he obtained by undercutting Titian's fee.

Titian's commitments outside Venice left abundant work for other artists who were kept busy decorating the churches, palaces, and scuole. **Palma Vecchio** was perhaps the best of a number of painters who migrated from Bergamo. One of his altarpieces, and possibly his finest work, can still be seen in situ: the St Barbara polyptych in S. Maria Formosa (c 1522–24). His follower, **Bonifazio Veronese** organised in the 1530s and '40s a productive workshop, and decorated the Palazzo dei Camerlenghi (canvases now in the Accademia and the Fondazione Giorgio Cini), and the sacristy of S. Sebastiano (1551–5).

**Paris Bordone**, who was also in some respects heir to Palma Vecchio, painted one major work in Venice, the Fisherman consigning the ring to the Doge (Accademia, 1534) which once decorated the Scuola di S. Marco. **Andrea Schiavone** was an artist of great originality, touched by Mannerism, whose painterly style may have anticipated and influenced the later work of Titian and Tintoretto. **Jacopo Bassano**, a pupil of Bonifazio Veronese, spent most of his career in Bassano (hence his name), and was the most celebrated member of a family business founded by his father and continued by his sons **Francesco** and **Leandro**. Their most characteristic production was a biblical scene treated as a farmyard pastoral, with peasants and herds of cows and sheep (see the Return of Jacob by Jacopo Bassano in the Sala dell' Anti-Collegio of the Ducal Palace).

Early in his career Jacopo Bassano responded to central Italian Mannerism which was making itself felt in the Veneto in the 1540s—the period of Titian's acceptance of certain traits and also of Andrea Schiavone's more complete absorption. Vasari visited Venice in 1541–2 and Francesco Salviati also came, in 1539–41, to execute a now lost altarpiece for S. Spirito. His pupil **Giuseppe Salviati** arrived in 1541 and settled here. He was an uneven painter but his fine altarpiece in the Frari (1548) is among the most Roman-looking paintings of its time in Venice, and in this respect he is the direct heir of Pordenone in the Venetian School. In the same period **Battista Franco** returned from Rome (1554) and painted for the Grimani family at S. Francesco della Vigna, before his death from a cold caught while frescoing Villa Malcontenta.

It was against this background that two artists of major importance emerge on the Venetian scene. **Jacopo Tintoretto** claimed to have been self-taught. The first clear statement of his style was the Miracle of the Slave (Accademia, 1548) with its acidic colours, posturing attenuated figures and dramatic foreshortening based on a study of Michelangelo's sculpture and in particular on Sansovino's 'Cantorie' in San Marco. From this point onwards, Tintoretto, with the greatest virtuosity, poured out vast canvases for such places as the Scuola di S. Rocco (1565–87) and the Madonna dell'Orto (1552–c 1575). He wilfully re-imagined traditional themes such as the Last Supper (with the table plunging into depth) and the Annunciation (set in an untidy carpenter's lean-to) and he gave the Crucifixion (Scuola di S. Rocco, 1565) an epic scale and a narrative richness that has never been surpassed. His few mythologies such as the recently cleaned quartet in the Sala dell'Anti-Collegio of the Ducal Palace, have an unexpected lyricism in both figures and landscape. He painted with the greatest bravura, conjuring up dynamic images with a few sweeping brushstrokes, though he was capable at times, and especially in his early career, of careful descriptions of form and texture.

Tintoretto's contemporary was **Paolo Veronese**. Born and trained in Verona, he settled in Venice around 1553. He was heir to Giulio Romano's *di sotto in su* treatment of ceilings and in 1555 he painted the ceiling of the sacristy at S. Sebastiano in this manner. He went on to decorate the entire church. The ceiling of the nave, with three scenes of Esther and Ahasuerus, the main altarpiece, the chancel canvases, and the frescoes, illustrate the full range of Veronese's power. He developed a genre of lavish banquet scenes suitable for refectories, and on a famous occasion in 1573 was questioned by the Inquisition for the intrusion of irrelevant detail in a Last Supper (now in the Accademia and called 'The Feast in the House of Levi'). Veronese's work presents an interesting contrast to that of Tintoretto. Though his figures are in restless movement, they remain normal in proportion and credible in their stance, whereas Tintoretto frequently disregarded laws of anatomy or gravity. Veronese's scenes are set in bright sunlight, in contrast to the dramatic tenebroso of Tintoretto's work. However, late in his career and possibly on Titian's example, Veronese toned down his colour and dimmed his light for religious paintings, especially of Christ's Passion. It was this manner that **Alvise dal Friso**, Veronese's pupil and nephew, adopted for his Life of Christ in the nave of S. Nicolò dei Mendicoli. In general Veronese's narrative sense is weaker, and the feeling he elicits less intense than Tintoretto's, but he can be considered Venice's first great decorator, and he profoundly influenced both Italian Baroque and Venetian Rococo painting.

Apart from Alvise dal Friso, Veronese had a number of pupils who followed him from Verona, including his bother **Benedetto Caliari**, his son **Carletto Caliari, Francesco Montemezzano**, and **Giulio del Moro** who was also a sculptor.

**Architecture and Sculpture in the Seventeenth Century**. The century opened with the appointment of **Bartolo Manopola** as 'proto' of the Ducal Palace—an architect content to continue the tradition of Sansovino and Scamozzi. His principal achievement was the completion of the courtyard facades of the Ducal Palace, including the Clocktower. The grandiose Palazzo Pisani at S. Stefano is attributed to him, and illustrates the cool 'cinquecentismo' that was never to disappear completely from Venetian palaces and which was to be revived in the 18C.

In 1624, the Palladian-style Duomo at Chioggia was begun by a young architect who was to dominate the century and to rank as Venice's only great Baroque architect: **Baldassare Longhena**. Longhena's contribution to the city equals that of Sansovino. Among his numerous palaces Ca' Pesaro (begun 1676) is notable for its great size. The facade is inspired by Sansovino's Palazzo Corner, and it is only in the exuberant detail that the Baroque asserts itself—the free-standing columns and deep recesses, the bizarre balustrades, and scarified monsters and masks. The Palazzo Belloni-Battagia (c 1650) is no less interesting with its 'beetle-browed' pediments and intricate bay-system. His other palaces include Ca' Rezzonico (begun 1667), and Palazzo Giustinian-Lolin (begun c 1624), an early work still tied to the cinquecento. Among Longhena's other commissions the facade of the Ospedaletto is remarkable for its grimacing and titanic telamones. His greatest achievement however was S. Maria della Salute. The design is profoundly indebted to the example of Palladio. The lateral facades copy those of the Zitelle, while inside the colour scheme and the arrangement of orders recall S. Giorgio Maggiore. The choice of the domed octagon is in the Renaissance tradition, while his skill in linking the appended chancel and retro-choir to the central space, by means of arches and piers that link up in vistas, is learned from Palladio's Redentore. But the total effect is dynamically Baroque: space plunges and soars away from the spectator, while outside, spiralling consoles link the mass of the church to the immense dome. The Salute occupied most of Longhena's career and was consecrated soon after his death, in 1687.

The central plan seems to have been a characteristic of the first half of the century. **Francesco Contino** (brother of Antonio) designed S. Angelo Raffaele in 1618 as a Greek cross, and (following Longhena's example) S. Maria del Pianto as an octagon (1647–59).

**Alessandro Tremignon** is known for one principal work—the facade of S. Moisè (begun 1668). This typifies Venice's two-storied Baroque church facades, in which abundant, exotic and usually profane statuary is given precedence over slack architectural form. This criticism may be made of the work of **Guiseppe Sardi**. After Longhena he was the principal architect of the century and likewise mediated between the cinquecento and Roman Baroque. For example his facade of S. Lazzaro dei Mendicanti (1673), based on the Zitelle, is an appropriate addition to Scamozzi's interior. His best works must be considered his facades for S. Maria degli Scalzi (1672–80) and S. Maria del Giglio (1680–3). The former, with its coupled columns, reflects the Roman High Baroque, but characteristically the explosive quality is defused—the facade is flat and the bays are static. This is improved upon slightly at S. Maria del Giglio, Sardi's last major work, where the deep crowning pediments have a peculiarly Venetian effect and recall Coducci's S. Zaccaria.

Longhena's closest follower was **Antonio Gaspari** who stepped into his shoes at S. Giorgio Maggiore, the Salute, and Ca' Pesaro. He continued the most conservative strain of Longhena's palace designs, although we know he was conversant with Roman Baroque. For example his oval plans for S. Maria della Fava were discarded in favour of a traditionally Palladian hall (begun 1711).

The demise of the sculptural tradition begun by Sansovino came with the deaths, early in the 17C, of Vittoria, Aspetti, and Campagna. This left a void that was not to be filled until the middle of the century, with the development of the ornamental Baroque facade. The only memorable figure of this 'interregnum' was the Genoese **Nicolò Roccatagliata** who worked mainly in bronze. He left a few works of high quality in Venice, in particular the Mannered statuettes of St Stephen and St George in S. Giorgio Maggiore (1595) and the crowded Deposition relief at S. Moisé (1633).

The emphasis that architects placed on statuary in the Baroque era inevitably galvanised activity. Itinerant artists from Rome and the North were attracted, bringing with them the Baroque style. For example, **Enrico Meyring** was responsible for the decoration of the facade of S. Moisè, and carved at the Scalzi a copy of Bernini's Ecstasy of S. Teresa (1699), **Michele Fabris Ongaro** collaborated with **Melchiorre Barthel** at the Cappella Valmarana in S Pietro di Castello (1670–74). Barthel was also responsible for the colossal Moors of Longhena's Pesaro Monument at the Frari.

Scenic effects were the principal object, and the quality of individual pieces was less important, especially if they were to be viewed from a great distance. Several sculptors were called in to work at the Salute, including **Michele Fabris, Francesco Penso il Cabianca** and **Bernardino Falcone**. **Thomas Ruer** was responsible for the Evangelists in niches around the main door, while the Sibyls and the Virgin were the work of **Francesco Cavrioli**.

A Flemish sculptor, **Juste Le Court** stands out as perhaps the most talented of the group that served the Baroque architects. He collaborated successfully with Sardi on the Cavazza tomb at the Madonna dell'Orto (begun 1657), and carved the proud and character-ful portraits of the Barbaro family for S. Maria del Giglio—a facade that highlights the extent to which architecture could be conceived as a vehicle for sculpture. A Flemish preoccupation with realistic surfaces can be seen in what is probably Le Court's principal work, the high altar of S. Maria della Salute (1670), and again his allegories of Winter and Autumn at Ca' Rezzonico have the charm of northern genre pieces.

The style of Bernini was brought to Venice in its purest form by **Filippo Parodi** who was his pupil from 1655–61. Parodi's admirable monument to Bishop Francesco Morosini (died 1678) at S. Nicolò da Tolentino has the colourism, the wind-swept drama, and the almost liquid drapery of Bernini's late style.

Unexpectedly, Venice's most famous furniture maker, **Andrea Brustolon** trained for a spell under Parodi, and his earliest works, the gilt-wood Angels in the sacristy of the Frari, are purely Baroque. Brustolon is best known for his imaginatively figurated furniture of which the masterpiece, the Venier suite, is preserved at Ca' Rezzonico. He was not the first woodcarver in Venice to indulge a bizarre fantasy. **Franscesco Pianta** carved a row of burlesque figures in the upper hall of the Scuola di S. Rocco. A third fine woodcarver of this time was **Giacomo Piazzetta** whose choir-stalls in the Cappella del Rosario at SS. Giovanni e Paolo are in a more sober style.

**Painting in the Seventeenth Century**. The impact of Tintoretto on the generation of painters active at the turn of the century was perhaps the greatest. Painters who had begun their careers close to Titian eventually turned their allegiance to Tintoretto, such as **Giovanni Contarini** and **Palma Giovane** (grand-nephew of Palma Vecchio), who completed Titian's Pietà in the Accademia. The latter was extraordinarily prolific, and both the quality of his work and his reputation have suffered as a consequence. Nevertheless some of his paintings are distinguished, such as the Cities of Northern Italy paying homage to Venice in the Sala dell Maggior Consiglio in which a Mannerist soldier stands wearing a bright pink cuirass.

In the work of **Andrea Vicentino, Leonardo Corona, Domenico Tintoretto** (son of Jacopo), **Antonio Vassilacchi l'Aliense** and others, it becomes clear that the legacy of the great 16C painters is losing its inspiration under the weight of vast and repetitive canvases. A comparison between Palma Giovane's Annunciation at the Madonna dell'Orto and the two Tintorettos that frame it, or between **Marco Vecellio's** Annunciation in S. Giacomo a Rialto and Titian's in S. Salvatore, reveals the extent to which the fire had gone out of Venetian brushwork and colour.

The prestige of the Venetian Renaissance established itself in the 17C, and we find **Padovanino**, the major local artist of his time, reworking the types and compositions of Titian, while his pupil, **Pietro Muttoni della Vecchia**, the author of a mock-heroic Crucifixion in S. Lio, acquired his nickname from imitating Old Masters.

The fame of Titian, Tintoretto and Veronese attracted to Venice several foreigners whose work is the most interesting and original in the Venetian seicento, and who played a large part in keeping the sluggish local school abreast of the times.

Among the earliest of these visitors were **Domenico Fetti** and **Johann Lys**. Fetti settled in Venice in 1622 and specialised in small, spirited genre paintings, and pastiches of Tintoretto and Veronese. Lys arrived in Venice in 1621 and stayed until his death from the plague eight years later. His paintings such as the Vision of St Jerome (S. Nicolò da Tolentino, c 1628) have warm and vibrant colours rendered with thick paint and a lively touch that present one of the first alternatives to the deadness of form and the opacity of shadow that lingered from the cinquecento.

**Bernardo Strozzi** also spent his last years here. In Genoa he developed a free handling of paint on the example of Rubens, a tendency reinforced by Lys' and Fetti's work when he arrived in Venice in 1630. But his figures remain substantial, and an element of realism in his 'props' and of coarseness in his characters stems ultimately from Caravaggio. This is apparent in such works as the St Lawrence (S. Nicolò da Tolentino) and the Feast in the House of the Pharisee (Accademia).

The stimulus that these artists gave to their successors was uneven in its effect. **Francesco Maffei** absorbed completely the iridescent handling of paint of Lys and Fetti, and his Guardian Angel in SS. Apostoli is one of the masterpieces of the century, while **Sebastiano Mazzoni** developed a vigorous style and a fertile imagination, based especially on Lys and Maffei, that make him one of the most original if not eccentric painters of the century (see his paintings in S. Benedetto and the Accademia). He was also the architect of a most un-Venetian palace: Palazzo Moro-Lin on the Grand Canal.

The local tradition remained inferior. Padovanino's pupils, in addition to Pietro della Vecchia, were **Pietro Liberi**, who despite his clumsy technique and muddy brown shadows, had some successes, and **Gerolamo Forabosco** whose Family rescued from Shipwreck in Malamocco is justly famous for its touching sincerity.

In the second half of the century it was once again the activity of foreign artists that pushed Venice into its High Baroque phase. In 1663 Pietro da Cortona himself sent his Daniel in the Lion's Den to the church of San Daniele (now in the Accademia). His follower, **Luca Giordano** visited Venice in 1653, when he was working in a realistic and shadowy style based on Caravaggio and Ribera, and it was this style that was taken up by two immigrants to Venice: **Gian Battista Langetti** and Langetti's follower **Johann Karl Loth**, whose forceful and densely shadowed altarpiece in S. Maria del Giglio exposes the weakness of his local rival **Antonio Zanchi**, whose canvases are to be seen in the same church.

Luca Giordano's later altarpieces for Venice, such as those for the Salute (1667–73) are lighter and more decorative, and directly influenced works such as the Birth of the Virgin in S. Stefano by **Nicolò Bambini** (a follower of Liberi). In this way, gradually the painters of the end of the century mastered large figure compositions in the Baroque spirit, which though derivative are competent.

**Antonio Molinari's** Battle of the Lapiths and Centaurs in Ca' Rezzonico (c 1698) renders the figures of Pietro da Cortona in a dark palette based on Zanchi. **Antonio Bellucci** and **Andrea Celesti** painted dynamically grouped figure compositions with the lively brushwork and luminous colour of Maffei. **Gregorio Lazzarini** represented a conservative trend that recalls Veronese (see his paintings for the Arco Morosini at the Ducal Palace). **Gian Antonio Fumiani** painted at S. Pantalon Venice's only worthy equivalent of Roman or Neapolitan Baroque celings (begun 1684); an infinity of dark toned figures on a cumbrous architecture of steps and platforms. But even before its completion in 1704 Sebastiano Ricci had begun to revolutionise Venetian painting with the first sunny Rococo ceilings.

**Architecture and Sculpture in the Eighteenth Century**. The close ties that existed between architecture and sculpture in the late 17C continued into the 18C. The churches of **Domenico Rossi** (nephew of Sardi) make extensive use of statuary. The entrance of S. Stae (begun 1709) is crowned by sturdy pieces of pediment on which free-flying sculptures are mounted. The same extravagant formula is used for the apsidal altars of Rossi's church of the Gesuiti (1715–28), and Rococo altars of equal fantasy can be seen in S. Stefano. The Gesuiti, as one might expect, is the most 'Roman' church in Venice. The plan depends from that of the Gesù in Rome, the headquarters of the Jesuit order, while the facade with its convex array of massed columns is almost unique in Venice. But one detail is peculiarly Venetian. This is the placing of statues over the lower range of columns, a device used by Longhena inside the Salute octagon. Rossi's Ca' Corner della Regina is restrained and muted compared to the nearby Ca' Pesaro. Its design was inspired by Sardi's Palazzo Flangini (Grand Canal, 1664–82) and exemplifies the return to the cinquecento tradition of architecture. An earlier example is the Corinthian portico at S. Nicolò da Tolentino by **Andrea Tirali** which was executed between 1706–14, while at S. Vitale, Tirali's facade (1734) is a slavish copy of S. Giorgio Maggiore.

**Giorgio Massari** was perhaps the leading architect of the period.

His oval church of the Pietà (1745–60) recalled a now-destroyed church by Sansovino (the Incurabili). The Gesuati (completed 1736) has a severe temple front facade after Palladio and an interior derived, even down to the design of individual bays, from the Redentore. At Palazzo Grassi the architect's personality is almost completely obscured by a cold classical reserve.

The first church to be seen by visitors to Venice who arrive by train belongs to this period: S. Simeone Piccolo (1718–36) designed by **Giovanni Scalfarotto**. The dome may be unpleasing but is nevertheless in the venerable tradition of Byzantium, while the portico and attic derive from the Pantheon.

The collaboration of sculptors and architects at the opening of the century continued to be fruitful. **Antonio Tarsia, Giovanni Bonazza** and **Marino Gropelli** worked on the scenario and reliefs of Tirali's grandiose Valier monument in SS. Giovanni e Paolo (1705); and went on to work at the Gesuiti (1715–28). **Giuseppe Torretto** worked on the reliefs of Massari's project for the Cappella del Rosario at SS. Giovanni e Paolo (1730). Torretto seems to have been the principal collaborator of Rossi, and his finest works are the sublime archangels at the east end of the Gesuiti (1715–28).

The Venetian-born German, **Gian Maria Morleiter** worked with Massari at the Gesuati, and produced there a noble gallery of prophets and saints in the spirit of Grand Opera. His altar statues at S. Maria del Giglio have a virtuosity of brittle and decorative drapery characteristic of German Rococo. They also illustrate the tendency of sculpture at this time to reassert its autonomy. The works of **Antonio Corradini**, such as the Virginity (1721) at the church of the Carmini, and of **Giovanni Marchiori**, such as the St Cecilia and David (1743) at the church of S. Rocco, have this independent quality: sweeping drapery and gesture are replaced by 'internal' design and a diligent, even virtuoso surface realism. Like architecture therefore, sculpture in the 18C returned to its classic phase, the cinquecento, although the Baroque experience was not to be effaced until the advent of a quite different movement: European neo-classicism. It was in the former ambience that the art of **Antonio Canova** was formed. His early (i.e. Venetian) work, such as the Daedalus and Icarus (Museo Correr, 1778–9) is self-contained and has a soft and realistic surface treatment in contrast to the Greek manner of his maturity in Rome. However, 'as with **Piranesi** (born nr. Mestre), Canova's career really belongs outside the context of Venetian art.

A versatile figure of the middle of the century was **Antonio Visentini**—view painter, academician, engraver, as well as architect. He was caught up with the entrepreneurial activities of Canaletto's English patron, Consul Joseph Smith, whose house on the Grand Canal, Palazzo Mangilli-Valmarana, Visentini remodelled.

In general there was little sculptural or architectural activity in the decades preceding Napoleon's arrival in 1797. **Tommaso Temanza** (nephew of Scalfarotto) designed Venice's first neo-classical building, the round church of S. Maria Maddalena (1763–8), but architects of this period were principally taken up with ephemeral constructions for 'feste', such as the Ascension Day Fair, and the visits of foreign Princes.

**Painting in the Eighteenth Century**. At the opening of the 18C Venice produced a generation of decorators, portraitists, landscape and view painters who achieved international importance, and developed a

Rococo style of grand decoration epitomised by Ricci and Tiepolo that lasted until the end of the century.

**Sebastiano Ricci** was born in Belluno, and after training under Mazzoni in Venice spent his early career travelling internationally, including England from 1712–16. An eclectic who learned the Baroque style of Pietro da Cortona and Luca Giordano, he adapted compositions and figures from such Old Masters as Titian, Correggio, Annibale Carracci and, especially, Paolo Veronese (see for example Ricci's altarpiece of 1708 in S. Giorgio Maggiore, in which the composition is based on Veronese's S. Zaccaria Madonna in the Accademia, with the reminiscence of Correggio in the figure of St Peter). Though he lacked the gravity of the cinquecento, he developed an idiom of ethereally graceful (and totally unreal) figures bathed in brilliant light which was to set the tone of Venetian Rococo and to influence the work of G.B. Tiepolo in particular. His earliest Venetian paintings in this manner still in situ decorate the ceiling of S. Marziale (c 1700–02), and several of his altarpieces can be seen in Venice (in the church of S. Rocco, for example) although as so often in this century the bulk of his painting exists elsewhere.

The work of **Giambattista Piazzetta** (son of Giacomo) provides a contrast to Ricci's effervescent style. Trained under G.M. Crespi in Bologna, Piazzetta seems to have been impressed by the visionary chiaroscuro of Guercino's work. In Venice from 1711, he executed one ceiling painting, the Apotheosis of St Dominic at SS. Giovanni e Paolo (completed 1727), and a number of altarpieces with impassioned saints and haughty Madonnas in cloudy zig-zagging compositions (see the St Philip Neri at S. Maria della Fava). His brown toned paintings contain passages of mundane realism that acquire extraordinary spirituality in the religious works and which gave rise to highly original genre paintings such as the Fortune Teller in the Accademia. Despite a melancholic temperament, he had a number of followers who adopted his tenebroso palette and compositional patterns, several of whom are represented in the church of the Pietà. Piazzetta became the first president of the Venetian Academy, founded in 1750, and exercised considerable influence on the work of both the Tiepolos.

**Gian Battista Tiepolo** was the greatest decorator of his age. His master Gregorio Lazzarini gave him, if nothing else, a training in vast figure compositions. His early work has both the chiaroscuro and the realism of Piazzetta (see his four mythologies in Room XVI of the Accademia, and the Sacrifice of Isaac in the Ospedaletto). An artist of the greatest virtuosity, he brightened his palette in the 1720s on the example of Sebastiano Ricci, and mastered the illusionism of the Roman Baroque ceiling painters, as well as a compositional sense and a repertoire of figure types and poses derived from the great Renaissance painters. Tiepolo's work is a more sincere expression of the Rococo than its French equivalent and his loyalty to the aristocratic milieu never failed. Venice has retained a handful of dazzling altarpieces and several great frescoes: at the Gesuati (1737–9), the Scuola dei Carmini (1740–7), the Pietà (1754–5), Ca' Rezzonico (1758), and, most complete of all, in Palazzo Labia (c 1744–5, in collaboration with the quadratura painter **Girolamo Mengozzi-Colonna**) where a sublime and Veronesian Cleopatra seems about to step down into the ballroom. In 1762 he settled in Madrid, where he died in 1770.

**Gian Domenico Tiepolo** has been understandably over-shadowed by his father, with whom he worked and travelled for much of his early career. In some ways he was no less original. He was a witty commentator on contemporary Venetian appearances and a painter of bizarre scenes from the Commedia dell'Arte (see his decorations in Ca' Rezzonico) as well as the author of disturbing religious works such as the Stations of the Cross at S. Polo.

The paler tones introduced by Ricci and G.B. Tiepolo affected the work of artists who were still composing ponderous figure compositions in the grand manner, such as **Girolamo Brusafero** and **Sante Piatti** whose paintings in S Moisé exemplify this. Ricci had a number of followers including **Gaspare Diziani**, and **Francesco Fontebasso**. **Gian Antonio Pellegrini** based his high-keyed colour and fluid light on Ricci, and had as much success abroad as Tiepolo. His Martyrdom of St Andrew at S. Stae makes clear the debt of Venetian Rococo to Johann Lys. **Giovanni Battista Pittoni** was another brilliant colourist while the Veronese **Antonio Balestra** stood apart from the Rococo of Ricci and Tiepolo in retaining a Roman density of form and design. **Francesco Zugno, Jacopo Marieschi** and **Jacopo Guarana** continued the style of Tiepolo to the end of the century, and the latter painted one of the last significant works of Rococo decoration in Venice—the music room at the Ospedaletto (c 1776).

Portraiture in this century was devoted principally to the unedifying male members of the patriciate. Nevertheless portraits by **Sebastiano Bombelli** of Udine, G.B. Tiepolo (whose portrait of Giovanni Dolfin in the Pinacoteca Querini-Stampalia is one of the most memorable of the century), **Alessandro Longhi**, and the highly successful **Rosalba Carriera**, who used pastels and has been called the first Rococo portraitist, are all worth seeking out.

Much of Rosalba's work was painted for a foreign clientele, including English milords, and Venice in the 18C enjoyed a thriving export business in easel paintings, especially the topographies and capriccios of **Canaletto** and **Francesco Guardi**, and the landscapes of **Marco Ricci** (nephew of Sebastiano), the Tuscan **Francesco Zuccarelli**, and his imitator **Giuseppe Zais**. Either Francesco Guardi or his brother **Gian Antonio Guardi** painted one of the greatest 'jewels' of the Venetian settecento—the Story of Tobias on the organ loft of S. Angelo Raffaele.

**Pietro Longhi** (father of Alessandro) painted for a Venetian market. He specialised in humourless genre paintings, interiors and conversation pieces, which make up for their incompetent drawing with the social interest of their subject matter. **Gabriel Bella** was a naive painter who documented Venetian sports and holidays in a remarkable cycle preserved in the Pinacoteca Querini-Stampalia.

**Venice since the fall of the Republic (1797).** The fall of the Republic was to be a catastrophe for Venetian art and architecture. Napoleon's bloodless conquest resulted initially in the destruction of several winged lions, symbols of Venice's past. For example, the group of Doge Foscari and the Lion on the Porta della Carta was smashed (later replaced by Luigi Ferrari, 1885), while the defaced remains of a lion can still be seen in Campo S. Maria Mater Domini. Large numbers of paintings, sculpture (including the four Golden Horses) and manuscripts were removed to Paris. (Most of these, with the exception of three Veroneses in the Louvre, were returned in 1816.) By the Treaty of Campo Formio (1797), Venice passed to the Austrians, and before departing in January 1798 the French 'spoiled' the Arsenal and sank the ships, including the purely ornamental ducal barge, the

its art. In 1932 the elegant stone bridge of the Scalzi was erected near the Railway Station, and the wooden bridge built at the Accademia. A year later the road was built across the lagoon adjacent to the railway bridge, and Piazzale Roma came into existence. In 1938 the Rio Nuovo was cut from the Grand Canal near Piazzale Roma through to Rio S. Pantalon. In the late 1940s the Hotel Danieli annex was built next to the Prisons on the Riva degli Schiavoni, and part of the Hotel Bauer-Grünwald was rebuilt in Campo S. Moisé—innovations that aroused such controversy that when in 1953 Frank Lloyd Wright designed Ca' Masieri, adjacent to Palazzo Balbi on the Grand Canal, building permission was refused.

Recent architecture in Venice includes the Cassa di Risparmio in Campo Manin, and the basketball stadium near the Arsenal. Perhaps the leading post-War Venetian architect was **Carlo Scarpa** who specialized in museum and exhibition installations. His mannered treatment of wall fixtures, frames and show cases recurs in the Accademia, the Museo Correr, and, most recently, in the Ca' d'Oro. He elegantly redesigned the ground floor, including the Sala Luzzato, of the Fondazione Querini Stampalia, and in 1985 the posthumous entrance way to the Architecture School of Venice, based on his design, was inaugurated at San Nicolò da Tolentino.

In 1946 Venice was the setting for the launching of the Fronte Nuovo, a movement that embodied the most avant garde tendencies in Italian painting of the time. Among the leading painters were the Venetians **Armando Pizzinato, Giuseppe Santomaso**, and **Emilio Vedova**, as well as the sculptor **Alberto Viani**. In 1952 the more abstracting tendencies split with the social realists and formed the Gruppo degli Otto which, with Santomaso and Vedova, also included **Giulio Turcato** and **Afro**. A contemporary movement launched by **Lucio Fontana** in the early 1950s was the Movimento Spaziale, which drew together several other talented artists working in Venice in the period including **Tancredi, Mario de Luigi, Virgilio Guidi** and **Edmondo Bacci**.

Modern art in Venice is also served by four distinguished institutions. In 1895 the Venice Biennale was founded. As the longest surviving event of its kind, it can claim still to be the most prestigious and renowned international exhibition of contemporary art, even since prize giving was abolished after 1964. In 1897 the Modern Art Gallery at Ca' Pesaro was created, partly to house acquisitions from the Biennale, and partly to exhibit Venetian painting of the 19C. In 1949 Peggy Guggenheim brought her collection of modern art permanently to Venice, and opened it to the public—a collection more representative of 20C art and higher in quality than that of Ca' Pesaro. Since 1979 this has been owned and administered by The Solomon R. Guggenheim Foundation which also runs The Solomon R. Guggenheim Museum in New York. Finally, in 1976 the so-called Biennale Archives were opened at ·Ca' Corner della Regina. This is an ambitious library of modern art covering film, photography, theatre and dance, as well as painting, sculpture and architecture.

Since 1966, an international campaign of restoration in Venice has done much to clear the disastrous backlog of maintenance and care that had built up since the fall of the Republic and also to counteract the hugely accelerated processes of decay caused by pollution. While most of this work followed the appeal for international aid by Unesco in 1966, the single most sensational achievement has been the restoration of the island of S. Giorgio Maggiore and the establishing of various philanthropic institutions there (1951–56) by Count Vittorio Cini. The restoration of Palazzo Labia by Italian Television (RAI) also predates the Unesco appeal. Since 1966, restoration has been carried out by voluntary committees from several countries, including France, the United States, West Germany, and of course, Italy itself.

Through ten different charities, through the expenditure of banks, companies, private individuals, parishioners, clergy, and more recently the 'Amici dei Musei e dei Monumenti' of Venice, Italy has done more 'private' restoration than any other country, excepting perhaps the United States. Meanwhile the contribution of public Italian funds and expertise, from the Municipality, Regional, and the State authorities, is impossible to calculate. Numerous Venetian monuments are still in need of salvation from ruinous damp and neglect, and one of the most serious problems is the corrosion of external sculpture. However, since the sinking of Venice has in the past few years been slowed down, if not actually stopped, these restorations have been fully justified, and the future of the city has begun to look much brighter.

# GLOSSARY

ALBERGO. Small room used for meetings on the upper floor of a Scuola.

ALTANA. Terrace made of wood on the roof of a Venetian house.

ANCONA. Retable or large altarpiece (painted or sculpted) in an architectural frame.

ANDRONE. Principal ground floor hall behind the water entrance of a Venetian palace.

ARCHITRAVE. The lowest part of an entablature, the horizontal frame above a door.

ARCHIVOLT. Moulded architrave carried round an arch.

ATLANTES (or *Telamones*). Male figures used as supporting columns.

ATRIUM. Forecourt, usually of a Byzantine church or a classical Roman house.

ATTIC. Topmost story of a classical building, hiding the spring of the roof.

BALDACCHINO. Canopy supported by columns, usually over an altar.

BARDIGLIO. Marble streaked with blue and white.

BASILICA. Originally a Roman building used for public administration in Christian architecture, an aisled church with a clerestory and apse, and no transepts.

BOTTEGA. The studio of an artist: the pupils who worked under his direction.

CAMPANILE. Bell-tower, often detached from the building to which it belongs.

CA' (CASA). Venetian term for palace (or house).

CHALICE. Wine cup used in the celebration of Mass.

CHIAROSCURO. Distribution of light and shade, apart from colour in a painting.

CIBORIUM. Casket or tabernacle containing the Host.

CIPOLLINO. Greyish marble with streaks of white or green.

CIPPUS (Pl. *Cippae*). Sepulchral monument in the form of an altar.

CLOISONNÈ. Type of enamel decoration.

CORBEL. A projecting block, usually of stone.

CORNU. Ducal horned beret in red velvet.

CRENELLATIONS. Battlements.

CUPOLA. Dome.

DIPTYCH. Painting or ivory tablet in two sections.

DUOMO. Cathedral.

EXEDRA. Semi-circular recess.

EX-VOTO. Tablet or small painting expressing gratitude to a saint.

GREEK CROSS. Cross with arms of equal length.

HERM. Quadrangular pillar decreasing in girth towards the ground, surmounted by a bust.

ICONOSTASIS. High balustrade with figures of saints, guarding the sanctuary of a Byzantine church.

INTARSIA. Inlay of wood, marble, or metal.

LATIN CROSS. Cross with a long vertical arm.

LOGGIA. Covered gallery.

LUNETTE. Semi-circular space in a vault or ceiling often decorated with a painting or relief.

MATRONEUM. Gallery reserved for women in early Christian churches.

MONSTRANCE. A vessel for displaying the Host.

NARTHEX. Vestibule of a Christian basilica.

NIELLO. A black substance used in an engraved design.

OGEE (ARCH). Shaped in a double curve, convex above and concave below.

OPUS ALEXANDRINUM. Mosaic design of black and red geometric figures on a white ground.

PALAZZO. Palace; any dignified and important building.

PALI. Wood piles used as foundations for buildings in Venice; and the mooring posts in front of palaces showing the colours of the livery of their proprietors.

PATEN. Flat dish on which the Host is placed.

PATERA (pl. *paterae*). Small circular carved ornament (often Byzantine), sometimes used as a decorative feature on facades in Venice.

PAVONAZZETTO. Yellow marble blotched with blue.

PAX. Sacred object used by a priest for the blessing of peace, and offered for the kiss of the faithful, usually circular, engraved, enamelled or painted in a rich gold or silver frame.

PENDENTIVE. Concave spandrel beneath a dome.

PIANO NOBILE. The main floor of a house, and usually the principal architectural feature of the facade.

PIETÀ. Group of the Virgin mourning the dead Christ.

PLUTEUS (pl. *plutei*). Marble panel, usually decorated; a series of them are often used to form a parapet to precede the altar of a church.

POLYPTYCH. Painting or panel in more than three sections.

PORTEGO. The central hall of a Venetian house, usually running the whole depth of the building.

PREDELLA. Small painting attached below a large altarpiece.

PRONAOS. Porch in front of the cella of a temple.

PROTO. 'Protomagister', chief architect.

PUTTO (pl. *putti*). Figure sculpted or painted usually nude, of a child.

QUADRATURA. Painted architectural perspectives.

QUATREFOIL. Four-lobed cusp (on an arch).

REREDOS. Decorated screen rising behind an altar.

ROOD-SCREEN. A screen below the Rood or Crucifix dividing the nave from the chancel of a church.

SCUOLA (pl. *Scuole*). Lay confraternity, dedicated to charitable works.

SOFFIT. Underside or intrados of an arch.

STILTED ARCH. Round arch that rises vertically before it springs.

STOUP. Vessel for Holy Water usually near the W door of a church.

STYLOBATE. Basement of a columned temple or other building.

TELAMONES, see *Atlantes*.

TENEBROSO. Dark-toned, shadowy.

TESSERA. Small cube of marble, glass, etc. used in mosaic work.

TRANSENNA. Open grille or screen, usually of marble, in an early Christian church.

TREFOIL. Three-lobed cusp (on an arch).

TRIPTYCH. Painting or tablet in three sections.

VILLA. Country house with its garden.

ZOIA. Doge's horned cap decorated with jewels for state ceremonies.

The terms QUATTROCENTRO, CINQUECENTO (abbreviated in Italy '400, '500, etc.), refer not to the 14C and 16C, but to the 'fourteen-hundreds' and 'fifteen-hundreds', i.e. the 15C and 15C, etc .

# HISTORICAL SKETCH OF VENICE

The inhabitants of the cities of the Roman Empire in the upper Adriatic who took refuge in the lagoon from the barbarian invasions (5–6C) decided to make their shelter a permanent home when they saw the Lombard rule firmly established on the mainland. The population of Altino migrated to Torcello which became the commercial centre; the patriarch of Aquileia moved to Grado; and the inhabitants of Oderzo moved to Cittanova, which, renamed Heraclea, became the political centre (later transferred to Malamocco). In the 6C and 7C the Venetian lagoon was subject to Byzantium and governed by 'maritime tribunes' who, though elected by the local nobility, were subject to the veto of the emperor. The traditional date of the election of the first 'dux' (doge) is 697; but it is more likely a leader from Heraclea was given this title c 726. At first nominated by the emperor, after 742 he was elected, though subject to ratification from Byzantium until the 10C. A decisive Venetian victory in 810 at Malamocco foiled the attempt by Pepin, son of Charlemagne, to capture the lagoon. The capital was now moved to the safer islands of the Rialto in the centre of the lagoon. At this time a treaty between the Western and Eastern Empires recognized Venice as an independent Byzantine province removed from the affairs of the Italian mainland. The building activity in the city was given further impetus in 828 when the body of St Mark was brought from Alexandria by Venetian merchants and the Basilica was erected to enshrine the city's new patron saint.

The political and commercial conquest of the East now began. Doge Pietro Orseolo II (991–1008), one of the greatest doges in the history of the Republic, established commercial terms with Constantinople and the Western Empire. By the end of the 11C Venice had quelled the pirates of the Narenta and acquired control of the Dalmatian coast, had prohibited a Norman landing in Albania, and were enjoying trading privileges throughout the Byzantine Empire. In the 12C Venice drew commercial profit from the Crusades, and established trading stations along the Balkan coast and as far East as the Sea of Azov and Palestine. Her ship-building activities were now concentrated in the Arsenal. Though remaining independent at first from Italian affairs, Venice joined the Lombard League against Barbarossa. The city was chosen as the scene for the reconciliation in 1177 of the Papacy with the Empire, when doge Sebastiano Ziani played host to Alexander III and Frederick Barbarossa. By the influence of doge Enrico Dandolo the Venetians led the ships of the Fourth Crusade to the conquest of Constantinople (1202–4) and the establishment of the Latin Eastern Empire, keeping for themselves the major part of the captured booty and territory. This outstanding success was capped by the conquest of the Cyclades and Crete. The rivalry that followed with Genoa, the other great Italian maritime power, lasted throughout the 13C and 14C and culminated in the war of 1378–80 when Venice was within an ace of destruction, but, thanks to the resource of Vettor Pisani, she defeated the enemy at Chioggia. In 1300, with a population of about 120,000, Venice was one of the largest cities in Europe. The plague of 1347–49 killed some 50 per cent or 60 per cent of the inhabitants.

*Detail of the bird's-eye view of Venice in 1500 by Jac. de' Barbari*

In the 15C Venice became the chief bulwark of Christendom against the Ottoman power. At first she tried to come to terms, but after the fall of Constantinople in 1453 she lost piece by piece her Eastern empire—Negropont, Argos, Lépanto, Scútari, the Morea, and finally Cyprus, which had been ceded to Venice by Caterina Cornaro (Cornér) in 1489. The heroic stand of this last island ended in the torture and death of Marcantonio Bragadin, the gallant defender of Famagusta, on 17 Aug 1571.

At the same time the Venetians were occupied in defending themselves on the Italian mainland and keeping open their river ports. The expansion of Venetian power on the mainland had begun with the conquest of the March of Treviso in 1338, and was followed by the voluntary surrender of Feltre, Belluno, Vicenza, and Bassano. Padua and Verona fell in 1406, Udine and the Friuli in 1420, Bergamo and Brescia in 1428, Legnano in 1440, Ravenna in 1442, Crema in 1454, Rovigo in 1484, and Cremona in 1499. All these conquests except Ravenna were retained until the fall of the Republic; but they were only won after a hard struggle directed especially during the dogeship of Fr. Foscari against Fil. Maria, last of the Visconti. At the age of 84 Foscari was at last forced by the Council of Ten to abdicate (1457). In the wars with the Visconti some of the most famous condottieri were employed: Gattamelata, Colleoni, Francesco Sforza, and Carmagnola, the last of whom was unjustly beheaded for treason in 1432. Besides her permanent conquests Venice held brief control of Rimini, Cesena, Imola, Rovereto, Gorizia, Trieste, and Fiume, and the extent of her power, which aroused the jealousy of Europe, led to the formation of the League of Cambrai in 1508. With almost all Europe against her, the skilful diplomacy of doge Leonardo Loredan led to squabbling among the allies, and Pope Julius II came to her assistance. In the 16C Venice had more inhabitants than in any other period of her history: the population rose to 190,000 before the plague of 1575–77 wiped out one third of the inhabitants.

The discovery of America and the circumnavigation of the Cape deprived Venice of her pre-eminent commercial position, and the slow decline of the Republic as a supreme power set in. The project to pierce the isthmus of Suez was checkmated by the war of 1508. In one of the most famous naval battles in history the Turks were finally defeated off Lépanto in 1571; 111 of the 208 Christian ships were Venetian. In a dispute between doge Leonardo Donà and pope Paul V over the rights of the civil power, the Pope, though he placed Venice under an interdict, was forced to give way, thanks largely to the able defence of the city's cause by Fra Paolo Sarpi. The war of Gradisca (1615–17), instigated by Austria, brought little good to the Republic and the defence of Crete against the Turks (1644–69) further exhausted her resources. The brief reconquest of the Morea in 1699 by Francesco Morosini (later elected Doge) lasted only till 1718. Meanwhile the commercial prowess of Venice had suffered irreparably with the emergence of the European States.

In the 18C the decadence of the Republic became evident. The worn-out political system was unable and unwilling to adapt itself to changed circumstances. On 17 May 1797, Napoleon entered the city without trouble and deposed the last of 120 doges, Lodovico Manin. By the treaty of Campo Formio (17 Oct 1797), Venice itself was ceded to Austria, and most of her territory on the terraferma was united with the Cisalpine Republic. The treaty of Pressburg (26 Dec 1805) restored Venice to Italy, but, with the fall of Napoleon, the whole of

Venetia reverted to Austria. The rising of 1848 led to the formation of a Republic under Daniele Manin, which offered a heroic resistance to Austria until 21 Aug 1849, being subjected to the first air raid in history when bombs were dropped from balloons by means of pre-set fuses. In 1866 Venice was finally reunited to Italy. During the First World War 620 bombs were dropped on the city, though without grave damage to artistic monuments.

The construction in the 1920s and 30s of a large commercial harbour and oil refinery at Marghera won back much of her pre-eminence in trade, although the consequences of pollution were disregarded, and the delicate physical balance between the lagoon, the open sea, and the mainland altered as a result. Restricted by her geographical limits Venice did not experience the post-war expansion typical of other big cities. Indeed, the old city suffers from a slow decrease in population. The expansion of Mestre on the mainland has, to a certain extent, answered a need for new economic outlets, and a referendum in 1979 confirmed the wish of the Venetians of the historical city and of Mestre to remain as one municipality.

The **Republican Constitution**, at first democratic, gradually became oligarchic, the power being concentrated in the hands of a few families. The appointment of Councillors and Senators limited the power of the Doge, and in 1044 the procedure for the election of the Doge was formalized in order to prevent nepotism. In 1172–3 the Maggior Consiglio, or Great Council, was formed, an assembly of nearly 500 Venetians who held office for one year only and were responsible for appointing all the chief officials of the State. In the 13C a complicated system was introduced for the election of the Doge. The 'Serrata del Maggior Consiglio' (1297), literally the 'locking' of the Great Council restricted to the nobility those eligible for election. In 1315 the members of the nobility were formerly registered in the 'Libro d'Oro' (Golden Book). The size of the Council varied; the greatest number it reached was 1700. The rebellion of the Tiepolos and Querini in 1310 against doge Pietro Gradenigo was quickly put down, but led to the appointment of the Council of Ten for the punishment of crimes against the State. This Council in 1355 beheaded doge Marin Falier, who had tried to turn his elective office into a despotic seigniory.

At the height of its power the government of the Republic was organized as follows: the *Executive Power* lay with the Doge, six Councillors, and three leaders of the Quarantia (a tribunal of 40 members), who together made up the 'Serenissima Signoria'; the *Legislative Power* was vested in the Maggior Consiglio, the Senate, and the Collegio, a sort of Parliamentary committee; the *Judicial Power* was managed by the Council of Ten, the Inquisitori di Stato, the Avogadori del Comune, the Quarantia (see above), the Signori di Notte, and other officials.

Among famous Venetians are Marco Polo (1256–1324), the first European to travel in the Far East; Marin Sanudo the elder (1270–1343) and Fra Mauro (15C) the geographers; Marin Sanudo the younger (1466–1536) and Pietro Bembo (1470–1547), the humanists (the latter was appointed official historian of the city); John Cabot (1420–98) and Sebastian Cabot (1477–1537), who explored the coast of America from Hudson's Bay to Florida and were the first to touch the American mainland; Fra Paolo Sarpi (1552–1623), the writer (comp. p 42); Carlo Goldoni (1707–93), writer of comedies; and five popes: Gregory XII, Eugenius IV, Paul II, Alexander VIII, and Clement XIII. Aldus Manutius (1450–1516), the celebrated printer and inventor of italic type, went to Venice in 1490, the first dated book issuing from his press in 1494. Marshal Marmont (1774–1852) died in exile in Venice, and W.D. Howells was U.S. Consul here in 1860–65. Frederick Rolfe, Baron Corvo, spent the last five years of

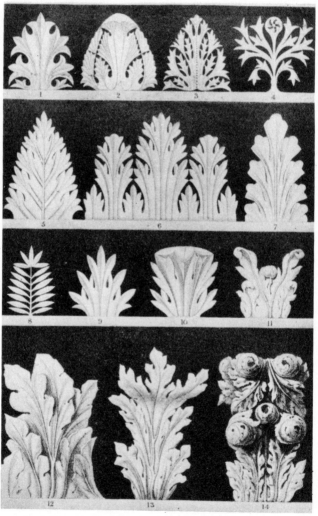

*Leafage of the Venetian capitals from the Byzantine to Gothic periods as observed by John Ruskin for 'The Stones of Venice' (1853)*

his life in Venice and died here in 1913. John Ruskin, one of the most scrupulous observers of the monuments of Venice visited the city on numerous occasions between 1835 and 1888.

Native composers include Giovanni Gabrieli (1557–1612) whose fame attracted Schütz as a pupil; Ant. Vivaldi (c 1677–1741); Tomaso Albinoni (1671–1750); Ermanno Wolf-Ferrari (1876–1948); and Gian Fr. Malipiero (1882–1973). Monteverdi directed the music at St Mark's for thirty years until his death in 1643 when he was followed by his pupil Cavalli (1602–76) who came to Venice from Crema as a chorister, and here followed his master's operatic lead. Cimarosa died in exile in Venice in 1801. Venetian also was Lorenzo Da Ponte 1749–1838), Mozart's librettist. Benjamin Britten composed 'Curlew River' (1964) and much of 'The Prodigal Son' (1968), during stays in Venice.

# List of Doges ＇ ２２０

| | | | |
|---|---|---|---|
| [697–717 | Paoluccio Anafesto] | 1026–1032 | Pietro Centranico |
| [717–726 | Marcello Tegalliano] | 1032–1043 | Domenico Flabanico |
| 726–737 | Orso Ipato | 1043–1071 | Domenico Contarini |
| 737–742 | Interregnum | 1071–1084 | Domenico Selvo |
| 742–755 | Teodato Ipato | 1084–1096 | Vitale Falier |
| 755–756 | Galla Gaulo | 1096–1102 | Vitale Michiel I |
| 756–764 | Domenico Monegario | 1102–1118 | Ordelafo Falier |
| 764–775 | Maurizio Galbaio | 1118–1130 | Domenico Michiel |
| 787–804 | Giovanni Galbaio | 1130–1148 | Pietro Polani |
| 804–811 | Obelario degli Antenori | 1148–1156 | Domenico Morosini |
| 811–827 | Agnello Participazio | 1156–1172 | Vitale Michiel II |
| 827–829 | Giustiniano Participazio | 1172–1178 | Sebastiano Ziani |
| 829–836 | Giovanni Participazio I | 1178–1192 | Orio Mastropiero |
| 836–864 | Pietro Tradonico | 1192–1205 | Enrico Dandolo |
| 864–881 | Orso Participazio I | 1205–1229 | Pietro Ziani |
| 881–887 | Giovanni Participazio II | 1229–1249 | Giacomo Tiepolo |
| 887 | Pietro Candiano I | 1249–1253 | Marin Morosini |
| 888–912 | Pietro Tribuno | 1253–1268 | Ranier Zeno |
| 912–932 | Orso Participazio II | 1268–1275 | Lorenzo Tiepolo |
| 932–939 | Pietro Candiano II | 1275–1280 | Jacopo Contarini |
| 939–942 | Pietro Participazio | 1280–1289 | Giovanni Dandolo |
| 942–959 | Pietro Candiano III | 1289–1311 | Pietro Gradenigo |
| 959–976 | Pietro Candiano IV | 1311–1312 | Marino Zorzi |
| 976–978 | Pietro Orseolo I | 1312–1328 | Giovanni Soranzo |
| 978–979 | Vitale Candiano | 1329–1339 | Francesco Dandolo |
| 979–991 | Tribuno Memmo | 1339–1342 | Bartolomeo Gradenigo |
| 991–1008 | Pietro Orseolo II | 1343–1354 | Andrea Dandolo |
| 1008–1026 | Otto Orseolo | 1354–1355 | Marin Falier |

| | | | |
|---|---|---|---|
| 1355–1356 | Giovanni Gradenigo | 1595–1605 | Marino Grimani |
| 1356–1361 | Giovanni Dolfin | 1606–1612 | Leonardo Donà |
| 1361–1365 | Lorenzo Celsi | 1612–1615 | Marcantonio Memmo |
| 1365–1368 | Marco Corner | 1615–1618 | Giovanni Bembo |
| 1368–1382 | Andrea Contarini | 1618 | Nicolò Donà |
| 1382 | Michele Morosini | 1618–1623 | Antonio Priuli |
| 1382–1400 | Antonio Venier | 1623–1624 | Francesco Contarini |
| 1400–1413 | Michele Steno | 1625–1629 | Giovanni Corner I |
| 1414–1423 | Tommaso Mocenigo | 1630–1631 | Nicolò Contarini |
| 1423–1457 | Francesco Foscari | 1631–1646 | Francesco Erizzo |
| 1457–1462 | Pasquale Malipiero | 1646–1655 | Francesco Molin |
| 1462–1471 | Cristoforo Moro | 1655–1656 | Carlo Contarini |
| 1471–1473 | Nicolò Tron | 1656 | Francesco Corner |
| 1473–1474 | Nicolò Marcello | 1656–1658 | Bertucci Valier |
| 1474–1476 | Pietro Mocenigo | 1658–1659 | Giovanni Pesaro |
| 1476–1478 | Andrea Vendramin | 1659–1675 | Domenico Contarini |
| 1478–1485 | Giovanni Mocenigo | 1675–1676 | Nicolò Sagredo |
| 1485–1486 | Marco Barbarigo | 1676–1684 | Alvise Contarini |
| 1486–1501 | Agostino Barbarigo | 1684–1688 | Mercantonio Giustinian |
| 1501–1521 | Leonardo Loredan | 1688–1694 | Francesco Morosini |
| 1521–1523 | Antonio Grimani | 1694–1700 | Silvestro Valier |
| 1523–1538 | Andrea Gritti | 1700–1709 | Alvise Mocenigo II |
| 1539–1545 | Pietro Lando | 1709–1722 | Giovanni Corner II |
| 1545–1553 | Francesco Donà | 1722–1732 | Alvise Mocenigo III |
| 1553–1554 | Marcantonio Trevisan | 1732–1735 | Carlo Ruzzini |
| 1554–1556 | Francesco Venier | 1735–1741 | Alvise Pisani |
| 1556–1559 | Lorenzo Priuli | 1741–1752 | Pietro Grimani |
| 1559–1567 | Girolamo Priuli | 1752–1762 | Francesco Loredan |
| 1567–1570 | Pietro Loredan | 1762–1763 | Marco Foscarini |
| 1570–1577 | Alvise Mocenigo I | 1763–1778 | Alvise Mocenigo IV |
| 1577–1578 | Sebastiano Venier | 1779–1789 | Paolo Renier |
| 1578–1585 | Nicolò Da Ponte | 1789–1797 | Lodovico Manin |
| 1585–1595 | Pasquale Cicogna | | |

# Topographical Notes

The irregular plan of Venice is traversed by some 100 canals of which the *Grand Canal* divides the city into two unequal parts. The other canals called *Rii* (sing. *rio*), with the exception of *Cannaregio*, have an average breadth of 4–5 metres and are often windy. They are spanned by c 400 bridges, mostly of brick or stone. The streets, nearly all narrow, are called *Calle*; the more important thoroughfares, usually shopping streets, are known as *Calle Larga, Ruga*, or *Salizzada* (the name given to the first paved streets in 1676). Smaller alleys are called *Caletta* or *Ramo*. A street alongside a canal is called a *Fondamenta*; a *Rio Terrà* is a street in the course of a filled-in rio. A *Sottoportego* (or *Sottoportico*) passes beneath buildings. *Piscina* is a place where a pool formerly existed; *Lista* a lane which led up to an ambassador's palace.

The only *Piazza* is that of St Mark; there are two *Piazzette*, one in front of the Doge's Palace, the other the Piazzetta dei Leoncini (now Giovanni XXIII). Other open spaces are called *Campo* (or *Campiello* or *Corte* according to their size). A notable feature of some of the campi is the *Vera da Pozzo*, or well-head, which stands above a cistern into which rain-water was collected through grilles in the pavement. Below ground level the water filtered through sand before reaching the central well shaft.—Numerous *Altane*, open wooden balconies survive on the housetops. The characteristic *Liagò*, protruding loggie, have now almost disappeared.—Some of the most curious corruptions of the Venetian dialect are: San Stae = Sant'Eustachio, San Marcuola = Santi Ermágora e Fortunato, and San Trovaso = Santi Gervasio e Protasio.—Houses are numbered consecutively throughout each of the six *Sestieri* into which the city was divided in the 12C (San Marco, Castello, Dorsoduro, San Polo, Santa Croce, and Cannaregio).

The city is supported on piles of Istrian pine, driven down about $7\frac{1}{2}$ metres to a solid bed of compressed sand and clay, and many of the buildings are built upon a foundation course of Istrian limestone which withstands the corrosion of the sea. Her prosperity as a port is due to the diversion of silt-bearing rivers to the N and S of the lagoon, still effected by channels dug in the 14–15C; and her very existence depends on the control of eroding waters of the Adriatic, which are allowed to flow into the lagoon by only three channels (pp 197, 198). This work, under special supervision as early as the 12C, has been performed since 1501 by a board presided over by the Magistrato alle Acque. Despite these precautions, the city suffered the worst flood for nearly a century in 1966. In 1985 it was decided to construct moveable barriers across the three entrances to the lagoon in order to regulate the high tides. The project will take at least five years to complete (comp. p 7). The *Acque Alte* are described on p 67.

# PRACTICAL INFORMATION

# I  Approaches to Venice

The Approaches from the North are described in 'Blue Guide Northern Italy'.

**Information Bureaux.** General information may be obtained in London from the *Italian State Tourist Office* (*E.N.I.T., Ente Nazionale Italiano per il Turismo*), 1 Princess St, W1, who distribute free an invaluable 'Traveller's Handbook' (revised c every year), an annual list of hotels in Venice, etc. The main information office of the official Venice tourist authorities is on the corner of Piazza San Marco and Calle Ascensione (No. 71C; Pl. 10; 2). They run subsidiary information offices at the Railway Station and at the Marghera exit from the Milan autostrada; and on the Lido (Viale S.M. Elisabetta) in summer. Hotel booking facilities on arrival are run by the Associazione Veneziano Albergatori (A.V.A.) at the Railway Station tourist information office and at Piazzale Roma (Autorimessa Comunale garage).

The weekly publication '**Un Ospite di Venezia**' ('A Guest in Venice') available (free) through information offices, hotels, and agencies gives up-to-date information for the visitor (especially useful for tariffs).

**Travel Agents** (most of whom belong to the Association of British Travel Agents) sell travel tickets and book accommodation, and also organize inclusive tours and charter trips to Venice. These include: *C.I.T.*, 10 Charles II St, SW1. (agents for the Italian State Railways), *Thomas Cook & Son*, 45 Berkeley St, W1, and other branches, *American Express*, 9 Suffolk Place, SW1, etc.

*Tour operators* who offer cheap air package holidays to Venice include: Brompton Travel, C.I.T., Prospect Tours, Heritage, Hayes and Jarvis, Pegasus, Pilgrim-Air, Serenissima, Sovereign, and Thomson.—By train, Venice can be reached by through train from Calais in summer, otherwise via Paris. The luxury *Venice Simplon Orient-Express* now runs twice a week from London via Paris and Milan to Venice (and continues to Florence).—A *European Bus Service* operates from London to Italy (information from the National Travel Office at Victoria Coach Station).

**Passports** or **Visitors Cards** are necessary for all British travellers entering Italy and must bear the photograph of the holder. American travellers must carry passports. British passports valid for ten years are issued at the Passport Office, Clive House, Petty France, London SW1, or may be obtained for an additional fee through any tourist agent. No visa is required for British or American travellers to Italy. Visitors are strongly advised to carry some means of identity with them at all times when in Italy.

**Currency Regulations.** Exchange controls have been suspended by the British Government since 1979. There are now no restrictions on the amount of sterling the traveller may take out of Great Britain. There are frequent variations in the amount of Italian notes which may be taken in or out of Italy. Since there are normally strict limitations the latest regulations should be checked before departure.

**Money.** In Italy the monetary unit is the Italian lira (pl. lire). Notes are issued for 500, 1000, 2000, 5000, 10,000, 20,000, 50,000 and 100,000 lire. Coins are of 5, 10, 20, 50, 100, 200, and 500 lire. The rate of exchange in 1985 is approximately 2,400 lire to the £ and 1,900 lire to the US dollar. Travellers' cheques are the safest way of carrying money while travelling. Certain credit cards are generally accepted. For banking hours, see p 61. Money can also be changed at exchange offices ('cambio'); usually open 7 days a week, at the airport and the station, and (usually at a lower rate) at some hotels, restaurants, and shops.

**Police Registration**. Police Registration is required within three days of entering Italy. For travellers staying at a hotel the management will attend to the formality. The permit lasts three months, but can be extended on application.

**Airport. Marco Polo**, at Tessera on the lagoon 9 kilometres N of Venice, is the airport for both international and internal air services. Direct flights from London, Paris, Munich, Dusseldorf, and Frankfurt. Internal services to Milan, Rome, etc. AIRPORT TERMINAL, Piazzale Roma (Pl. 4; 7; coach service run by A.T.V.O. in connection with scheduled flights). Bus No 5 (A.C.T.V.) runs between Piazzale Roma and the airport every hour. Motor-boats to connect with British Airways, Alitalia, and Air France flights usually leave from the Giardinetti (Pl. 10; 4), although the service was temporarily suspended in 1985. They are run by the Cooperativa San Marco Motoscafi (Tel 35775). The trip takes c 30 min. and is more expensive than the bus but it is the most pleasant way of arriving in the city from the airport.—At night, radio taxis are available at the airport to Piazzale Roma.

**Railway Station. Stazione Santa Lucia** (Pl. 4; 6), near the W end of the Grand Canal. Venice was first connected by rail to the mainland in 1846; the station was rebuilt in 1955. It has a restaurant, an 'albergo diurno' (day hotel; comp. p 53), a left luggage office (open always), a bank, etc. Water-buses (vaporetti and motoscafi), motor-boat taxis, and gondolas from the quay outside. Some of the water-bus services (comp. p 58) and the taxis (unless specifically requested) for San Marco and the Lido take the less attractive short cut by the Rio Nuovo avoiding the first bend of the Grand Canal.

**Car Parks**. Venice was connected to the mainland by a road bridge in 1933. Motorists approaching the city have to leave their vehicles in a multi-story garage or an open-air car park (unless they are going on to the Lido in which case they board the car ferry at Piazzale Roma; comp. p 59). There are no free car parks. Charges vary according to the size of the vehicle; the rates are per day. *Parking space is very limited* especially in summer (the garages are used also by Venetian residents); visitors are strongly advised to approach Venice when possible by rail rather than by road. Automatic signs on the motorway approaches indicate the space available at the time of arrival in the various car parks and garages.

**Piazzale Roma** (Pl. 4; 5, 7). The most convenient car park (multi-story garages) with a landing-stage (served by vaporetto No. 1, 2, and 5) on the Grand Canal, and a taxi-stand. The garage at the end of the bridge is the *Autorimessa Comunale di Venezia* (municipal car park) used almost exclusively by Venetian residents. Other garages here charge considerably more. It is forbidden to park outside in

Piazzale Roma; cars are towed away by the police to Via Torino, Mestre (Tel 780730).—**Isola del Tronchetto** (beyond Pl. 4; 5; comp. Atlas 14). Garage and open-air parking. Direct vaporetto service (No. 34; summer only) every 15 min. to San Marco (in under 20 min.). Bus service (17) to Piazzale Roma (every 20 min.).—**San Giuliano** (comp. Atlas 16). Open-air parking only. Direct vaporetto service (No. 24; summer only) every 15–30 min. to Fondamenta Nuove (Pl. 6; 4) in 30 min. Bus service to Piazzale Roma.—**Fusina** (comp. Atlas 16). Open-air parking only. Direct vaporetto service (No. 16; summer only) every 30 min. to the Zattere (Pl. 9; 6) in 20 min. These last two parks are open only in summer, at Easter and carnival time.

If the car parks are full it is necessary to leave cars on the mainland in Mestre or Marghera, both connected by frequent bus or train services to Venice.

The road approaches to Venice are described in 'Blue Guide Northern Italy'. The city is connected by motorway (autostrada) with Milan (via Brescia, Verona, Vicenza, and Padua), and with Rome, Florence, and Bologna (via Ferrara and Padua); both these routes meet at 'Padova Est' and the exit for Venice is at 'Mestre'. On the motorway from Trieste the most convenient exit for Venice is at 'Mestre Est'.

**Bus Station**, Piazzale Roma (Pl. 4; 7). Services from Padua, Treviso, the Brenta, etc.; see p 60.

**Approaches by Water**. Steamers and cruise ships anchor at the quays alongside Rive dei 7 Martiri (Pl. 12; 3, 6) or at the Stazione Marittima (San Basilio; Pl. 8; 4) on the Giudecca canal (near the landing-stage of motoscafo No. 5; see p 150). Steamer services operate from Turkey, Yugoslavia, Greece, etc. For the 'Burchiello' motor-launch from Padua, see p 60.

Private Boats can sometimes find moorings at the Diporto Velico Veneziano, Sant'Elena (Pl. 13; 6); the port on the Isola di San Giorgio Maggiore (Cini Foundation); or near the Punta della Dogana on the Giudecca canal (information from the Compagnia della Vela, Giardinetti, San Marco). The *Port Authority Office* (Capitaneria di Porto) is on the Fondamenta delle Farine (Pl. 10; 4).

**Porters** (distinguished by their badges) are available in various parts of the city. Although tariffs are fixed the price for each piece of luggage should be established before hiring a porter.

# II  Hotels

Most of the numerous hotels in Venice are near Piazza San Marco; others are to be found near the Rialto bridge, by the Station, or in Dorsoduro. These are all listed with charges in the annual (free) publication of the *Azienda Autonoma Soggiorno Turismo*, 'Venezia: Alberghi*, (available from tourist information offices). Since Venice has a great number of visitors, *it is essential to book well in advance*, especially in summer, at Easter, and at Carnival time; to confirm the booking a deposit should be sent.

Venice is divided into 'Sestiere' (comp. p 47). When writing to a hotel the only address necessary is the name of the Sestiere (San Marco, Dorsoduro, etc.) and the number, as given in the list below.

Many of the luxury five-star and four-star hotels are near San Marco, on the Grand Canal, or on Riva degli Schiavoni. Numerous more simple hotels, often in attractive and quieter positions, are also situated near these areas. One of the most pleasant parts of the city in which to stay is the Dorsoduro, an area less crowded with tourists. The hotels near Piazzale Roma and the station (mostly in Lista di Spagna; Pl. 4; 4 and 5; 3) are convenient (and easy to reach with luggage) but in a much less attractive part of the town. Most of the agents who meet travellers at the station cater for these hotels. They should be borne in mind by those who arrive late at night in Venice since they are closest to the station.

Information about hotels in Venice may be obtained in London from the E.N.I.T. office, and, on arrival, at the official tourist information offices at the Station and on the autostrada. There are booking facilities, run by the Associazione Veneziana Albergatori (A.V.A.), at the Station and at Piazzale Roma (in the Autorimessa Comunale garage).

Every hotel has its fixed charges agreed with the official Tourist Board. In all hotels the service charges are included in the rates. VAT is added at a rate of 9 per cent (14 per cent in 5-star hotels). However, the total charge is exhibited on the back of the door of the hotel room. Prices are raised from 15 March–31 Oct, and 20 Dec–2 Jan. Breakfast should by law be an optional extra but it is now often included in the price of a room. Hotels are now obliged by law (for tax purposes) to issue an official receipt to customers who should not leave the premises without this document ('ricevuta fiscale').

In 1985 a new classification of hotels was introduced indicated by 'stars', as in the rest of Europe. At the same time the official categories of 'Pensione' and 'Locanda' were abolished. There are now five official categories of hotels from the luxury 5-star hotels to the most simple 1-star hotels. In the following list the category has been given. Hotels with more than 100 rooms (100 R) have been indicated. Venice has about 200 hotels and it has been thought necessary to give only a small selection; omission does not imply any derogatory judgement. Some hotels are closed in winter. Rooms to let in private houses can also be found sometimes by asking locally.

## Accommodation in Venice and Environs

5-STAR LUXURY HOTELS. *On Riva degli Schiavoni*: **Danieli** (a; Pl. 11; 1), Castello 4196 (250 R); *On the Grand Canal near San Marco*: **Gritti Palace** (b; Pl. 10; 3), S. Marco 2467; **Bauer Grünwald** (c; Pl. 10; 4), S. Marco 1459 (210 R), **Europa & Regina** (h; Pl. 10; 4), S. Marco 2159 (199 R); *On the Giudecca*: **Cipriani** (d; Pl. 11; 5), Giudecca 10 (with a swimming pool).

4-STAR HOTELS. *Near San Marco*: **Monaco & Grand Canal** (e; Pl. 10; 4), S. Marco 1325; **Luna** (f; Pl. 10; 2, 4), S. Marco 1243 (125 R); **Cavalletto & Doge Orseolo** (n; Pl. 10; 2), S. Marco 1107; **Saturnia & International** (i; Pl. 10; 3), S. Marco 2399; **Splendid Suisse** (g; Pl. 6; 8), S Marco 760 (166 R).—*On Riva degli Schiavoni* : **Gabrielli Sandwirth** (j; Pl. 11; 2), Castello 4110 (110 R); **Londra Palace** (k; Pl. 11; 1), Castello 4171; **Metropole** (l; Pl. 11; 2), Castello 4149.—*Near Piazzale Roma*: **ETAP Park Hotel** (m; Pl. 4; 6), S. Croce 245 (100 R).—*Near the Station*: **Principe** (gg; Pl. 4; 4), Cannaregio 146.

3-STAR HOTELS. *Near San Marco*: **Ala** (o; Pl. 10; 3), S. Marco 2494; **Concordia** (p; Pl. 11; 1), S. Marco 367; **Bonvecchiati** (q; Pl. 10; 2), S. Marco 4488; **Boston** (r; Pl. 10; 2), S. Marco 848; **Casanova** (s; Pl. 10; 2), S. Marco 1284; **Flora** (t; Pl. 10; 3), S. Marco 2283a; **La Fenice et des Artistes** (u; Pl. 10; 1), S. Marco 1936; **Montecarlo** (v; Pl. 11; 1), S. Marco 463; **San Marco** (w; Pl. 10; 2), S. Marco 877;

**Bel Sito & Berlino** (x; Pl. 10; 3), S. Marco 2517; **Patria e Tre Rose** (y; Pl. 10; 2), S. Marco 905; **Panada** (ii; Pl. 10; 2), S. Marco 656; **Do Pozzi** (hh; Pl. 10; 3), S Marco 2373; **Kette** (nn; Pl. 10; 2), S. Marco 2053.—*Near Riva degli Schiavoni:* **Savoia & Jolanda** (z; Pl. 11; 1), Castello 4187; **Bisanzio** (aa; Pl. 11; 2), Castello 3651.—*In San Polo* (on the Grand Canal): **Carpaccio** (bb; Pl. 5; 8), S. Polo 2765.—*Near the Rialto:* **Giorgione** (cc; Pl. 6; 6), Cannaregio 4587; **Malibran** (an; Pl. 6; 6), Cannaregio 5864; **San Cassiano-Ca' Favretto** (ao; Pl. 6; 5), S. Croce 2232.—*On Dorsoduro:* **American** (zz; Pl. 9; 6), Dorsoduro 628.—*Near the Station:* **Al Sole Palace** (dd; Pl. 4; 8), S. Croce 136; **Austria e de la Ville** (ee; Pl. 5; 3), Cannaregio 227; **Continental** (ff; Pl. 4; 4), Cannaregio 166, 119; **Santa Chiara** (ap; Pl. 4; 6), S. Croce 548; **Gardena** (ab; Pl. 4; 6), S. Croce 239.

2-STAR HOTELS. *Near San Marco:* **Astoria** (jj; Pl. 10; 2), S. Marco 951; **Città di Milano** (kk; Pl. 10; 2), S. Marco 590; **Gallini** (ll; Pl. 10; 1), S. Marco 3673; **Firenze** (mm; Pl. 10; 2), S. Marco 1490; **Lisbona** (oo; Pl. 10; 4), S. Marco 2153; **San Moisè** (pp; Pl. 10; 2), S. Marco 2058; **Ateneo** (qq; Pl. 10; 1), S. Marco 1876; **Noemi** (rr; Pl. 10; 2), S. Marco 909; **Serenissima** (ss; Pl. 10; 2), S. Marco 4486; **Scandinavia** (ar; Pl. 6; 8), Castello 5240.—*Near the Rialto:* **Da Bruno** (tt; Pl. 6; 8), Castello 5726a; **Marconi & Milano** (uu; Pl. 6; 7), S. Polo 729.—*Near Riva degli Schiavoni:* **La Residenza** (ag; Pl. 11; 2), Castello 3608; **Paganelli** (vv; Pl. 11; 2), Castello 4182; **Pellegrino & Commercio** (ww; Pl. 11; 1), Castello 4551; **Trovatore** (xx; Pll. 11; 1), Castello 4534.—*In the NW part of the city:* **Madonna dell' Orto** (yy; Pl. 5; 1), Cannaregio 3499.—*On Dorsoduro:* **Accademia** (ah; Pl. 9; 4), Dorsoduro 1058; **La Calcina** (ai; Pl. 9; 6), Dorsoduro 780; **Seguso** (aj; Pl. 9; 6), Dorsoduro 779; **Agli Alboretti** (al; Pl. 9; 4), Dorsoduro 882/4; **Tivoli** (ad; Pl. 9; 1, 2), Dorsoduro 3838.—*Near the Accademia Bridge:* **San Stefano** (aq; Pl. 10; 1), S. Marco 2957.—*Near Piazzale Roma and the Station:* **Nazionale** (ac; Pl. 4; 4), Cannaregio 158; **Abbazia** (Pl. 4; 4), Cannaregio 66.—*On the Giudecca:* **Casa Frollo** (af; Pl. 10; 6), Giudecca 50.

1-STAR HOTELS. *On Dorsoduro:* **Montin** (at; Pl. 9; 3), Dorsoduro 1147; **Alla Salute-da Cici** (ak; Pl. 10; 5), Dorsoduro 222; **Casa de' Stefani** (am; Pl. 9; 1), Dorsoduro 2786, and numerous others.

**Hotels on the Lido.** The Lido (comp. p 195) is a resort with numerous hotels, most of them closed in winter. Some of them have swimming-pools, tennis courts, etc. Travellers wishing to explore the monuments of Venice are strongly advised to choose a hotel in the city itself. 5-STAR HOTEL. *Excelsior,* Lungomare Marconi 41.—4-STAR HOTELS. *des Bains,* Lungomare Marconi 17, *Quattro Fontane,* 16 Via 4 Fontane, *Villa Mabapa,* 16 Riviera S. Nicolò.—3-STAR HOTELS. *Biasutti Adria Urania-Nora,* Via E Dandolo 24; *Cappelli,* 5 Via Perasto; *Helvetia,* Gran Viale 4/6; *Rigel,* Via E Dandolo 13; *Villa Otello,* Via Lepanto 12.—Also 2-star and 1-star hotels.

The island of **Torcello.** The *Locanda Cipriani* (Isola di Torcello 29) is a 3-star hotel (6 rooms; closed in winter).

**Mestre** and **Marghera,** the nearest places to Venice on the mainland, are industrial towns, both with a number of hotels, but these provide no substitute for a stay in Venice itself.

On the coast N of the Lido the resorts of **Cavallino** and **Lido di Jesolo** are both well supplied with hotels.—At the S. end of the lagoon, **Chioggia** and **Sottomarina** (see pp 198, 201) also have a number of hotels.

**Youth Hostel** and **Students' Hostels.** *Italian Youth Hostels Association* (Associazione Italiana Alberghi per la Gioventù), 61 Lungotevere Maresciallo Cadorno, Roma. In Venice, the A.I.G. has offices in Via 2 Aprile, S. Marco 5042 (Tel. 704414). A 'Guide for Foreign Students' giving detailed information on students' hostels, students' facilities, etc., can be obtained from the Italian Ministry of Education, Viale Trastevere, Rome (500 l.). The *Venice Youth Hostel* (Ostello per la Gioventù) is on the Giudecca (Fondamenta Zitelle 86; Pl. 10; 6, 8), in a good position (380 beds). Bookings should be made in advance in writing. —*Students' Hostels* (Casa dello Studente), Dorsoduro 3482/g. and

Foresteria dell' Istituto di Ca' Foscari.—Other hostels, some run by religious organisations, are shown on an annual list supplied by the Tourist Information Offices. Among the Institutes which offer lodgings for young tourists in the summer period are the following: *Domus Cavanis*, Sant'Agnese (Tel. 87374); *Domus Civica*, S Polo 3082 (Tel. 27139; for girls only; open in July, Sept, and early Oct); and the *Istituto Salesiani*, Giardini di Castello (Tel. 85586).

**Camping**. A current list of camping sites is prepared every year by the offical Venice Tourist Offices. Guides to sites and general information is published by the *Federazione Italiana del Campeggio*; available from the *Centro Nazionale Campeggiatori Stranieri*, Casella Postale 649, Florence 50100. The sites nearest Venice on the mainland are on the outskirts of *Mestre* and *Marghera*, near Marco Polo airport ('Alba d'Oro', at *Ca' Noghera*), at *Tessera*, and at *Fusina*.—On the mainland N of the Lido there are numerous camping sites along the coast at *Punta Sabbioni*, *Cavallino*, *Lido di Jésolo*, *Eraclea Mare*, *Cáorle*, and *Bibione*.—In thte S. part of the lagoon, *Chioggia* and *Sottomarina* are also supplied with camping sites.

ALBERGO DIURNO, 'day hotel', off Calle Ascension (Pl. 10; 2), and at the Railway Station, with bathrooms, hairdressers, cleaning services, and other amenities (no sleeping accommodation).

# III  Restaurants and Cafés

Restaurants (*Ristoranti*, *Trattorie*) of all kinds and categories abound in Venice. The least pretentious restaurant often provides the best value. Prices on the menu generally do not include a cover charge (*coperto*, shown separately on the menu) which is added to the bill. The service charge is now almost always automatically added at the end of the bill. Tipping is therefore not strictly necessary, but a few hundred lire are appreciated. The menu displayed outside the restaurant indicates the kind of charges the customer should expect. However, many simpler establishments do not offer a menu, and here, although the choice is usually limited the standard of cuisine is often very high. Lunch is normally around 1 o'clock and is the main meal of the day, while dinner is around 8 or 9 o'clock. Restaurants are now obliged by law (for tax purposes) to issue an official receipt to customers, who should not leave the premises withuot this document ('ricevuta fiscale').

Many of the numerous restaurants near San Marco cater to the international tourist market; simpler trattorie (often better value) are to be found away from this area (in the smaller campi, etc.). Although some restaurants serve excellent fish (always more expensive than meat) the general standard of Venetian cooking can be disappointing.

In the list below a selection of restaurants has been given grouped according to price range.

1. Luxury-class well-known restaurants, mostly with international cuisine. Not cheap, and frequented also by travellers on expense accounts.

*Al Conte Pescaor*, 544 Piscina S. Zulian (Pl. 6; 8)
*Al Graspo de Ua*, Calle dei Bombaseri (San Bartolomeo, Pl. 6; 7)
*A la vecia cavana*, 4624 Rio terrà SS. Apostoli (Pl. 6; 6)
*Antico Martini*, Campo San Fantin (Pl. 10; 1)
*Harry's Bar*, Calle Vallaresso (Pl. 10; 4)
*Quadri*, 120 Piazza San Marco (Pl. 10; 2)
*Taverna La Fenice*, Campiello della Fenice (Pl. 10; 1)
*Do Forni*, 470 Calle Specchieri (Pl. 11; 1)

The restaurants in the following luxury-class hotels have superb positions:
*Gritti* (Pl. 10; 3)
*Danieli* (Pl. 11; 1)
*Cipriani* (Pl. 11; 5)

2. First-class Restaurants.

*Alle Poste Vecie*, 1608 Pescheria (Pl. 6; 5)
*Al Campiello*, Calle dei Fuseri (Pl. 10; 2)
*Antico Panada*, 656 Calle Larga S. Marco (Pl. 10; 2–Pl. 11; 1)
*Città di Milano*, Campiello San Zulian (Pl. 10; 2)
*Corte Sconta*, Calle del Pestrin (Pl. 12; 1)
*Da Arturo*, Calle degli Assassini (Pl. 10; 1)
*Da Fiore*, Calle del Scaleter (Pl. 5; 8)
*Da Raffaele*, Fondamenta delle Ostreghe (Pl. 10; 3)
*Fiaschetteria Toscana*, Sottoportico del Remer (S Giovanni Crisostomo, Pl. 6; 6)
*Harry's Dolci*, near Sant'Eufemia on the Giudecca (Pl. 9; 5; in a splendid position run by Cipriani, also a 'snack bar')
*La Colomba*, Piscina di Frezzeria (Pl. 10; 2)
*La Furatola*, Calle Lunga San Barnaba (Pl. 9; 3)
*Malamocco*, Campiello del Vin (Pl. 11; 1)
*Madonna*, Calle della Madonna (Pl. 6; 7)
*Noemi*, Calle dei Fabbri (Pl. 10; 2)

3. Well-known restaurants and trattorie.

*Al Gaffaro*, 164 Fondamenta Minotto (Pl. 4; 8)
*Antica Besseta*, Salizzada Zusto (near San Giacomo dell'Orio; Pl. 5; 5)
*Cantinone Storico*, 661 Fondamenta Bragadin (Pl. 9; 4, 6)
*Da Ignazio*, Calle dei Saoneri (Pl. 5; 8)
*Montin*, Fondamenta di Borgo (Pl. 9; 3)
*Pordenone*, Calle d. Madonetta (S Polo; Pl. 5; 8)

4. Simple trattorie of good value.

*Alla Rampa*, Via Garibaldi (Pl. 12; 4)
*Altanella*, Calle dell'Erba (Pl. 9; 8)
*Antica Mola*, Fondamenta degli Ormesini (Pl. 5; 2)
*Città di Vittoria*, 1591 Frezzeria (Pl. 10; 2)
*San Trovaso*, Fondamenta Priuli (Pl. 9; 4)

5. 'Osterie' (who sell wine by the glass and good simple food) and cheap eating places (usually crowded and often less comfortable than normal trattorie).

*Al Mascaron*, Calle Lunga Santa Maria Formosa (Pl. 7; 7)
*Al Milion*, behind the church of San Giovanni Crisostomo (Pl. 6; 6)
*Al Volto*, Calle Cavalli (Riva del Carbon; Pl. 6; 7)
*Do Mori*, off Ruga Vecchia San Giovanni Elemosinario; (Pl. 6; 7)
*Fiaschetteria Toscana*, Sottoportico del Remer (S Giovanni Crisostomo; Pl. 6; 6)
*Osteria Antico Dolo*, near Calle del Paradiso, San Polo (Pl. 6; 7)
*Osteria ai Postali*, 821 Rio Marin, Santa Croce (Pl. 5; 5)

There are a number of self-service restaurants in the centre of the city (notably in the Frezzeria). Pizzas and other good hot snacks are served in a *Pizzeria*, *Rosticceria*, and *Tavola Calda*. Some of these have no seating accommodation and sell food to take away or eat on the spot. There are several pizzerie with tables outside on the Zattere (Pl. 9; 6). Sandwiches ('panini') can be ordered from some *Alimentari* (grocery shops), and *Fornai* (bakeries) often sell individual pizze, cakes, etc.

**Restaurants in the Venetian Lagoon**: Rte 15. **Murano** has a number of simple trattorie.—Rte 16. **Burano** has good fish restaurants, notably *Da Romano*. On **Mazzorbo**, *alla Maddalena*, a first-class restaurant, serves wild duck. **Torcello** has a luxury-class restaurant at the *Locanda Cipriani*, and two other trattorie, recently opened.—Rte 17. On the **Lido**: *al Porticciolo*, and *da Valentino*, among others; *Da Nane al Canton*, and *Da Memo* at **San Pietro in Volta**.—Rte 18. **Chioggia** has good fish restaurants.

**Cafés** (*Bar*) which are open from early morning to 8 or 9 o'clock at night (those with tables outside remain open longer on summer evenings), serve numerous varieties of excellent refreshments which are usually eaten standing up. The cashier should be paid first, and the receipt given to the barman in order to get served. It has become customary to leave a small tip of 100 lire for the barman. If the customer sits at a table the charge is considerably higher (about double) and he will be given waiter service (and should not pay first). Black coffee (*caffè* or *espresso*) can be ordered diluted (*lungo*), with a dash of milk (*macchiato*), with a liquor (*corretto*), or with hot milk (*cappuccino* or *caffè-latte*). In summer cold coffee (*caffè freddo*) and cold coffee and milk (*caffè-latte freddo*) are served.

The two most famous cafés in the city are *Florian* and *Quadri* in Piazza San Marco, with tables outside and orchestras; customers are charged extra for their magnificent surroundings. *Harry's Bar* (Pl. 10; 4) is the most celebrated cocktail bar. The *Danieli* and *Gritti* hotels also have renowned foyer bars.

Among the best cafés for ice-cream ('*Gelaterie*') are *Nico*, on the Zattere (Pl. 9; 6), and *Paolin* in Campo Santo Stefano (Pl. 9; 2). The best cake-shops ('*Pasticceria*') include *Colussi* in the Calle Lunga San Barnaba (Pl. 9; 3), *Marchini* in Calle del Spezier (Pl. 10; 1, 3); *Vio* in Rio Manin, and *Rosa Salva*, Merceria San Salvador and Campo S. Luca.

**Food and Wine**. The chief speciality of Italian cookery is the *pasta asciutta*, served in various forms with different sauces and sprinkled with cheese. *Risotto* is also a favourite Venetian first course. *Zuppa di pesce*, fish stew, is almost a meal in itself. Raw Parma ham (*prosciutto crudo*) is particularly good (the best quality is known as 'San Daniele') in Venice as elsewhere in northern Italy; it is often served with melon or green figs. Among the main dishes is *Fegato alla Veneziana*, calf's liver thinly sliced and fried with onions. The chief speciality of Venetian cooking however is fish, often served grilled, boiled, or fried (*Fritto misto*, usually fried octopus, squid, cuttlefish, prawns, etc.). Among the more unusual dishes are *Seppie*, cuttlefish, usually cooked in their own ink and served with polenta; *Sampiero*, John Dory; *Anguilla alla Veneziana*, eels cooked in lemon and tunny fish; *Baccala mantecato*, salt cod simmered in milk; and *Sardelle in saor* (fried sardines marinated in vinegar and onions, served cold). Venetian confectionery, cakes, and pastries are renowned.

**Wines**. It is often advisable to accept the 'house wine' (*vino della casa* or *vino sfuso*); white and red usually available. This varies a great deal, but is normally a 'vin ordinaire' of average standard and reasonable price. Bottled wines normally served in Venice include wines from the Verona area (*Valpolicella*, *Soave*, and *Bardolino*), and from the Friuli region (*Pinot*, *Merlot*, *Tocai*, and *Cabernet*). Excellent white wines from the Alto Adige are also sometimes available (particularly good are those from *Tramin*, *Lake Caldaro*, and *Novacella*). *Prosecco* and *Cartizze*, sparkling white wines from Conegliano, are popular as aperitifs.

The MENU which follows includes many dishes that are likely to be met with:

**Antipasti**, Hors d'oeuvre

*Prosciutto crudo o cotto*, Ham, raw or cooked
*Prosciutto e melone*, Ham (usually raw) and melon
*Salame*, Salami
*Salame con funghi e carciofini sott'olio*, Salami with mushrooms and artichokes in oil
*Tonno*, Tunny fish
*Bresaola*, Cured beef
*Salsicce*, Dry sausage
*Frittata*, Omelette
*Verdura cruda*, Raw vegetables
*Carciofi o finocchio in pinzimonio*, Raw artichokes or fennel with a dressing
*Antipasto misto*, Mixed cold hors d'oeuvre
*Antipasto di mare*, Seafood hors d'oeuvre
*Sarde in saor*, Fried sardines, served cold with vinegar and onions

**Minestre e Pasta**, Soups and Pasta

*Minestra, zuppa*, Thick soup
*Brodo*, Clear soup
*Stracciatella*, Broth with beaten egg
*Minestrone alla toscana*, Tuscan vegetable soup
*Taglierini (or Tagliolini) in brodo*, Thin pasta in broth
*Spaghetti al sugo* or *al ragù*, Spaghetti with a meat sauce
*Spaghetti al pomodoro*, Spaghetti with a tomato sauce
*Penne all'arrabbiata*, Short pasta with a rich spicy sauce
*Tagliatelle*, Flat spaghetti-like pasta, almost always made with egg
*Lasagne*, Layers of pasta with meat filling and cheese and tomato sauce
*Cannelloni*, Rolled pasta 'pancakes' with meat filling and cheese and tomato sauce
*Ravioli*, Pasta filled with spinach and ricotta cheese (or with minced veal)
*Tortellini*, Small coils of pasta, filled with a rich stuffing served either in broth or with a sauce
*Fettuccine*, Ribbon noodles
*Spaghetti alla carbonara*, Spaghetti with bacon, beaten egg, and black pepper sauce
*Spaghetti alla matriciana*, Spaghetti with salt pork and tomato sauce
*Spaghetti alle vongole*, Spaghetti with clams
*Cappelletti*, Form of ravioli often served in broth
*Gnocchi*, A heavy pasta made from potato, flour, and eggs
*Gnocchi alla parigina*, Pasta made from maize
*Risotto*, Rice dish
*Risotto di mare*, . . . with fish
*Risi e bisi*, Risotto cooked with peas and ham
*Polenta*, Yellow maize flour, usually served with a meat or tomato sauce

**Pesce**, Fish

*Zuppa di pesce*, a variety of fish cooked in a light tomato sauce (or soup)
*Fritto misto di mare*, a variety of fried fish and crustaceans
*Fritto di pesce*, Fried fish
*Pesce arrosto, Pesce alla griglia*, Roast, grilled fish
*Pescespada*, Sword-fish
*Aragosta*, Lobster (an expensive delicacy)
*Calamari*, Squid
*Sarde*, Sardines
*Coda di Rospo*, Angler fish
*Dentice*, Dentex
*Orata*, Bream
*Triglie*, Red mullet
*Sgombro*, Mackerel
*Cefalo*, Grey mullet
*Baccalà*, Salt cod
*Sampiero*, John Dory
*Anguilla (alla Veneziana)*, Eel (cooked in lemon and tunny fish)

*Sogliola*, Sole
*Tonno*, Tunny fish
*Trota*, Trout
*Cozze*, Mussels
*Gamberi*, Prawns
*Polipi*, Octopus
*Seppie*, Cuttlefish
*Cannocchie* (or *Pannocchie*), Mantis shrimp

**Pietanze**, Entrèes

*Vitello*, Veal
*Manzo*, Beef
*Agnello*, Lamb
*Maiale* (*arrosto*), Pork (roast)
*Pollo* (*bollito*), Chicken (boiled)
*Petto di Pollo*, Chicken breasts
*Pollo alla Cacciatora*, Chicken with herbs, and (usually) tomato and pimento sauce
*Costoletta alla Bolognese*, Veal cutlet with ham, covered with melted cheese
*Costolette Milanese*, Veal cutlets, fried in breadcrumbs
*Saltimbocca*, Rolled veal with ham
*Bocconcini*, As above, with cheese
*Scaloppine al marsala*, Veal escalope cooked in wine
*Ossobuco*, Stewed shin of veal
*Coda alla vaccinara*, Oxtail cooked with herbs and wine
*Stufato*, Stewed meat served in pieces in a sauce
*Polpette*, Meat balls (often served in a sauce)
*Involtini*, Thin rolled slices of meat in a sauce
*Spezzatino*, Veal stew, usually with pimento, tomato, onion, peas, and wine
*Cotechino e Zampone*, Pig's trotter stuffed with pork and sausages
*Stracotto*, Beek cooked in a sauce, or in red wine
*Trippa*, Tripe
*Fegato* (*alla Veneziano*), Calf's liver thinly sliced and fried with onions
*Tacchino arrosto*, Roast turkey
*Cervello*, Brains
*Rognoncini trifolata*, Sliced kidneys in a sauce
*Animelle*, Sweetbreads
*Bollito*, Stew of various boiled meats
*Coniglio*, Rabbit

**Contorni**, Vegetables

*Insalata verde*, Green salad
*Insalata mista*, Mixed salad
*Pomodori*, Tomatoes
*Funghi*, Mushrooms
*Spinaci*, Spinach
*Broccoletti*, Tender broccoli
*Piselli*, Peas
*Fagiolini*, Beans (French)
*Carciofi*, Artichokes
*Asparagi*, Asparagus
*Zucchini*, Courgettes
*Melanzane*, Aubergine
*Melanzane alla parmigiana*, Aubergine in cheese sauce
*Peperoni*, Pimentoes
*Peperonata*, Stewed pimentoes, often with aubergine, onion, tomato, potato, etc.
*Finocchi*, Fennel
*Patatine fritte*, Fried potatoes

**Dolci**, Sweets

*Torta*, Tart
*Monte Bianco*, Mont Blanc (with chestnut flavouring)

*Saint Honorè*, Rich meringue cake
*Gelato*, Ice cream
*Cassata*, Ice cream cake
*Zuppa inglese*, Trifle

**Frutta**, Fruit

*Macedonia di frutta*, Fruit salad
*Fragole con panna*, Strawberries and cream
*Fragole al limone* . . . with lemon
*Fragoline di bosco*, Wild strawberries
*Mele*, Apples
*Pere*, Pears
*Arance*, Oranges
*Ciliege*, Cherries
*Pesche*, Peaches
*Albicocche*, Apricots
*Uva*, Grapes
*Fichi*, Figs
*Melone*, Melon
*Popone*, Water melon

# IV  Transport

**Water-buses**. An excellent service is run by A.C.T.V. (*Azienda del Consorzio Trasporti Veneziano*; formerly A.C.N.I.L.). Their headquarters are in Corte dell'Albero (next to the Sant'Angelo landing-stage on the Grand Canal). A plan of the transport in the city is given on Atlas pages 14–15. Tickets can be bought at most landing-stages; the most convenient way is to purchase a book of 10 or 20 tickets which have to be stamped at automatic machines on the landing-stages before each journey. If tickets are bought on board the fare is considerably higher. The '**Vaporetti**' (220 pers.) are more comfortable and provide better views for the visitor than the smaller and faster '**Motoscafi**' (130 pers.). The fare is the same on most lines (including the 'Accelerato', No. 1) but it is more on the 'Diretto' (No. 2 and No. 4). A tourist ticket ('Biglietto Turistico') may be purchased at any landing-stage which gives free transport on any line for one day. It is also possible to purchase a Venice 'pass' ('Carta Venezia') which entitles the holder to travel at greatly reduced fares. This can only be obtained in person at the A.C.T.V. office (comp. above) and must bear the photograph of the holder (it is valid for 3 years). Season tickets are also available at the A.C.T.V. office. Suitcases must be paid for. Most of the services run at frequent intervals (every 10 min.); when a boat is particularly crowded it is worth waiting for the next one. Timetables are displayed at all landing-stages; the summer timetable comes into force on 1 June and operates until the last day of September.

#### Water buses: Vaporetti and Motoscafi

**1** 'Accelerato', the line most frequently used which runs along the Grand Canal. It operates every 10 min. by day, and also throughout the night c every hr. It takes c 1 hr with 19 stops between Piazzale Roma and the Lido: *Piazzale Roma* (Car Park)—*Ferrovia* (Railway Station)—*Riva di Biasio*—*San Marcuola*—*San Stae* (Ca' Pesaro)—*Ca' d'Oro*—*Rialto*—*San Silvestro*—*Sant'Angelo*—*San Tomà* (Frari)—*Ca' Rezzonico*—*Accademia*—*Santa Maria del Giglio*—*Santa Maria della Salute*—*San Marco* (Vallaresso)—*San Zaccaria*—*Arsenale*—*Giardini*—*Sant'Elena*—*Lido*.

**2** 'Diretto', the motoscafo which takes the short cut to the Station and Piazzale Roma along the Rio Nuovo (every 10 min.; night service at less frequent intervals, in summer only). *Rialto—San Marcuola—Ferrovia—Piazzale Roma—San Samuele—Accademia—San Marco (Vallaresso)—San Zaccaria—Sant' Elena—Lido.*

**5** 'Circolare sinistra' and 'circolare destra'. Two services which provide a left circular and a right circular route of the city: *Murano—San Michele (Cimitero)—Fondamente Nuove—Ospedale Civile—Celestia—Campo della Tana (Arsenal)—San Zaccaria—Isola di San Giorgio Maggiore—Zitelle—Redentore—Sant' Eufemia—Zattere—San Basilio—Sacca Fisola—Santa Marta—Piazzale Roma—Ferrovia—Ponte Guglie (Cannaregio canal)—Ponte Tre Archi—Sant' Alvise—Madonna dell'Orto—Fondamente Nuove—San Michele (Cimitero)—Murano.*

**6** *Riva Schiavoni—Lido* (direct), by steamer (offering fine views of the city on the approach from the Lido).

**8** *Monumento Vitt. Emanuele—S. Zaccaria—Isola di S. Giorgio—Zitelle—Redentore—Traghetto—Zattere—S. Eufemia—S. Basilio—Sacca Fisola—S. Marta.*

**9** 'Traghetto,' the ferry across the Giudecca canal: *Zattere—Giudecca* (near Sant'Eufemia).

**10** 'Ospedali', the service which runs to the minor islands in the southern part of the lagoon (some of which are hospitals). *Monumento Vittorio Emanuele—Grazia—San Servolo—San Lazzaro—San Clemente.*

**11** The service for Pellestrina and Chioggia (bus connections are used for part of the journey) which runs c every hour. *Lido—Alberoni—Santa Maria del Mare—Pellestrina—Chioggia.* The trip takes about 1½ hrs.

**12** The regular service for Burano and Torcello islands, every 1–1½ hrs in c 40 min. *Fondamente Nuove—Murano* (Faro)*—Mazzorbo—Torcello—Burano—Treporti.*

**13** *Fondamente Nuove—Murano* (Faro)*—Vignole—Sant'Erasmo.*

**14** (Steamer service) *Riva Schiavoni—Sant' Elena—Lido* (Santa Maria Elisabetta; in winter only).*—Lido* (San Nicolò)*—Punta Sabbioni.*

**20** *Monumento Vitt. Emanuele—S. Servolo—Isola di S. Lazzaro degli Armeni.*

**34** (express service every 20–25 min.) *Tronchetto—Piazzale Roma—Station—San Marco* (via the Grand Canal).

**Car Ferry** (No. 17) from *Piazzale Roma* (Tronchetto) via the Giudecca canal to the *Lido* (and 3 times a day continuing to *Punta Sabbioni*) c every hour; to the Lido in ½ hr, to Punta Sabbioni in 1 hr 10 min. On the Lido the boat docks near San Nicolò (N of S.M. Elisabetta).

SUMMER SERVICES

**3** *Tronchetto* (car park)*—San Marco.*

**4** 'Turistico', a service for visitors from Piazzale Roma along the Grand Canal to the Lido (but with fewer stops than the Accelerato, No. 1). Every 20 min. in c 40 minutes. *Piazzale Roma—Ferrovia—Rialto—San Tomà* (Frari)*—Accademia San Marco (Vallaresso)—San Zaccaria—Giardini* (when the 'Biennale' is open)*—Lido.*

**15** *Riva Schiavoni—Punta Sabbioni* (direct).

**16** *Fusina* (car park)*—Zattere* (direct).

**18** (A service for the Lido beaches) *Fondamente Nuove—Murano—Lido* (San Nicolò)*—Lido* (Santa Maria Elisabetta).

**21** (A service for the Lido beaches) *Riva Schiavoni—Giardini—Sant'Elena—Lido.*

**24** *San Giuliano* (car park)*—Fondamente Nuove* (direct).

**Taxis** (motor-boats) charge by distance, and tariffs are officially fixed. However, it is always wise to establish the fare before hiring a taxi.

It is also possible to hire a taxi for sightseeing (hourly tariff). Taxi-stands on the quays in front of the Station, Piazzale Roma, Rialto, San Marco, etc. *Radio taxis*: Tel. 32326 and 22303.

**Gondolas** are now almost exclusively used for pleasure (mostly by visitors) and not as a means of transport (although some ferries still operate across the Grand Canal; comp. below). Few noble Venetian families still maintain a private gondola. They are of ancient origin and peculiar build. The curious toothed projection forward, called the *Ferro*, is supposed to represent the six sestiere of the city, and Dorsoduro. In 1562, in order to minimize the rivalry between noble houses, it was decreed that all gondolas should be painted black. The wooden shelter, or *Felze*, which used to protect passengers in bad weather is now no longer used. The cries of the gondoliers as they round a corner are peculiar to themselves. A small tip should be given to the *Ganzèr* armed with a boat-hook who pulls the gondolas to the shore and helps passengers to alight at hotels.

Gondolas are for hire for 50 minute periods and the tariffs are fixed, but it is advisable to establish the fare before starting the journey. Night surcharge (after 19). Gondola stands at the station, Piazzale Roma, Calle Vallaresso (San Marco), Riva degli Schiavoni, etc.

**Gondola ferries** (*Traghetti*) cross the Grand Canal in several places, either straight (diretto) or diagonally (traversale). They are a cheap and pleasant way of getting about in Venice and provide the opportunity to board a gondola to those who cannot afford to hire one (passengers usually stand for the short journey). At present they run at Campo Santa Maria del Giglio (for the Salute area); San Barnaba (near Ca' Rezzonico for San Samuele); San Toma (for the Frari); Riva del Carbon (for Riva del Vin in the Rialto area); Santa Sofia (near Ca' d'Oro for the Rialto markets), San Marcuola and the Fontego dei Turchi; and at the Railway Station. They normally operate from 6 or 8–19 or 22 including fest. (with the exception of San Barnaba, Riva del Carbon and the Railway Station which operate on a reduced timetable).

### Local Transport

The BUS STATION is at Piazzale Roma (Pl. 4; 7). Services run by A.C.T.V., SIAMIC, and the Società Veneta Autoferrovie. Local A.C.T.V. bus service to *Tronchetto* (No. 17; ev. 20 min.); to *Mestre* (Nos. 2, 4, 7, 8, 12, & 13); to *Marghera* (No. 6); to the *Airport* (No. 5); to *Malcontenta*; and to *San Giuliano* and *Fusina*. For *Padua*, SIAMIC services via the autostrada every half hour, and Società Veneta services via the Brenta every hour.—SIAMIC buses to *Chioggia* and *Sottomarina* (via Mestre); to *Asiago* (via Padua, Vicenza, and Thiene or via Padua and Bassano); to *Este* (via Padua, Vicenza, and Thiene or via Gorizia; to *Rovigo* and *Monselice*; to *Trieste*; and to *Vicenza*.—A.C.T.V. services also run to *Treviso, Castelfranco, Piazzola sul Brenta*. etc.

On the **Lido**, A.C.T.V. bus services operate (the same tickets as for the vaporetti are stamped at automatic machines on board). From Piazzale Santa Maria Elisabetta (at the vaporetti landing-stage) *Service A* to San Nicolò al Lido, and via Lungomare Marconi, to the Casinò and Excelsior Hotel; *Service B* to the public bathing beaches at San Nicolò, and to Malamocco; *Service C* to Alberoni via Malamocco. *Bus No. 11* runs the entire length of the Lido (via Malamocco and Alberoni) and has a connecting ferry from Alberoni (Santa Maria del Mare) to San Pietro in Volta and Pellestrina (comp. p 194).

The '**Burchiello**' motor-launch (named after a 17C boat which followed the same route) operates in summer (April–Oct) between Padua and Venice along the Brenta canal, stopping at Villa Pisani (Nazionale) at Stra, Mira, Oriago, and

Malcontenta. It leaves Venice on Tues, Thurs, & Sat at 9.20 and arrives in Padua at 18 (return by coach). The departure from Padua is at 8.10 arriving in Venice at 17.15 (on Wed, Fri, & Sun). Inclusive price with lunch and return by coach. It is operated by CIT in Padua and in Venice, P.za S. Marco; Tel. 85480. It is one of the pleasantest ways of arriving in Venice.

# V  Useful Addresses

**Information Bureaux and Tourist Agents**. The main information office of the official Venice Tourist authorities is in Calle Ascensione 71c, San Marco (Tel. 26356). *Municipal Tourist Office*, Ca' Giustinian, San Marco 1364a. *Wagons-Lits/Cook*, Piazzetta dei Leoncini (San Marco 289–305); *American Express*, Salizzada San Moisè (San Marco 1474); *C.I.T.*, Piazza San Marco 48/50; *Ventana*, Piazzetta dei Leoncini (San Marco 4843).

**Head Post Office**. *Fondaco dei Tedeschi* (Pl. 6; 7, 8), at the foot of the Rialto bridge, with the telephone exchange and telegraph and telex office (8.30–19) and the poste restante, 'Fermo Posta' (open 8–17).—Branch Post Offices (open 8–14) in Calle Ascensione (end of Piazza San Marco) and on the Zattere.

**Public Offices**. *Municipio* (Town Hall; with a police station and Lost Property Office), Palazzi Farsetti and Loredan, Riva del Carbon (Pl. 6; 7); *Questura* (Central Police Station), Fondamenta San Lorenzo 5055.—*Airport* (Marco Polo), Tel. 661111.—*Railway Station*: Information, Tel. 715555; Lost Property Office, Tel: 716122. *A.C.T.V.* Lost Property, Tel. 780310.—Hospitals: Ospedale Civile, Santi Giovanni e Paolo; Ospedale Giustinian, Fondamenta Ognissanti (Dorsoduro); Ospedale al Mare, Lido. For emergencies Tel. 113. For ambulance, Tel. 30000. Some chemists (Farmacie) remain open all night and on holidays (listed in the local newspaper).—Port Authority Office (Capitaneria di Porto), Fondamenta delle Farine (Tel. 22716, 703044).

**Airline Offices**. *Alitalia*, San Marco 1463; *British Airways*, Riva degli Schiavoni, Castello 4191; *T.W.A.* San Marco 1471; *Air France*, Riva degli Schiavoni, Castello 4158.

**Shipping Companies**. *Adriatica*, Zattere 1411; *Adriatic Shipping Company*, San Marco 2098; *Bassani*, Via XXII Marzo, San Marco 2414.

**Banks** (usually open Mon–Fri 8.30–13.30, 14.45–15.45, Sat & holidays closed). *Banca Commerciale Italiana*, Via XXII Marzo 2188; *Banca d'Italia*, San Marco 4799; *Credito Italiano*, Campo San Salvador; *Banca d'America e d'Italia*, Via XXII Marzo 2216; *Cassa di Risparmio di Venezia*, Campo Manin, San Marco 4216; *American Express Bank*, San Marco 1336.

**Consulates**. *British*, Palazzo Querini, Accademia (Dorsoduro 1051; Tel. 27207); *American*, Via Roma 9, P.O. Box 604, Trieste (Tel. 040-68728).

**Learned Institutions and Cultural Societies**. *Ateneo Veneto*, Scuola di San Fantin 1897; *Giorgio Cini Foundation*, Isola di San Giorgio Maggiore; *German Institute*, Palazzo Barbarigo della Terrazza, Ramo

Pisani; *Istituto Veneto di Scienze, Lettere, ed Arti,* Palazzo Loredan, Campo Santo Stefano 2945; *Conservatorio di Musica 'B. Marcello',* Palazzo Pisani, Santo Stefano 2810; *Fondazione Levi,* Palazzo Giustiniani-Lolin, San Marco 2893; *Istituto Ellenico di Studi Bizantini e post-Bizantini,* Ponte dei Greci 3412; *La Biennale di Venezia,* Ca' Giustinian, San Marco 1364; *Archivio Storico delle Arti Contemporanee (La Biennale),* The 'Biennale' archives and art and media library, Palazzo Corner della Regina; *Società Italiana Dante Alighieri,* Fondamenta dell'Arsenale (with Italian language courses); *Università Internazionale dell'Arte,* Palazzo Fortuny, San Marco 3780 (with courses in history of art, etc.); *Istituto di Studi Teatrali,* Casa Goldoni, San Tomà; *Italia Nostra,* San Marco 1260; *UNESCO,* San Marco 63; *Amici dei Musei,* San Marco 63; *Venice in Peril Fund,* c/o The British Centre, Campo S. Luca 4267/A (Tel. 86612); *World Monuments Fund, Venice Committee,* Scuola Grande di San Giovanni Evangelista, San Polo 2454; *Centro Europeo di Formazione degli Artigiani,* Isola di San Servolo.

**Libraries**. *Nazionale Marciana,* San Marco 7; *Archivio di Stato,* Campo dei Frari 3002; *Fondazione Querini-Stampalia,* Santa Maria Formosa 4778; *Correr,* Piazza San Marco; *'Biennale' archive and library,* see above.

# VI  Churches

The opening times of churches vary a great deal but the majority are open from 7.30 to 12. In the afternoon many remain closed until 16 or even 17 and close again at 18 or 19; some do not repoen at all in the afternoon. A few churches open for services only. The sacristan will show closed chapels, crypts, etc., and a small tip should be given. Many pictures are difficult to see without lights which are often coin operated (100 lire coins). Some churches now ask that sightseers do not enter during a service, but normally visitors may do so, provided they are silent and do not approach the altar in use. At all times they are expected to cover their legs, and arms, and generally dress with decorum. Churches in Venice are very often not orientated. In the text the terms N and S refer to the liturgical N (left) and S (right), taking the high altar as at the E end.

**Roman Catholic Services**. On Sun and, in the principal churches, often on weekdays, Mass is celebrated up to 12 o'clock and from 17.30 until 19 in the evening. High Mass, with music, is celebrated in San Marco at 10. At 10.30 the Gregorian chant is sung at San Giorgio Maggiore. Confessions are heard in English on Sunday (7–10) in San Marco, the Gesuiti, the Scalzi, Santi Giovanni e Paolo, the Redentore, San Giorgio Maggiore, and on the islands of San Francesco del Deserto and San Lazzaro degli Armeni.—*Diocesan Tourist Office,* Piazzale Roma 469/a (next to the church of Sant' Andrea).

**Church Festivals**. On saints' days mass and vespers with music are celebrated in the churches dedicated to the saints concerned. On the Feast of St Mark (25 April) special services are held and the Pala d'Oro exposed on the high altar (also displayed at Christmas and

Easter). For the Feasts of the Redentore (3rd Sun in July) and of Santa Maria della Salute (21 Nov), see p 64.

**Non-Catholic churches**. *Anglican*, St George's, Campo San Vio; *Lutheran*, Campo Santi Apostoli; *Methodist*, Santa Maria Formosa 2170; *Greek Orthodox*, Ponte dei Greci.—*Jewish Synagogue*, Ghetto Vecchio.

# VII  Amusements

September is traditionally the best month in Venice for cultural activities. Concerts, exhibitions, and conferences throughout the year are advertized in the local press, on wall posters, in the A.C.T.V. landing-stages, and in 'Un Ospite di Venezia' ('A Guest in Venice'), a weekly publication available (free) through hotels, agencies, and the tourist offices. Concerts are often given in churches, and organ recitals are held in St Mark's in July and August.

**Theatres**. LA FENICE (Pl. 10; 1), Campo San Fantin, one of the most famous opera-houses in Italy (comp. p 130). Opera, ballet, and concerts are held throughout the year exc in Aug when the theatre is closed. *Malibran*, behind San Giovanni Crisostomo, for ballet, and also opera and concerts.—PROSE THEATRES: *Goldoni*, Calle Goldoni; *Del Ridotto*, Calle Vallaresso; *L'Avogaria*, Calle de l'Avogaria, Dorsoduro 1607.—The OPEN-AIR THEATRE next to *Palazzo Grassi* is being restored. Concerts (open to the public) are held at *Palazzo Labia* (comp. p 174).

**Exhibitions** are held in the Accademia Gallery, Museo Correr, Palazzo Ducale, Palazzo Grassi, Ca' Pesaro, the Cini Foundation, etc.

The **Biennale** (held in even years) is one of the most famous international exhibitions of Modern Art, first held in 1895. It is held in the Giardini Pubblici (see p 182) in permanent pavilions. At the same time other exhibitions are held in various parts of the city (San Lorenzo, the salt warehouses on the Zattere, the old ship-yards on the Giudecca, etc.). Every other year smaller exhibitions are held in conjunction with the Biennale.—The 'Biennale' also organizes a famous FILM FESTIVAL usually held in summer on the Lido.

**Casinò Municipale** open in summer at the Lido with gaming rooms, night club, and theatre. Play (roulette, chemin de fer, etc.) begins at 15 and continues until about 4.30 in the morning. Direct motor-boat services from 13.45 am from the Station, Piazzale Roma, and San Marco (Giardinetti) every $\frac{1}{2}$ hr. Similar direct services back to Venice from the Casinò.—In winter (Oct–March) the Casinò operates at Palazzo Vendramin on the Grand Canal.

**Annual Festivals**. Since 1980 **Carnival** time, the week in February before Lent, has been celebrated in Venice by ever increasing numbers of Italians and foreigners. At this time the city is invaded by merry-makers in fancy dress and masks. Numerous theatrical and musical events take place, both in theatres, and in the calli and campi. On some days during Carnival week the city more than doubles its population. The festivities end on Shrove Tuesday when a huge ball is held in Piazza San Marco.

The '**Vogalonga**' (literally 'long row') takes place on a Sunday in May. First held in 1975 it has become a very popular Venetian event. The 'Vogalonga' is open to anyone prepared to row from the mouth of the Giudecca canal around the E end of Venice (Sant' Elena) up past Murano, through the Mazzorbo canal, around Burano, past San Francesco del Deserto and back down Sant' Erasmo and Vignole, through the main canal of Murano, and back to Venice via the Cannaregio canal and the Grand Canal to the Punta della Dogana; a course of 32 kilometres. Any type or size of boat may participate with any number of oarsmen in each boat. A small participation fee is paid on enrolment. The departure is at 9.30 (best seen from the Zattere or Riva degli Schiavoni and the Giardini) and the first boats usually arrive back in the city at 11 or 11.30 (seen from the Cannaregio canal and the Grand Canal). It is a non-competitive course and the last oarsmen usually return around 3 o'clock. Usually some 1500 boats and over 5000 people took part in the event in a remarkable variety of boats, some of them elaborately decorated.

On the **Festa del Redentore** (3rd Sun in July) a bridge of boats is usually constructed across the Giudecca canal; its vigil is celebrated with acquatic concerts and splendid fireworks (best seen from the Giudecca, the Zattere, or from a boat). Motor-boats are excluded from the Basin of St Mark's after 9 pm.

The **Festa della Salute** (21 Nov) is also usually celebrated by a bridge of boats across the Grand Canal at the Dogana.

The **Regata Storica** (first Sun in Sept) starts with a procession on the Grand Canal of the historic 'bissone', boats of a unique shape richly decorated. This is followed by the most famous of the Venetian regattas in which two-oar 'gondolini' are rowed by expert Venetian oarsmen. Other 'Regate' are held at regular intervals throughout the summer.

The **Festa della Sensa** takes place on the Sunday after Ascension Day. This was celebrated throughout the Republic when the Doge ceremonially cast a ring into the lagoon at San Nicolò al Lido (comp. p 197) symbolizing the marriage of Venice with the sea. For the occasion, the doge was transported from Venice in the elaborate 'Bucintoro' (comp. pp 88, 179). It is now celebrated by the Mayor and Patriarch and other Venetian authorities. They depart from the Bacino di San Marco and proceed to San Nicolò al Lido.

**Sport**. SEA-BATHING on the Lido. The big hotels on the sea-front have their own private beaches and the other hotels share a bathing establishment on the Lungomare Marconi. Beach huts at some of these may be hired by the day. The public beaches are at the extreme N and S. ends of the island, at San Nicolò and Alberoni.—SWIMMING-POOLS at the Excelsior and Hotel des Bains on the Lido, and at the Cipriani hotel on the Giudecca.

GOLF-COURSE (18 holes) at Alberoni at the S. end of the Lido.—TENNIS COURTS at the larger hotels on the Lido, and at Lungomare d'Annunzio.—The CIGA Yacht Club hires sailing boats and gives sailing courses in Spring and Summer.—BOATS may sometimes be hired by the hour at the boatyard in Venice on Rio degli Ognissanti and Rio di San Trovaso (Dorsoduro).—HORSE-RIDING on the Lido.

# VIII Museums, Collections and Monuments

Below will be found a table giving the hours of admission to the various museums, galleries, scuole, and monuments in Venice in force in 1985. Many of the museums and galleries are closed on Mondays; on Sundays and public holidays some are open for two or three hours in the morning, when admission is usually free. *Opening times vary and often change without warning*; those given below should therefore be accepted with reserve. All museums etc. are closed on the main public holidays: 1 Jan, Easter, 1 May, 15 Aug, and Christmas Day. On other holidays (see p 67) they open only in the morning (9–13). There is a standard time-table for the whole year for all State-owned museums and galleries, namely weekdays 9–14,

Sunday and fest. 9–13, although there are plans to prolong these opening hours. A current list of the opening times is usually available at the Tourist Information offices in Venice.

In 1980–85 the admission charges to state galleries and museums were greatly increased (they had remained unchanged since 1958). At the same time, museum cards for tourists and other facilities for free admission (such as membership of Italia Nostra, T.C.I., holders of the International Student Identity Card, etc.) were abolished. However, there remain four days a month when entrance is free: 1st and 3rd Sat, and 2nd and last Sun in the month.

## Hours of Admission to the Museums, Collections and Monuments

| Name | Open (see note b) | Page |
|---|---|---|
| Accademia Galleries | (s) 9–14; Sun 9–13; closed Mon | 134 |
| Aquarium | 9–19; closed Tues | 112 |
| Archaeological Museum | (s) 9–14; Sun 9–13; closed Mon | 100 |
| Basilica of San Marco | see p72 | |
| Treasury & Pala d'Oro | see p72 | |
| Loggia, Galleries, and Museo Marciano | see p72 | |
| Burano: Scuola di Merletti | 9–18 exc Tues | 194 |
| Ca' del Duca | April–Oct, Mon, Wed, & Fri 9.30–12; Sat 15–18 | 103 |
| Ca' d'Oro | (s) 9–14; Sun 9–13; closed Mon | 167 |
| Ca' Pesaro | see Galleria d'Arte Moderna | |
| Ca' Rezzonico | see Museo del Settecento Veneziano | |
| Campanile di San Giorgio Maggiore | daily 9–12, 14.30–19.30; winter: 9–12, 14–17 | 183 |
| Campanile di San Marco | summer 10–19.30; Spring 10–18, or 19; winter 10–16 or 17, closed Christmas Day, and 1–31 Jan | 89 |
| Casa Goldoni | 8.30–13.30 exc. Sun | 152 |
| Cini Collection | daily exc Mon 14–19 | 143–4 |
| Correr Museum | 10–16; Sun 9–12.30; closed Tues | 86 |
| Doges' Palace | see Palazzo Ducale | |
| Franchetti Gallery | see Ca' d'Oro | |
| Galleria d'Arte Moderna (Pal Pesaro) | temporarily closed; 10–16; Sun 9.30–12.30; closed Mon | 152 |
| Goldoni's House | see Casa di Goldoni | |
| Guggenheim (Peggy) Collection | April–Oct, daily exc Tues, 12–18; Sat 12–21 | 144 |
| Icons, Museum of | see Museo Dipinti Sacri Bizantini | |
| Murano Glass Museum | see Museo Vetrario di Murano | |
| Museo Civico Correr | see Correr Museum | |
| Museo Communità Israelitica | 10–12.30, 15–17.30; closed Sat, & Sun pm | 175 |

| | | |
|---|---|---|
| **Museo Diocesano di Arte Sacra** | 10.30–12.30 exc fest. | 117 |
| **Museo Dipinti Sacri Bizantini** | 9–12.30, 15.30–17 or 18; Sun 9–12; closed Tues | 113 |
| **Museo dell'Estuario (Torcello)** | 10–12.30, 14–17.30; winter; 10.30–12.30, 14–16; closed Mon | 193–4 |
| **Museo Fortuny** | 8.30–13.30; closed Mon | 133 |
| **Museo del Settecento Veneziano (Ca' Rezzonico)** | 10–16; Sun 9–12; closed Fri | 141 |
| **Museo Storico Navale** | 9–13; Sat 9–12; closed Sun | 179 |
| **Museo Vetrario di Murano** | 10–16; Sun 9–12.30; closed Wed | 189 |
| **Natural History Museum** | 9–13.30; Sun 9–12; closed Mon | 154 |
| **Naval Museum** | *see* Museo Storico Navale | |
| **Oratorio dei Crociferi** | Fri, Sat, & Sun only; April, May, June & Oct 10–12; July–Sept 16.30–18.30; closed Nov–March | 171 |
| **Oriental Museum** | temporarily closed; (s) 9–14; Sun 9–13; closed Mon | 152 |
| **Palazzo Ducale** | April–May 9.30–17.15; June–Oct 8.30–19; Nov–March 9.30–15.45 | 90 |
| **Pinacoteca Manfrediniana** | *See* Seminario Patriarcale | |
| **Querini-Stampalia Gallery** | 10–15.30; winter: 10–14.30; closed Mon; Sun 10–14.30 | 118 |
| **Scuola dei Carmini** | 9–12; 15–18; closed fest. | 140 |
| **Scuola di San Giorgio degli Schiavoni** | 10–12.30, 15.30–18; Sun 10.30–12.30; closed Mon | 113 |
| **Scuola di San Giovanni Evangelista** | 9.30–12.30; closed Sat & Sun | 164 |
| **Scuola Grande di San Rocco** | 9–13; 15.30–18.30 | 162 |
| **Seminario Patriarcale** | By appointment | 147 |
| **Torcello Museum** | *see* Museo dell'Estuario | |
| **Torre dell'Orologio** | 9–12, 15–18; winter 9–12, 15–17; Sun 9–12; closed Mon | 86 |

## Notes

(s) state-owned museums

b The opening hours for Sundays apply also to holidays (giorni festivi)

# IX  General Information

**Season**. The climate of Venice is conditioned by its position on the sea; although it is subject to cold spells in winter and oppressive heat on some summer days, there is almost always a refreshing sea air. September and October are perhaps the pleasantest months in which to visit the city, since Spring can be unexpectedly wet until well after Easter. In winter thick sea mists can shroud the city for days at a time (making it impossible to see from one side of the Grand Canal to the other). The most crowded times of the year in Venice are summer (July and August), Easter, and the last days of Carnival. The presence of thousands of visitors at these times can mar a visit; but it is always possible to escape from the crowds which tend to congregate around Piazza San Marco and the Rialto bridge.

ACQUE ALTE ('High Waters'). Exceptionally high tides occur several times a year (usually between Nov and April) and flood many of the low-lying areas of the city (up to about 50cm). A watch is kept on the level of the lagoon and warning notices posted up in the A.C.T.V. landing-stages. When an 'acqua alta' is imminent sirens are sounded throughout the city. The period of the high water usually lasts 2 or 3 hours, and duck-boards are normally laid out in Piazza San Marco, by the landing-stages, and in other thoroughfares. However, it is not possible to get about the city on these occasions without wellington boots.

**Plan of Visit**. The 20 itineraries in the Guide correspond to at least 20 days (leisurely) sight-seeing. For visitors with only a short time at their disposal, the following areas and monuments in the city should not be missed:
1. Piazza San Marco, Basilica of San Marco, and the Palazzo Ducale (Rte 1).
2. The Grand Canal (Rte 2)
3. The Accademia Gallery (Rte 7) and a walk in the Dorsoduro (Rte 8; including the church of San Sebastiano)
4. Ca' Rezzonico (Rte 7) or the Ca' d'Oro (Rte 11), both palaces on the Grand Canal; the church of the Frari and the Scuola Grande di San Rocco (Rte 10)
5. The Scuola di San Giorgio degli Schiavoni (Rte 3); the church of Santi Giovanni e Paolo (Rte 4); the church of Santa Maria dei Miracoli (Rte 11)
6. The church of the Madonna dell'Orto and a walk in the NW part of the city (Rte 12)
7. The church of San Giorgio Maggiore and the Giudecca (Rte 14)
8. The islands of Murano, Burano, and Torcello (Rtes 15 and 16)

**Public Holidays**. The main holidays in Italy, when offices, shops, and schools are closed, are as follows: New Year's Day, 25 April (Liberation Day, and the Festival of St Mark), Easter Monday, 1 May (Labour Day), 15 Aug (Assumption), 1 Nov (All Saints' Day), 8 Dec (Conception), Christmas Day, and 26 Dec (St Stephen).

**Telephones and Postal Information**. Stamps are sold at tobacconists (displaying a blue 'T' sign) and post offices. There are numerous public telephones all over the city in the campi, and in bars and restaurants, etc. These are operated by coins or metal discs known as 'gettone' which are bought from tobacconists, bars, some newspaper stands, and post offices (and are considered valid currency). Most cities in Europe can now be dialled direct from Italy (prefix for London, 00441).

**Newspapers**. The local Italian newspapers in Venice are the *Gazzettino* and *Nuova Venezia* (with theatres, cinemas, etc). Other national papers include *Corriere della Sera, La Stampa, Paese Sera,* and *La Repubblica*. Foreign newspapers are obtainable at most kiosks.

**Working Hours**. Government offices usually work weekdays from 8–13.30 or 14. Shops are normally open from 8 or 9–13 and 16.30 or 17–19.30 or 20, although recently the local authority in Venice has allowed shops to adopt whatever opening hours they wish. Most of the year, some food shops are closed on Wednesday afternoon (in July and August they are closed instead on Saturday afternoon); although now many of them close only on Sunday. Clothes shops, hairdressers, etc. are usually closed on Monday morning. For banking hours, see p 61.

# EXPLANATIONS

**Type**. Smaller type is used for historical and preliminary paragraphs, and (generally speaking) for descriptions of greater detail or minor importance.

**Asterisks** indicate points of special interest or excellence.

**Populations** are given in round figures according to the latest official figures.

**Italian words** have been used in the text for topographical descriptions (i.e. *campo, calle, rio, fondamenta*, etc.); these are explained on p 47. Names of streets, canals, etc. are written up in the Venetian dialect and often change when re-painted; the names found in situ have generally been used in the text but it should be borne in mind that the form of a word can be changed by a letter or two.—Water-buses are referred to as *vaporetti*, (sing., *vaporetto*) and *motoscafi* (sing., *motoscafo*).

**Abbreviations**. In addition to generally accepted and self-explanatory abbreviations, the following occur in the guide:

| | |
|---|---|
| A.C.T.V. | Azienda del Consorzio Trasporti Veneziano (the company that runs the Venetian transport system) |
| Adm | Admission |
| C | century |
| C.I.T. | Compagnia Italiana Turismo |
| E.N.I.T. | Ente Nazionale Italiano per il Turismo |
| exc | except |
| fest | *festa*, or festival (i.e. holiday) |
| incl | including |
| fl | floruit (flourished) |
| l | lira (pl. lire) |
| m | metre(s) |
| min. | minutes |
| Pal. | Palazzo |
| Pl. | atlas plan |
| R | room(s) |
| Rte | route |
| SS. | Saints (in English): Santissimo, -a (in Italian) |
| T.C.I. | Touring Club Italiano |

For abbreviations of Italian Christian names, see p 205; for glossary see p 37.

References in the text (Pl. 1; 1) are to the 16-page Atlas at the back of the book, the first figure referring to the page, the second to the square. Ground plan references are given as a bracketed single figure or letter.

*Venice as Justice (detail from the Porta della Carta)*

# VENICE

**VENICE** in Italian **Venézia**, with 334,000 inhabitants, stands on an archipelago of 117 islets or shoals, 4km from the mainland and 2km from the open sea, whose force is broken by the natural breakwater of the Lido. The population of the commune includes Mestre; that of the historic centre being now only about 80,000 compared with the 200,000 it had when the Republic was at its zenith. A unique position, the grace of her buildings, the changing colours of the lagoon, and not least the total absence of wheeled transport, make Venice the most charming and poetic city in the world. The Republic of the 'Serenissima' founded in the 8th century survived until 1797, and was one of the most glorious in history. The influence of the East on the Venetian Empire was essential to its character. The monuments in the city today, contained geographically within virtually the same limits as in the height of the Republic, are testimony to her remarkable civilisation. Alarm for the survival of the city which is subject to periodic floods from exceptionally high tides (the 'acque alte') has been somewhat quelled since the construction of a new aqueduct and the control of the three entrances into the lagoon. A special law was passed in 1973 and, renewed in 1984, by the Italian government to safeguard the city, and committees funded from various countries have been working in conjunction with the Italian authorities for over twenty years on the restoration of buildings.

# 1    Piazza San Marco, the Basilica of San Marco, and the Palazzo Ducale

**\*\*Piazza San Marco** (Pl.10;2), the piazza par excellence, is without an equal in the world. It is enclosed on three sides by the uniform facades of stately public buildings; in the arcades beneath (hung with draped curtains on sunny days), the elegant cafés have tables outside grouped around their orchestra podiums. The colonnades open out towards the east end of the Piazza and the fantastic facade of the Basilica of San Marco. In front of the church tall flagstaffs (from which the standard of the Republic and the tricolour are flown) rise from elaborate pedestals cast in bronze by Aless. Leopardi (1505). Near the Piazzetta Giovanni XXIII (or dei Leoncini) the gay Torre dell' Orologio provides an entrance from the Piazza to the Merceria, the main pedestrian thoroughfare of the city which leads to the Rialto. Opposite, beyond the tall isolated campanile, the Piazzetta with the Palazzo Ducale opens on to the water-front, the entrance to the city in Republican days.

Some of the most important events in the history of the Venetian Republic were celebrated in the Piazza and it remains the centre of Venetian life. It is of unrivalled charm at all seasons and however crowded or deserted. Napoleon commented that it was 'the finest drawing room in Europe'. The pavement in trachyte and Istrian stone was laid in 1722 by Andrea Tirali. The famous pigeons of St Mark still flock to the square, and until recently were fed here at the public charge as in Republican days. In the period of the 'acque alte' (high waters), the square is one of the first places in the city to be flooded; the duck-boards used on these occasions are usually stacked in readiness.

The **\*\*Basilica of San Marco** (Pl.11;1) stands high in importance among the churches of Christendom. Founded in 832 its sumptuous architecture retains the original Greek-cross plan derived from the great churches of Constantinople, and in particular, from the (destroyed) 6C church of the Holy Apostles. Its five domes are Islamic in inspiration. This famous shrine has been embellished over the centuries by splendid mosaics, marbles, and carvings. It contains outstanding art treasures, the origins of some of which are still not known with certainty (the bronze horses, the columns which support the baldacchino in the Sanctuary, etc). Every detail of its decoration is worthy of close study; numerous different styles and traditions have been blended in a unique combination of Byzantine and Western art. As the Doge's Chapel the basilica was used throughout the Republic's history for State ceremonies; it became the cathedral of Venice only in 1807. The name and symbol of St Mark (a winged lion) have been emblematic of Venice since the ninth century.

**Admission**. The Basilica is open daily 6.30–19.30 (tourists are asked to visit the church 10–16.30).—The TREASURY and PALA D'ORO (inclusive ticket) are open from 9.30–16.30 ; fest. & Sun 14–16.30.—The LOGGIA on the facade, the GALLERIES, and the MUSEO MARCIANO are open 10–16.30; fest. & Sun 14–16.30.

**History**. According to legend St Mark the Evangelist on a voyage from Aquileia to Rome anchored off the islands of the Rialto where he had a vision of an angel who greeted him with the words 'Pax tibi, Marce evangelista meus. Hic requiescet corpus tuum'. This portent was fulfilled in 828 when two Venetian merchants brought the body of St Mark from Alexandria and placed it in charge of doge Giustiniano Participazio who caused the first church on this site to be built. This was consecrated in 832. Damaged by fire in a popular rising (976) against doge Pietro Candiano IV, it was radically restored if not rebuilt by doge Pietro Orseolo I. Doge Domenico Contarini began a new building in 1063, which was continued by doge Dom. Selvo (1071-84). This church consecrated in 1094 by doge Vitale Falier is thought to have had basically the same form as the first church, and is that which exists today.

The mosaic decoration begun at the end of the 11C is the work of centuries. After 1159 the walls were faced with marble from Ravenna, Sicily, Byzantium, and the East. During the Fourth Crusade (1204) many of the greatest treasures which now adorn the Basilica (including the four bronze horses) were transported from Constantinople. The sculptural decoration of the upper facade dates from the end of the 14C and beginning of the 15C. In the 16C Jacopo Sansovino carried out important restoration work to consolidate the structure of the building; a task which continues to this day.

The music school of the Ducal Chapel of St Mark became famous towards the end of the 15C. Andrea Gabrieli was appointed organist in 1566, and his nephew the composer Giovanni succeeded him in 1585. The Flemish choirmaster Adriano Willaert remained here from 1527 until the end of his life. Monteverdi directed the music at St Mark's from 1613 until his death in 1643.

The roman and arabic numerals in the text refer to the Plan on pp 76–77; the letters refer to the Plan of the mosaics on p 79.

**Exterior**. The sumptuous **\*Main Facade** is in two orders, each of five arches, those below supported by clusters of numerous columns and those above crowned by elaborate Gothic tracery, pinnacles, sculptures, and tabernacles. A balcony with water-spouts separates the two orders: here stand copies of the famous bronze horses. LOWER ORDER OF THE FACADE. The columns are of different kinds of marble,

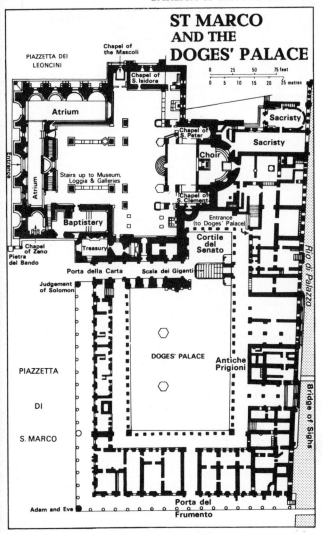

**ST MARCO AND THE DOGES' PALACE**

PIAZZETTA DEI LEONCINI

Chapel of the Mascoli

Chapel of S. Isidore

0    25    50    75 feet

0    5    10    15    20    25 metres

Atrium

Sacristy

Sacristy

Chapel of S. Peter

Choir

Atrium

Stairs up to Museum, Loggia & Galleries

Chapel of S. Clement

Entrance

Baptistery

Entrance (to Doges' Palace)

Cortile del Senato

Chapel of Zeno

Pietra del Bando

Treasury

Porta della Carta    Scala dei Giganti

Judgement of Solomon

DOGES' PALACE

Antiche Prigioni

PIAZZETTA

DI

S. MARCO

Rio di Palazzo

Bridge of Sighs

Adam and Eve

Porta del Frumento

many from older buildings, and most of them have fine capitals. Between the arches are six bas-reliefs: Hercules carrying the Erymanthean boar, St Demetrius, Hercules and the Hydra, St George, the Virgin Orans, and the Angel Gabriel; the first is a Roman work; the second was made by a Byzantine craftsman in the late 12C, and the others are 13C in the Veneto-Byzantine style. At either end of the facade, between the columns, are statuettes of water-carriers.

At the left end of the facade a huge single column with a fine capital supports three porphyry columns. In the arch above the DOOR OF SANT' ALIPIO (I) is a *Mosaic of the Translation of the body of St

*Mark to the Basilica* (1260–70). This is the only original mosaic left on the facade, and is the earliest representation known of the exterior of the basilica (the bronze horses are already in place). Beneath is a fine arched lunette with early-14C bas-reliefs of the Symbols of the Evangelists and five pretty screened arches, Islamic in style. The architrave above the door is formed by a long 13C Venetian bas-relief in the palaeochristian style. Superb capitals surmount the columns on either side of the door which dates from 1300 (by Bertuccio).—SECOND DOORWAY (II). The mosaic of Venice venerating the relics of St Mark dates from 1718 (cartoon by Seb. Ricci). Above the door is a window with Gothic tracery surrounded by fine carvings of Christ and two Prophets on a mosaic ground. These doors are also by Bertuccio.—The CENTRAL DOORWAY (III; covered for restoration since 1982) is crowned by a mosaic of the Last Judgement (1836). Among the columns flanking the doorway are eight in red porphyry. The three *Arches* have beautiful carvings dating from c 1235 (first inner arch) to c 1265 (third outer arch). These constitute one of the most important examples of Romanesque carving in Italy, showing the influence of Benedetto Antelami (the details are difficult to see).

The main outer arch has, on the soffit, carvings showing Venetian trades (boat building, fishing, etc), and, on the outer face, Christ and the Prophets. The middle arch depicts the Months on the soffit and the Virtues on the outer face. The smallest arch shows Earth, the Ocean, and animals on the soffit, and, on the outer face, scenes of daily life from youth to old age.—The Byzantine doors date from the 6C. In the lunette is a marble carving of the Dream of St Mark by the school of Antelami (13C).

The FOURTH DOORWAY (IV) has a mosaic of Venice welcoming the Arrival of the Body of St Mark (by Leop. dal Pozzo from cartoons by Seb. Ricci, early 18C), and 13C reliefs above a Gothic window.—Above the FIFTH DOORWAY (V), Mosaic of the Removal of the Body of St Mark from Alexandria (also by dal Pozzo). The Moorish window has Byzantine reliefs and mosaics.

The UPPER ORDER OF THE FACADE. The central window is flanked by arches filled with mosaics (left to right, Descent from the Cross, Descent into Hell, Resurrection, and Ascension) rearranged by Luigi Gaetano (1617–18) from designs by Maffeo da Verona. Before the central window stand copies made in 1980 of the famous gilded bronze horses, now displayed in the Museo Marciano (comp. p 85).

The facade is crowned by fine Gothic sculpture (better seen from the balcony, comp. p 85), begun by the Dalle Masegne and continued by Lombard and Tuscan artists (including the Lamberti). Between the arches are figures of water-carriers by a Lombard master of the 15C. The central arch has fine carving by Piero di Niccolò Lamberti. Above is the gilded lion of St Mark, and, crowning the arch, a statue of St Mark (by Niccolò Lamberti). The two outer tabernacles contain the annunciatory angel and the Virgin annunciate recently attrib. to Jac. della Quercia. At the SW angle of the balcony, overlooking the Piazzetta, is a porphyry head (8C), said to be a portrait of Justinian II (d. 711).

The **South Facade** (towards the Palazzo Ducale) continues the design of the W facade. The first doorway (VI), which was blocked by the construction of the Cappella Zen (see p 82) was formerly one of the main entrances to the basilica and the first to be seen from the water-front. The columns are surmounted by two marble griffins (12–13C).—The second arch (VII) contains the bronze doors (14C) of the Baptistery and a Gothic window.—The two upper arches are finely decorated; between them and above a small 10C door, is a Byzantine mosaic of the Madonna in prayer (13C), in front of which two lamps are lighted nightly in fulfillment of a vow of a sea-captain. The Gothic sculpture which crowns the arches is partly the work of Niccolò Lamberti.—The two rectangular walls of the Treasury (VIII) stand beside the Porta della Carta of Palazzo Ducale. These are richly adorned with splendid marbles and fragments of ambones and plutei (9–11C). The front of the bench at the foot of the wall bears an inscription of the late 13C with one of the earliest examples of the Venetian dialect. On the corner are two delightful sculptured groups in porphyry known as the 'Tetrarchs', thought to represent Diocletian and three other emperors, Egyptian works of the 4C.

The two isolated pillars in front of the Baptistery door are tradition-ally thought to have been brought by Lorenzo Tiepolo from the church of St Saba in Acre (now part of Israel) after his victory there over the Genoese in 1256. A more recent hypothesis suggests they were brought from Constantinople at the time of the Fourth Crusade. They are a rare example of Syrian carving of the 5C–6C. At the SW corner of the facade is the 'Pietra del Bando', a stump of a porphyry column also from Acre, from which decrees of the Signoria were promulgated from 1256 onwards. It was hit when the campanile collapsed (see p 89), but saved the corner of the church from serious damage.

**North Facade** (facing the Piazzetta dei Leoncini). This was probably the last to be finished. Between the arches and in the bays are interesting bas-reliefs, including one showing Alexander the Great conducted to Heaven by two griffins (between the first two arches). The last of the four arches, the Porta dei Fiori (IX) has beautifully carved 13C arches enclosing a Nativity scene.—The upper part of the facade has statues by Nic. Lamberti, and fine water-carriers by Piero di Niccolò Lamberti (also attrib. to Jac. della Quercia). Beyond the Porta dei Fiori the projecting walls of the Mascoli and St Isidore Chapels bear Byzantine bas-reliefs. Here is the sarcophagus of Daniele Manin (X; d. 1857 in Paris), ruler of the short-lived Republic (1848–49).

The **Narthex** provides a fitting vestibule to the Basilica. It could formerly be approached also from the S side before the construction of the Cappella Zen (comp. above). The slightly pointed arches, probably the earliest of their kind in Italy, support six small domes. The fine columns of the inner facade were either brought from the East or are fragments of the first basilica. The lower part of the walls is encased in marble; the upper part and the pavement are mosaic. The *Mosaics of the domes and arches represent stories from the Old Testament, and are mainly original work of the 13C.—FIRST BAY (XI). *Mosaics (1200–1210) of the story of Genesis to the Death of Abel. The mosaics are in poor condition and have suffered from restorations.

The carefully worked out iconographical scheme is thought to have been inspired by the Cotton Bible (probably late 5C) miniatures. The 24 episodes are divided into three bands; in the centre of the dome, Creation of the Sky, Earth, and Firmament; in the middle band, Creation of the Sun, Moon, Animals, and Man; third band, Stories of Adam and Eve.—In the pendentives are four winged seraphs.

The Door of San Clemente, cast in the East, is traditionally supposed

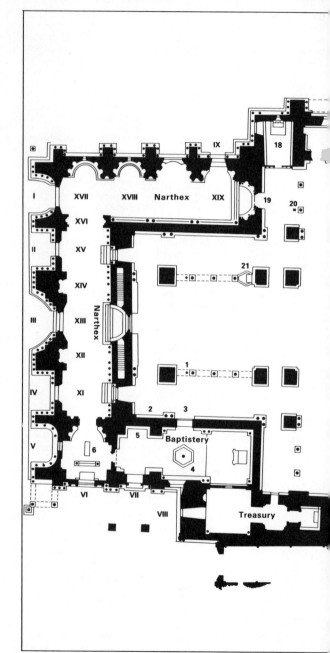

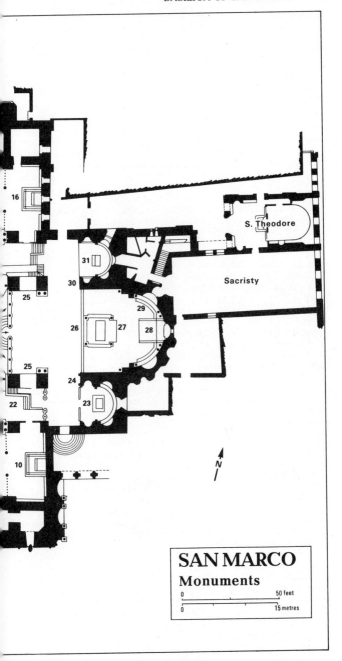

S. Theodore

Sacristy

16

31

30

25

29

26    27    28

25

24

22    23

10

N

**SAN MARCO**
Monuments

0                    50 feet

0                    15 metres

to be a gift from the Byzantine emperor Alexius Comnenus. It is decorated with figures of Saints (with their names in Greek). The capitals of the columns flanking the doorway are beautifully decorated with birds.—The FIRST ARCH (XII) has mosaics showing the story of Noah and the Flood. Here is the tomb, made up of Byzantine fragments, of doge Vitale Falier (d. 1096) who consecrated the basilica in 1094, and who was responsible for much of the work on it. This is the oldest funerary monument which survives in the city.—SECOND BAY (XIII), in front of the main door. Two tiers of niches contain unrestored *Mosaics, the earliest in the basilica (c 1063). They represent the Madonna with the apostles Peter, Paul, James, Andrew, Simon, Thomas, Philip, and Bartholomew, and, beneath, the four Evangelists. In the semi-dome, St Mark in Ecstasy (cartoon attrib. to Lotto, 1545). Two Byzantine angels stand on the columns flanking the great door which was executed by order of Leone da Molino (1113–18) and modelled on the Byzantine doors of San Clemente (see above). The slab of red Verona marble with a white marble lozenge in the pavement traditionally marks the spot where Barbarossa did obeisance before Alexander III in 1177. The little door on the right leads up to the Museo Marciano, the Loggia, and the Galleries of the Basilica (see p 85).

The SECOND ARCH (XIV) has mosaics showing the Death of Noah and the Tower of Babel. The tomb of the wife of doge Vitale Michiel (d. 1101) is made up of plutei and transennae of the 11C.—THIRD BAY (XV). In the dome and the arch above the door, mosaics of the story of Abraham (c 1230) and, in the pendentives, four tondoes with Prophets. In the lunette above the door, Byzantine mosaic of St Peter.—THIRD ARCH (XVI). Mosaics of SS. Alipio and Simon, and, in the centre, a tondo with Justice (c 1230).—FOURTH BAY (XVII). Tomb of doge Bart. Gradenigo (d. 1342) by a Pisan sculptor. The N wing of the narthex was probably added before 1253. The mosaics along this side of the narthex were partly re-made in the 19C; they portray the story of Joseph and, in the pendentives, the Prophets.—In the FIFTH BAY (XVIII) is the recomposed tomb of doge Marin Morosini (d. 1253), with a 13C relief—The SEVENTH BAY (XIX) has mosaics with the Story of Moses. Here is a bust of pope John XXIII, by Giac. Manzù.

**Interior**. Five great domes cover the Greek-cross of the interior, alternating with barrel vaults; each of the four arms has vaulted aisles in which the numerous columns with exquisite foliated capitals support a gallery (formerly the matroneum), fronted by a parapet of ancient plutei (dating from the 6C–11C). The Sanctuary, where the religious and political ceremonies of the Republic were held, is raised above the crypt, and separated from the rest of the church by a rood screen. The whole building is encased by eastern marbles below, and splendid mosaics on a gold ground above, illuminated high up by small windows (the rose window in the S transept and the arch opened at the W end are later additions which alter the delicate effect of dim lighting). At the centre of the nave hangs a huge Byzantine chandelier, while red lamps decorate the side chapels. The 12C *PAVEMENT, which has subsided in places, has a geometric mosaic of antique marble with representations of beasts, birds, etc. The light in the interior of the church changes constantly; it should be visited at different times of the day.

The **\*\*Mosaics** (some of which can be studied more closely from the Galleries above, see p 86) which cover a huge area of the basilica were begun after 1063. They were badly damaged in a fire of 1106, and work continued on them up until the 20C. The original medieval iconographical scheme has been largely preserved. Some mosaics were renewed, often following the original designs, others were repaired. In the 12C and 13C the Venetian school of mosaicists flourished, much influenced by Byzantine prototypes, and the decoration of the interior was completed by 1277. In the 14C and 15C mosaics were added to the Baptistery and other chapels, with the help of Tuscan artists including Paolo Uccello and And. del Castagno. In the early 16C many well-known Venetian painters (Titian, Salviati, Tintoretto, Palma Giovane, etc.) provided cartoons for mosaicists

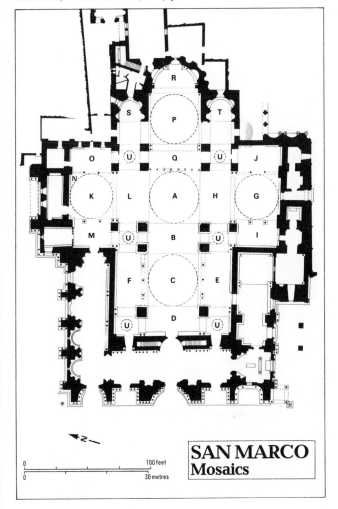

SAN MARCO
Mosaics

0                    100 feet
0                    30 metres

including the Zuccato brothers and the partial replacement of the mosaics took place. In this way paintings were reproduced in mosaic, and the art of true mosaic decoration was lost. From 1715–45 Leopoldo Dal Pozzo carried out restoration work and added new mosaics. Many of the mosaics were cleaned in the 1970s when a remarkable survey of them was undertaken by Otto Demus.

The central ˙DOME OF THE ASCENSION (A) is the work of Venetian masters of the late 12C. Around the Ascension in the centre are the Virgin and two angels and the twelve Apostles; between the windows, the sixteen Virtues of Christ; in the pendentives, the Evangelists above four figures representing the rivers of Paradise. The ˙Mosaics on the Arch (B) towards the nave also date from the late 12C and portray Scenes of the Passion: Kiss of Judas; Crucifixion; Marys at the Tomb (15C copy); Descent into Limbo; and the Incredulity of St Thomas. Over the nave rises the ˙DOME OF THE PENTECOST (C), dating from the early 12C and probably the first of the five domes to be decorated with mosaics. The fine composition shows the Descent of the Holy Spirit; between the windows, the Converted Nations; in the pendentives, four colossal angels. Lower down above the W door into the Narthex, is a brightly coloured ˙Lunette (D) ˙of Christ enthroned between the Madonna and St Mark (13C; restored). In the barrel vault stretching to the facade (also seen through glass from the narthex and from the Gallery above, p 85) are scenes of the Last Judgement, from a cartoon by Tintoretto, Aliense, and Maffeo da Verona (1557–1619; restored in the 19C), and Paradise, a Mannerist work of 1628–31, and, on the arch, the Apocalypse and Vision of St John, by the Zuccato brothers (1570–89; restored).

In the right aisle (E), Frieze of five mosaic ˙Rectangles with the single figures of the Madonna and the prophets Isaiah, David, Solomon, and Ezekiel (c 1230; well restored in the 19C). On the wall above, ˙Agony in the Garden, a splendid large composition, the earliest 13C mosaic in the basilica. On either side of the windows, and in the arch above, Lives of the Apostles (end of 12C, beginning of 13C).—In the left aisle (F), Frieze of five mosaic ˙Rectangles with the single figures of a beardless Christ and the prophets Hosea, Joel, Micah and Jeremiah. On the wall and arch above, the Life of Christ and the Apostles, replaced in 1619–24 from cartoons by Tizianello, Padovanino, Aliense, and Palma Giovane.

RIGHT TRANSEPT. The DOME OF ST LEONARD (G) has just four lone figures of Saints: St Nicholas, St Clement, St Blaise, and St Leonard (early 13C); in the spandrels, four female Saints: St Dorothea (13C), SS. Erasma and Euphemia (both 15C), and St Thecla (by Vinc. Bastiani, 1512). In the arch towards the nave, ˙Scenes from the Life of Christ (early 12C): Entry into Jerusalem, Temptations of Christ, Last Supper, and the Washing of the Feet. The first narrow arch in front of the rose window is decorated with four Saints (Anthony Abbot, Bernardino of Siena, Vincent Ferrer, and Paul the Hermit), fine works dating from 1458 (showing Tuscan influence). On the right wall (I): ˙Prayers for and the Miraculous rediscovery of the Body of St Mark (second half of the 13C, but restored), with interesting details of the interior of the basilica, and portraits of doge Vitale Falier and doge Ranieri Zen (1253–68). In the vault (difficult to see), Scenes from the Life of the Virgin (17C). On the arch above the Altar of the Sacrament (J), the Parables and Miracles of Christ (end of 12C or beginning of 13C; restored). The mosaics on the end wall were renewed in the early 17C from cartoons by Pietro Vecchia (scenes from the Life of St Leonard).

LEFT TRANSEPT. The *DOME OF ST JOHN (K) was executed in the first half of the 12C. The Greek cross in the centre is surrounded by Stories from the Life of St John the Evangelist. On the arch (L) towards the nave, 16C mosaics of the Miracles of Christ (cartoons by Iac. Tintoretto, Gius. Salviati, and Veronese). Left wall (M): on the arch, Scenes from the Life of the Virgin and the Infant Christ (end of 12C, beginning of 13C). The cycle was continued with the story of Susanna on the W wall in the 16C (from cartoons by Palma Giovane and Jac. Tintoretto). In the archivolt (N; difficult to see above the marble wall of the Chapel of St Isidore), Miracles of Christ (end of 12C, beginning of 13C, restored), and, on the end wall, the huge Tree of Jesse (by Vinc. and Dom. Bianchini, on a cartoon by Salviati, 1542). The arch (O) over the Altar of the Madonna of Nicopeia has Baroque mosaics of Miracles of Christ by Pietro Vecchia (1641–52). The E wall of the transept has the Communion of the Apostles, and Christ at Emmaus from cartoons by L'Aliense and Leandro Bassano (1611–17).

The *DOME AT THE EAST END of the church over the Presbytery (P) is a superb work of the 12C showing the Religion of Christ as foretold by the Prophets with the bust of Christ Emmanuel holding a half-revealed Scroll (remade c 1500), surrounded by the Virgin between Isaiah and Daniel and eleven other Prophets. In the spandrels, Symbols of the Evangelists. In the arch above the Rood-screen (Q) are 16C Scenes from the Life of Christ (cartoons by Tintoretto). In the apse at the E end (R), Christ Pantocrator, signed and dated 1506, but copied from its 12C prototype. Below, between the windows, the four Patron Saints of Venice: St Nicholas, *St Peter, *St Mark, and St Hermagorus, among the earliest mosaics of the basilica (probably completed before 1100). In the arches above the singing galleries to the left and right (S and T) are Scenes from the Life of SS. Mark and Peter (beginning of 12C, partly restored). The mosaics on the end walls are partly hidden by the organs; they represent Scenes from the Life of SS. Peter, Mark and Clement.

The little domes and arches at the piers forming the side aisles (marked 'U' on the Plan) are also beautifully decorated with mosaics of Saints, etc (13C, but many of them restored or re-worked). Other important mosaics in the Baptistery and the chapels of St Isidore and of the Mascoli are described below with the rest of the church (p 84).

**The Lower Part of the Church**. RIGHT AISLE. Stoup (1) of Oriental porphyry (the carved base is now in the Museum, see p 86). On the S wall (2) is a Byzantine relief (12C) of Christ between Mary and St John the Baptist. A door (3) leads into the **Baptistery** (restored 1982–84). The Font, designed by Sansovino (c 1545), has a lid with bronze reliefs (recently restored) by his pupils Tiziano Minio and Desiderio da Firenze; the statue of St John the Baptist above was executed by Fr Segala (1575). On the wall behind is the fine Gothic sarcophagus (4) of doge Andrea Dandolo (d. 1354), by Giovanni de' Santi. This doge, a friend of Petrarch, took a degree at Padua University and was a famous man of letters. He was the last doge to be buried in St Mark's. To the right (5), near a 13C statuette of an angel, is the sarcophagus of doge Giov. Soranzo (d. 1328). At the E end a slab in the pavement marks the resting place of Jac. Sansovino (d. 1570) whose remains were transferred from the Seminario in 1929. The huge block of granite (with an ancient inscription) is said to have

been brought from Tyre in 1126. It has been raised to reveal traces
(recently discovered) of a rectangular font for total immersion with
fresco fragments, thought to have belonged to the first church. On
the wall are three reliefs of the Baptism of Christ, and SS. George
and Theodore on horseback (13–14C). On the left wall fresco fragments were exposed in 1963 (the Virgin in prayer and two angels,
probably part of an Ascension scene) dating from the 13C. The
Baptistery mosaics, carried out for doge Andrea Dandolo (c 1343–54,
comp. above) illustrate the life of St John the Baptist and the early
Life of Christ. They are fine works (especially noteworthy is the
*Banquet of Herod, above the door into the church, which shows the
influence of Paolo Veneziano).

The adjoining **Cappella Zen** (6; reopened in 1985 after restoration) was built
in 1504–22 in honour of cardinal G. Battista Zen who had left his patrimony to
the Republic on condition he was buried in the Basilica. The construction of
the chapel blocked up the original entrance to the Narthex from the Piazzetta.
The fine *Doorway into the Narthex remains: beneath a mosaic of the Madonna
between two archangels (the Madonna dates from the 19C, but the two angels
are 12C) are niches with mosaics (early 14C) alternating with fine statuettes of
Prophets (Antelami school). Tullio Lombardo was largely responsible for the
construction of the fine 16C chapel, which is filled with remarkable bronze
sculptures (all of which have recently been restored). The Tomb of cardinal
Zen (d. 1501), and the altar, were started by Leopardi and Ant. Lombardo and
finished by Paolo Savin. The monumental statue of the Madonna ('of the Shoe')
is a classical work by Ant. Lombardo (1506). Here, too, are some interesting
bas-reliefs (11C–13C), and two red marble lions (Romanesque, thought to have
been formerly outside the entrance to the Basilica). The barrel vault mosaics
(late 13C, restored) relate to the Life of St Mark.

RIGHT TRANSEPT. On one of the corner piers (7) is a bas-relief of the
Madonna and Child (known as the Madonna 'of the Kiss' since it has
been worn away by the kisses of the faithful), thought to date from
the 12C. The door into the Treasury (8) has a pretty ogee arch with
a 13C mosaic of two angels holding a reliquary of the True Cross,
and a carved frieze and a 14C statuette of the Risen Christ.

The **Treasury** (adm see p 72; ticket should be retained for adm to
the Pala d'Oro) contains a rich store of booty from the sack of
Constantinople in 1204. Many of its most precious possessions were
melted down in 1797, but it retains one of the most important
collections of Byzantine goldsmiths' work of the 12C. It is in the
process of rearrangement.

In the anteroom is a fine silver statuette of St Mark (by Fr. Franceschi,
1804).—On the left is the SANCTUARY (now usually kept locked), with many
precious reliquaries, mostly Byzantine. Above the altar frontal made of oriental
alabaster is a relief of Christ among the Apostles, and, even higher, a tondo of
Christ between two angels (13C).—On the right is the TREASURY proper, in a
room with exceptionally thick walls thought to have been a 9C tower of the
Palazzo Ducale. At the entrance is the marble Chair of St Mark (Alexandrine,
6–7C), a gift from the emperor Heraclius to the patriarch of Grado in 630. A
case on the left (temporarily removed) contains four Byzantine *Icons. Nearby
is a 13C Crucifix; two elaborate altar frontals (13C and 14C) and two silver gilt
candelabra. On either side of the window: a marble monstrance (6–7C) and the
sword of doge Francesco Morosini (a gift from pope Alexander VIII). On the
right wall, a showcase contains Byzantine works (10–11C), including a rock
crystal bowl with classical figures (Corinthian?), chalices, etc. In the two cases
by the door, 16C paxes; and (bottom shelf), Gothic reliquary casket which
belonged to Charles VIII of France; Byzantine chalices (one in metal); and huge
precious gems.

Ber. *Gothic!*

In the four central showcases: 1. *Coffer in the shape of a Byzantine church with five domes (from Georgia, 11–12C?); reliquary caskets; chalices; and bowls in precious stones including one in turquoise (a gift in 1472 from the Shah of Persia).—Case 2. Chalices, including one in onyx made by a Byzantine master in imitation of a classical work; alabaster bowl.—Case 3. Glass phial with incised decoration (Saracen, 10C); oriental vases; *Gospel cover in gilded silver (12C, from Aquileia); red onyx chalice with enamel panels (10C, Byzantine); two Roman situlae.—Case 4. *Paten in oriental alabaster and enamel, richly decorated (Byzantine, 10–11C); (second shelf) Byzantine chalice; (third shelf) rare chalice in agate-onyx, probably a Roman work of the 1C AD with Byzantine additions (restored).

The door (9) in this transept is the main entrance to the church from Palazzo Ducale (now usually kept closed). Above the door is a 13C mosaic lunette of St Mark. In the passageway fresco fragments (including the Maries at the Tomb) have recently been uncovered. Above is a huge Gothic rose window inserted in the 15C. The *Altar of the Sacrament* (10) has a tabernacle borne by columns of porphyry and pavonazzetto. It is flanked by two bronze candelabra (by Maffeo Olivieri, 1527). On the two pilasters are rectangles of fine marble inlay; the one on the left marks the place where St Mark's body was hidden during reconstruction work on the church, and miraculously re-discovered on 24 June 1094 (illustrated in the mosaic on the opposite wall, comp. p 80). A lamp burns perpetually here. On the wall to the right of the altar is a relief of St Peter enthroned (and two bishop Saints in mosaic beneath the arch); to the left of the altar, Byzantine relief of the Madonna and Child. The mosaic pavement here bears palaeochristian motifs. On the nave pier (11) is the *Altar of St James*, a charming work in the 15C Lombardesque style (with a beautifully carved frontal).

Here is the entrance to the Sanctuary (see below). From the polygonal pulpit (12) the Doge traditionally showed himself to the people after his coronation in the sanctuary. Above it, Madonna and Child, statue attrib. to Giovanni Bon. The Presbytery is raised above the crypt on a stylobate of sixteen little marble arches at the foot of the Rood Screen. The *ROOD SCREEN (13) with eight columns of dark marble, bears the great Rood, a work in silver and bronze by Iac. di Marco Benato of Venice (1394), and marble *Statues of the Virgin, St Mark the Evangelist, and the Apostles, signed by Jacobello and Pier Paolo Dalle Masegne (1394). The second pulpit (14) is really two pulpits one above the other, supported by precious marble columns and surrounded by parapets of verde antico. It is crowned by a little oriental cupola. The fine stairway can be seen from the left transept.—At the spring of the pendentives of the central cupola are four gilded marble *Angels (Romanesque works showing the influence of Antelami). In the pavement is a large rectangle of veined Greek marble on the site of the old choir (11–12C).

LEFT TRANSEPT. On the nave pier (15) is the *Altar of St Paul* by Ant. Rizzo. The **Chapel of the Madonna of Nicopeia** (16) contains a precious *Icon said to have been brought from Constantinople in 1204. It is the most venerated image in the basilica and considered the Protectress of Venice. It was carried by the Byzantine emperor into battle at the head of his army and dates from the 12C. It is surrounded by a fine enamelled frame encrusted with jewels. It was badly damaged in 1979 when the jewels were stolen (they were later recovered) and it has been restored. Candelabra by Camillo Alberti (1520) flank the altar. On the right is a Byzantine bas-relief of the

Madonna and Child, and, on the left, other interesting bas-reliefs.—At the end of the transept is the **Chapel of St Isidore** (17; sometimes closed) constructed by doge Andrea Dandolo in 1354–55 (note the charming stoup near the door). Behind the altar, in a niche, a sarcophagus bears a reclining statue of the saint (by the school of de' Santi, 14C), with an angel bearing a censor. The arch is richly carved; on the outside are statuettes of the Annunciation. The upper part of the walls and the barrel vault of the chapel are completely covered by mosaics in a beautiful decorative scheme depicting the history of the saint.—The adjacent **Chapel of the Madonna dei Máscoli** (18; closed by a screen) is so named because it became the chapel of a confraternity of male worshippers in 1618. Set in to the end wall encased in splendid marbles is a carved Gothic altar (1430), with statues of the Madonna and Child between SS. Mark and John, by Bart. Bon. The *Mosaics (1430–50) on the barrel vault depict the Life of the Virgin. They are one of the most important 15C mosaic cycles, and one of the earliest examples of Renaissance art in Venice. They were carried out under the direction of Michele Giambono, using cartoons by And. del Castagno and probably also Jac. Bellini. The Birth and Presentation of the Virgin (left wall) bear the signature of Giambono; on the right wall are the Visitation and Dormition of the Virgin. On the wall outside the chapel (right) is a Byzantine relief of the Madonna in prayer.

Above the door (19) leading out to the Narthex is a pretty carved ogee arch with a late 13C mosaic. The Greek marble stoup (20) has Romanesque carvings. On the nave piers are a Byzantine Madonna in prayer, and a large bas-relief of the Madonna and Child (named after a gun placed here as an ex-voto).

The NORTH AISLE contains the little *Chapel of the Crucifix (21), with a pyramidal marble roof surmounted by a huge oriental agate and supported by six columns of precious marble with gilded Byzantine capitals. It contains a painted wood Crucifix thought to have been brought from the East in 1205. Nearer the W door is a Stoup of 'bardiglio' marble.

The **Sanctuary**. The entrance (22) is from the right transept beneath a transenna bearing Gothic statues of the Madonna and four female Saints. Ahead is the Chapel of St Clement (23) with sculptures by the Dalle Masegne. Here tickets are shown for admission (comp. p 82) to the Sanctuary and Pala d'Oro. On the side pier is a fine Gothic tabernacle (24). The singing galleries in the chancel (25) have bronze reliefs by Sansovino (1537–44; martyrdom and miracles of St Mark). The baldacchino (26) of the high altar is borne by four *Columns of eastern alabaster sculpted with New Testament scenes which are extremely interesting both from an artistic and from an historic point of view. It is still uncertain whether these are Byzantine works of the early 6C or even 5C, or Venetian works of c 1250. On the side walls of the sanctuary are six Gothic statues of Saints. The sarcophagus of St Mark is preserved beneath the altar (seen through a bronze grate). On the marble balustrades are the four Evangelists by Sansovino (c 1552) and four patriarchs by Girol. Paliari (1608–1614). Over the altar (covering the back of the Pala d'Oro) has been placed an altarpiece attrib. to Michele Giambono. Behind this is the *Pala d'Oro (27), glowing with precious stones, enamel, and old gold. This is one of the most remarkable works ever produced by Medieval goldsmiths.

The first Pala was ordered in Constantinople by Pietro Orseolo I (976–978).

Enriched in 1105 (in Constantinople) for doge Ordelafo Falier, it was enlarged by doge Pietro Ziani in 1209, and finally re-set in 1345 by Gian Paola Boninsegna. In the upper part, the archangel Michael is surrounded by roundels with sixteen Saints; on either side, six scenes: Entry into Jerusalem, Descent into Limbo, Crucifixion, Ascension, Pentecost, and Dormition of the Virgin (these last perhaps from the church of the Pantocrator in Constantinople).—Lower part: in the centre, the Pantocrator (a 12C work also from Constantinople?) surrounded by 14C Venetian panels. These in turn are flanked by 39 niches with enamels from Constantinople, and, in the border, 27 scenes from the Life of the Evangelists, thought to survive from the Pala of doge Falier. The precious stones used to decorate the work include pearls, sapphires, emeralds, amethysts, rubies, and topaz. The enamels are worked in the cloisonné technique.

The APSE, with two fine gilded capitals from Orseolo's basilica, has three niches. In the central one (28) is an altar with six precious columns, including two of unusually transparent alabaster. The gilded door of the tabernacle is by Sansovino, and the statues of St Francis and St Bernardino by Lorenzo Bregno. The Sacristy door in the left-hand niche (29) is also by Sansovino, with bronze *Reliefs (Entombment, Resurrection, and, in the frame, heads of the artist, of Aretino and Titian).—Beyond a Gothic pier tabernacle (30), with sculptures by the Dalle Masegne, is the *Chapel of St Peter* (31), with a large 14C relief of St Peter with two small kneeling Procurators. The two columns have superb Byzantine capitals; behind the altar is the entrance to the Sacristy.

In the charming Renaissance SACRISTY (adm rarely granted), by Giorgio Spavento (1486–90) are decorative mosaics by the Zuccato, and others after Titian and Padovanino, and inlaid cupboards.—The CRYPT (rarely open) is supported by 50 ancient columns. Here the body of St Mark was placed in 1094.
   From a small door to the right of the main W door (entered from the Narthex; see Plan XIII) is access (by very steep stairs) to the **Museo Marciano, the Loggia, and Galleries** (adm see p 72).—The first room of the Museum is to the left at the top of the stairs. Here are displayed mosaic fragments, 16C illuminated choirbooks, and a double bass made by Gaspare da Salò in the second half of the 16C.—R II. 14C mosaic fragments from the Baptistery.—R III. Altar frontal of the Dead Christ between two angels and Symbols of the Evangelists, a Byzantine embroidery of the 11–12C; Persian carpets (16–17C); Lion of St Mark in gilded wood (16C); Madonna 'del Latte', a Venetian work of the end of the 13C or beginning of the 14C.—From the organ gallery (the organ, made in Crema, was donated to the church in 1958 by Count Cini) is access to the LOGGIA on the facade which commands a fine view of the Piazza and allows a close examination of the Gothic sculpture on the upper part of the facade. The bronze horses are replicas (comp. below).
   Beyond the organ, R IV contains the Cover for the Pala d'Oro painted by Paola Veneziano and his sons Luca and Giovanni (1345). Beneath a brick cupola here are the four famous gilded bronze *HORSES. After their restoration in 1979 the controversial decision was taken to replace them on the facade of the basilica by replicas and exhibit them permanently here. The horses were brought to Venice from Constantinople (where they probably adorned the Hippodrome) at the time of the Fourth Crusade in 1204, and they were already in place on the facade of the Basilica by the middle of the century. They remained a symbol of Venetian power throughout the Republic. Discussion continues about their origin; recent scholarship tends to assign them to the 2C AD, and therefore to a Roman rather than a Greek sculptor. They are the only quadriga known to survive from classical times. Petrarch recorded his admiration for the horses when he sat beside the Doge on the loggia in 1364 watching a tournament in the Piazza. In 1797 they were carried off to Paris by Napoleon where they remained until 1815 (the sculptor Canova being instrumental in their return). In 1917–19 they were removed for safety (to Rome) and again in 1940–45.

The last room has been closed while the tapestries are being restored. The magnificent series of Tapestries with ten scenes from the life of Christ (c 1420) are attrib. to a design by Nicolò di Pietro. Also here are four tapestries worked by Giov. Rost (1551) to a cartoon attrib. to And. Schiavone; marble fountain with marine carvings (2C AD?, formerly the base of a stoup in the basilica); Christ and the Apostles by Maffeo da Verona, another case for the Pala d'Oro.—The *GALLERIES offer a superb opportunity to study the mosaics (care should be taken not to trip on the iron girders placed here by Sansovino in an attempt to consolidate the structure of the church).

To the left of the Basilica is the PIAZZETTA GIOVANNI XXIII (formerly 'dei Leoncini' or 'di San Basso'), with a well-head and two red marble lions presented by doge Alvise Mocenigo in 1722. Here stands the *Palazzo Patriarcale*, built in 1834–43 by Lor. Santi. The church of *San Basso*, with a facade by Longhena (1675), is sometimes open for exhibitions.—Above the entrance to the Merceria (p 127) rises the **Torre dell' Orologio**, probably by Mauro Codussi (1496–99); the wings were added in 1506 perhaps by Pietro Lombardo. Above the great clock-face, brightly decorated with gilding and enamels is the figure of the Madonna (during Ascension week and on Epiphany the Magi come out of the side doors every hour and bow before her). On top of the tower two bronze figures (1497), known as the 'Mori', strike the hours. The tower may be climbed (no lift) to see the mechanism of the clock (No. 147, under the archway; adm see p 66).—The rest of the N side of the Piazza is occupied by the arcades of the **Procuratie Vecchie** by Mauro Codussi, reconstructed after a fire in 1512 by Gugl. dei Grigi Bergamasco, Bart. Bon the Younger and Sansovino. These were built as the residence and offices of the Procurators who had charge of the fabric of St Mark's, and still serve as offices. They are fronted by three open galleries, of which the lowest has 50 arches, the upper two 100. Beneath the portico is the Caffè Quadri.— Sansovino's church of San Geminiano at the W end of the Piazza between the two Procuratie, was pulled down in 1807 by Napoleon, who replaced it by the so-called ALA NAPOLEONICA of the Palazzo Reale, a building by Gius. Soli (1810), the two lower floors of which copy the Procuratie Nuove, while on top is a heavy attic fronted by statues of Roman emperors.

The **Procuratie Nuove**, on the S, were planned by Sansovino to continue the design of his Libreria Vecchia (p 99) which faces the Doges' Palace. Up to the tenth arch from the left they are the work of Scamozzi (1582–86), and they were completed by Longhena c 1640. They were a later residence of the Procurators (see above), and became a royal palace under Napoleon. In the portico beneath is one of the city's most celebrated cafès, the Caffè Florian, named after its first proprietor in 1720, Floriano Francesconi. It retains a charming old-fashioned interior decorated in 1858 by Lod. Cadorin. In 1920 the Procuratie Nuove were presented to the city by the royal family, and since 1923 they have been occupied by the *Museo Correr (Pl.10;2; adm see p 65), the city museum of art and history, which was founded by the wealthy citizen Teodoro Correr (1750–1830). The entrance is usually on the right of the central passage of the portico beneath the Ala Napoleonica. However, when exhibitions are being held in the Ala Napoleonica the entrance may be from the Procuratie Nuove (No. 52, near the Caffè Florian), and some rooms closed. In this case the itinerary starts at Room 16 (see below).

From the central door an imposing staircase mounts to the FIRST FLOOR. The first rooms of the museum retain their neo-classical decoration and they provide

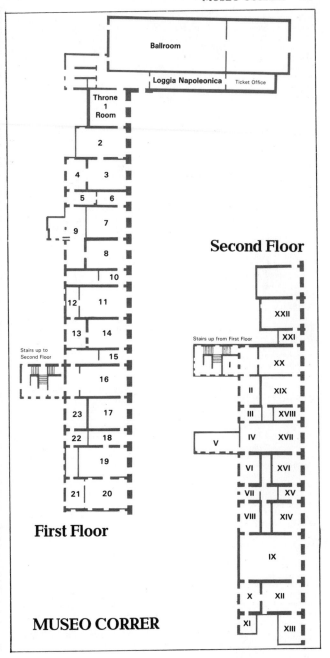

**Ballroom**

Loggia Napoleonica    Ticket Office

Throne
1
Room

2

4    3

5    6

7

9

8

10

12    11

13    14

Stairs up to
Second Floor

15

16

23    17

22    18

19

21    20

**First Floor**

**Second Floor**

XXII

XXI

Stairs up from First Floor

I

XX

II    XIX

III    XVIII

V    IV    XVII

VI    XVI

VII    XV

VIII    XIV

IX

X    XII

XI    XIII

**MUSEO CORRER**

an appropriate setting for some important works by *Ant. Canova*. From the landing an antechamber leads into the BALLROOM by *Lor. Santi* (1822) with decorations by *Gius. Borsato*. It is now used as a conference and exhibition hall. The LOGGIA NAPOLEONICA has old views and plans of Venice including 17C works by *Joseph Heintz the Younger*. ROOM 1, the THRONE ROOM, is decorated by *Gius. Borsato* and *G.B. Canal*. Here have been hung fine neo-classical *Frescoes recently detached from rooms in the Procuratie Nuove by *Giov. Carlo Bevilacqua* and panels with mythological scenes and dancers, early works by *Fr. Hayez* (1817). The works by *Canova* include Daedalus and Icarus, a marble group, bozzetti, and a (painted) portrait of Amedeo Svaier.—R 2, the Dining Room preserves its decoration by *Giov. Carlo Bevilacqua* and *Gius. Borsato*. The early 19C French circular table has mythological scenes in Sèvres porcelain. A case contains more bozzetti by *Canova*, and here is hung a painting of Amore and Psyche by him. ✦

The following rooms are devoted to the **Historical Collections**. ROOM 3. *Aliense*, Landing of Caterina Cornaro, queen of Cyprus (1489).—R 4. Relief in Istrian stone of St Mark between SS. Roch and Sebastian (as protectors from the plague) from the entrance porch of the Lazzaretto Vecchio by *Gugl. Bergamasco* (1525); high relief of the 15C of the Madonna enthroned between a Doge and Magistrates from the island of Poveglia.—RR 5 & 6. Documents and portraits of the Doges, and representations of their ceremonies.—R 7. Elaborately carved bookcases of the 17C, and an 18C chandelier made in Murano.—RR 8–10. Another fine chandelier and robes and portraits, including (in R 9) Santa Giustina with the Treasurers, by *Jac.* and *Dom. Tintoretto*, and a Portrait of doge Fr. Foscari by *Lazzaro Bastiani*.—R 11. Coins, a very complete collection from the 9C to the fall of the Republic; standards.

A passage (R 12) leads to R 13, with mementoes of the Battle of Lépanto (1571); *Aless. Vittoria*, Bust of Francesco Duodo, in terracotta.—R 14. The Bucintoro (p 179), including decoration from the vessel of 1729 by *Ant. Corradini*.—R 15. The Arsenal.—R 16. Commerce and navigation (including a wood gilt statue, an 18C copy of one venerated in a temple in Canton and thought to be an effigy of Marco Polo); Persian and Chinese ceramics.—R 17. Arms and armour; 16C Flemish tapestry (Marriage of the Virgin).—R 18. Eastern arms, notably a Persian shield of gold and silver (16C).—RR 19–23 are devoted to Fr. Morosini, the admiral who conquered the Peloppenese and was doge in 1688–94. The exhibits include a finely carved lamp from his galley, his bust by *Fil. Parodi*, and an equestrian portrait by *Giov. Carboncino*.

On the SECOND FLOOR the **Museo del Risorgimento** (usually closed) continues the history of Venice to the present day. Of the fifteen rooms, five of them are concerned with 1848–49.

The **Quadreria**, or Picture Gallery, is arranged strictly chronologically. ROOM I. Veneto-Byzantine period, including a late-13C painted coffin from a monastery on the Giudecca, and a relief of the Crucifixion.—R II. Triptychs and polyptychs of the 14C, including works by *Paolo Veneziano*.—R III. *Lor. Veneziano*.—R IV. Gothic fragments and frescoes; kneeling statuette of doge Antonio Venier by *Jacobello Dalle Masegne*.—R V. *Stef. Veneziano* and Gothic painters of the 14C.—R VI. International Gothic painters of the 15C: *Stefano da Zevio* (?), Angel musicians; *Fr. de' Franceschi*, Martyrdom; *Michele Giambono*, Madonna and Child; *Jacobello del Fiore*, Madonna; 'Master of the Jarves marriage-chest', painted frontal of a marriage-chest, with a story from Boccaccio.—R VII. *Cosmè Tura*, *Pietà; Ferrarese painter*, c 1450, Profile of a man.—R VIII contains fine works by the Ferrarese School: *Baldassarre Estense*, Portrait of a man; *Angelo Maccagnino*, Profile of a lady; works by *Leonardo Boldrini*; *Bart. Vivarini*, Madonnas.—R IX. Gothic woodcarving; decorative arts, ladies' apparel, etc.—R X. Flemish painters: *Pieter Bruegel*, Adoration of the Magi.—R XI. *Antonello da Messina*. *Pietà, painted during his short stay in the city c 1476 (very ruined). *Hugo van der Goes*, Crucifixion; *Dirk Bouts*, Madonna.

R XII. Flemish and German painters: *Herri met de Bles*. Temptations of St Anthony; *Jos Amman von Ravensburg*, Saints; *Barthel Bruyn*, Portrait of a woman; *Lucas Cranach* (attrib.), Resurrection.—R XIII. *Giov. Bellini*, Crucifixion; *Gentile Bellini*, doge Giovanni Mocenigo; *Giov. Bellini*, Transfiguration, Pietà, Madonna and Child, Portrait of a young Saint crowned with laurel leaves, Crucifixion (also attrib to *Jac. Bellini*).—Beyond R IX (comp. above) is R XIV.

*Alvise Vivarini*, St Anthony of Padua; *Cima da Conegliano*, Madonna and Child with SS. Nicholas and Laurence (very ruined); *Benedetto Diana* (attrib), Ecce Homo; *Bart. Montagna*, Holy Family and donors; *Marco Basaiti*, Madonna and Child with donor; *Bart. Montagna*, S Giustina.—R XV. *Vitt. Carpaccio*, *Two Venetian Ladies, c 1507. For long known as the two 'courtesans', it is now thought they may represent a mother and daughter of the Torelli family. Also by *Carpaccio*, St Peter Martyr. —R XVI. Further works by *Carpaccio*, and by minor painters of the early 16C, including a Portrait of a Young Man in a red hat. Also, *Lazzaro Bastiani*, Annunciation; *Giov. Mansueti*, St Martin and the beggar.—R XVII. Works of the same period: *Giov. Dalmata*, Bust (Carlo Zen?); *Il Riccio* (attrib), Bust of a young man; *Boccaccio Boccaccino*, Madonnas; *Lor. Lotto*, Madonna crowned by two angels. Cases of ivories and enamels.—R XVIII. 16–17C Greco-Venetian school.—RR XIX–XXII. 15–16C Ceramics.

The last section of the museum (usually closed when exhibitions are in progress) illustrates Venetian history by means of the minor arts. The exhibits include small bronzes (by *Tullio Lombardo, Il Riccio, Aless. Vittoria*, and others): Madonna and Child, a relief by *Jac. Sansovino*. Materials (17–18C) and lace. Model of the Bucintoro; household objects; ladies' apparel; a display relating to gondolas. In the last two rooms are plans and maps, including a huge wood engraving (with the original six *Blocks) of Venice in 1500 by *Jac. de' Barbari*. This bird's eye view shows in detail how the city appeared and is of fundamental importance to historians of Venice.

The courtyard of the museum contains a fine collection of well-heads (9–11C).

At the corner of the Procuratie Nuove rises the **Campanile of San Marco**, over 98½ metres high, first built in 888–912, and completed in 1156–73. It was later restored, the last time by Bart. Bon the Younger in 1511–14. On 14 July 1902, it collapsed without warning causing little damage (except to the Loggetta, see below) and no human casualties. From the proceeds of a world-wide subscription an exact reproduction of the original was immediately begun and opened on 25 April 1912.

The brick tower of the campanile is surmounted by a bell-chamber with four-light windows of Istrian stone, and a square story decorated with two winged lions and two figures of Venice beneath the symbol of Justice; the spire at the top is crowned by an angel. The bell-chamber (adm see p 65), reached by a lift, commands a magnificent *View of the town and lagoon, the Euganean hills, and the Alps. Only one of the old bells survived the collapse of the tower; the others were presented by Pius X. Galileo experimented with his telescope

*Piazza San Marco after the collapse of the Campanile in 1902*

from the top of the campanile in 1609—At its base instruments record the level of the tides in the lagoon.

At the base of the campanile is the *Loggetta, a fine work in red Verona marble by *Jac. Sansovino* (1537–49), which was crushed by the fall of the tower, but has been carefully restored. It was originally a meeting-place of the 'nobili' or patricians. After 1569, owing to its strategic position, a military guard was posted here during the sessions of the Great Council. Its form is derived from the Roman triumphal arch and its sculptures celebrate the glory of the Republic. Three arches, flanked by twin columns, are surmounted by an ornate attic. White Carrara mable, Istrian stone, and verde antica have been used for the decorative details. Between the columns are niches with bronze statues of Pallas, Apollo, Mercury, and Peace, all by *Sansovino*. The three reliefs in the attic show Venice (represented by the figure of Justice), Jupiter, and Venus (allegories of Crete and Cyprus). The two admirable little bronze gates are by *Ant. Gai* (1733–34). Inside is a Madonna and Child, also by *Sansovino*; a charming work, it was recomposed (except for a young St John) from shattered fragments.

The *Piazzetta (Pl.11;1), with the Doge's Palace on the left, and the old Library on the right, extends from St Mark's to the water-front on the Bacino di San Marco. Near the water's edge are two huge monolithic columns brought to Venice from the east by doge Vitale Michiel II, and erected here at the end of the 12C. One bears a winged lion adapted as the symbol of St Mark from a Persian, Syrian, or even Chinese chimera; the other a statue of St Theodore and his dragon, the first patron saint of Venice. The torso is a fragment of a Roman statue of the time of Hadrian, and the head a fine portrait in Parian marble (the original has been replaced by a copy).

The **Doges' Palace**, or *Palazzo Ducale* (Pl.11;1; adm see p 66), the former official residence of the doges and the chief magistrates, was founded on this site in the 9C. The present building dates from the 14C and the two facades overlooking the Bacino di San Marco and the Piazzetta are magnificent examples of florid Gothic architecture. The decoration of the interior by Venetian painters of the 16C–17C (after fires in 1574 and 1577) survives intact. Restoration of some of the exterior sculpture was begun in 1984.

**History**. The palace was begun in the 9C and was rebuilt in the 12C under doge Sebastiano Ziani; this in turn was destroyed by fire. In 1340 a big sum of money was voted to build a room large enough to contain the 1212 members of the Maggior Consiglio. This was built overlooking the Bacino di San Marco and was inaugurated in 1419. The building extended as far as the seventh column on the Piazzetta. Shortly afterwards, in 1422, the Maggior Consiglio decided to demolish part of the old building in order to extend the facade in the same style towards the Basilica of San Marco. It is thought the building was constructed by a group of master-masons, including Filippo Calendario (d 1355), under the direction of officials of the Republic. After another conflagration in 1483, *Ant. Rizzo* began the chief interior facade and the Scala dei Giganti, and the work was continued by *P. Lombardò, Giorgio Spavento*, and *Scarpagnino*. Again burned in 1574 and 1577, it was restored by *Ant. Da Ponte*, and the courtyard and facade overlooking the Rio di Palazzo were completed in the 17C on the old lines by *Bart. Monopola*. The palace contained a vast number of public offices, law courts, etc., as well as the doge's residence.

The numbers in the text refer to the Plans on pp 95, 97. A guide giving details of every painting is displayed in each room.

The **Main Facade** (overlooking the Bacino di San Marco) is a superb

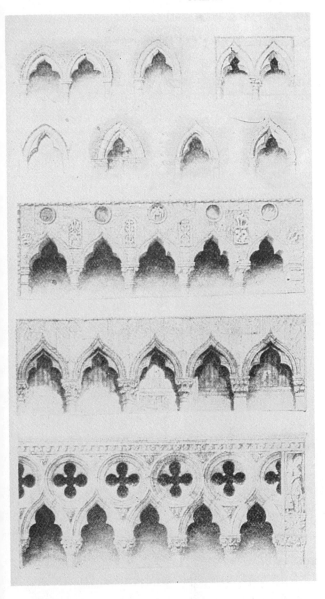

The development of the style of the windows of early Gothic
Venetian palaces showing their conclusion (bottom line) in the
façade of the Doges' Palace (John Ruskin, 'The Stones of Venice',
1853)

Gothic work. Each arcade of the portico supports two arches of the loggia decorated with quatrefoil roundels. This in turn is surmounted by a massive wall 12½ metres high lightened by a delicate pattern of white Istrian stone and pink Verona marble. Marble ornamental crenellations crown the facade. The windows along this side belong to the immense Sala del Maggior Consiglio. In the centre is a balconied window built in 1404 by *Pier Paolo Dalle Masegne*, crowned with a statue of Justice. On the corner nearest to the Ponte della Paglia are statues of the Drunkenness of Noah, and the archangel Raphael above (covered for restoration in 1985); on the corner nearest to the Piazzetta, Adam and Eve, with the archangel Michael above. Of uncertain attribution, these carvings date from the mid 14C. The *Capitals (36 in all, including those on the W facade) are superb examples of Medieval carving; some were replaced by copies c 1880. The level of the pavement used to be two steps lower so that the bases of the columns of the portico were exposed, altering the proportion of the lower facade.

*The Porta della Carta: left, before, and right, after restoration*

The **Facade towards the Piazzetta**. The original building (comp. above) reached as far as the seventh column (marked by a tondo of Justice on the loggia). In 1424 it was extended in the same style (and using the same building materials) as far as the Basilica, and the Porta della Carta was added in 1438. In the centre is a balconied window (1536), similar to that on the front of the building. The capitals here, as on the main facade, are superbly carved (note the one beneath the tondo of Justice with scenes of courtly love). On the corner nearest the Basilica is the *Judgement of Solomon, with the archangel Gabriel above, a beautiful sculptural group recently attributed to *Jac. della Quercia* (c 1410; covered for restoration in 1985).—The *PORTA DELLA CARTA (1438–1443; restored 1976–79) is an extremely graceful gateway in the florid Gothic style, by *Giov.* and *Bart. Bon.* It is thought to owe its name to the state archives ('cartae') which used to be kept near here. The fine *Statues of Temperance, Fortitude, Prudence and Charity are attrib. to the *Bon* workshop. The gateway is crowned by a figure of Venice as Justice attrib. to *Bart. Bon* (see p 70). The group of doge Francesco Fóscari kneeling before the Lion of St Mark is a good reproduction (1885) of the original destroyed in 1797.

The fine Renaissance facade on Rio di Palazzo, built of Istrian stone, can be seen from Ponte della Paglia or Ponte della Canonica (p 117). Begun by *Ant. Rizzo*, it was continued by the *Lombardo* family, by *Scarpagnino*, and finally completed in the 17C by *Bart. Monopola*.

The **Cortile** (courtyard) is approached by a vaulted passage through the Porta della Carta. The magnificent E side (opposite the entrance) was rebuilt after the fire by *Antonio Rizzo* (1483–98). It consists of four stories with richly carved decoration by the *Lombardo* family. The right-hand end was finished by *Scarpagnino* (1546–53). The lower stories of the other two sides of the courtyard were completed in the same style by *Bart. Monopola* in the 17C. In the centre are two splendid well-heads in bronze signed by *Alfonso Alberghetti* (1559) and *Niccolò dei Conti* (1556).

On the last side towards the Basilica is a Baroque facade by *Monopola* incorporating a clock, and the side of the ARCO FOSCARI which faces the Scala dei Giganti. This triumphal arch was begun by the *Bon* family and completed by *Ant. Bregno* and *Ant. Rizzo*; on the side facing the main courtyard is a statue of the condottiere Fr. Maria I della Rovere, duke of Urbino (1490–1538) by *Giov. Bandini* (1587), and (right) a Page attrib. to *Ant. Rizzo* (both now replaced by copies; originals inside the palace, see p 97). The main front of the arch bears statues of the mid-15C, and bronze copies of two fine marble statues of Adam and Eve by *Rizzo* (originals inside the palace; see p 97).

The ceremonial *SCALA DEI GIGANTI, designed by *Ant. Rizzo* (1484–1501), is decorated with delicate reliefs and elaborate sculpture. The colossal statues of Neptune and Mars (which gave the staircase its name) are late works by *Jac. Sansovino*. On the wide landing at the top the doges used to be crowned with the jewelled 'beretta'.—The smaller Cortile dei Senatori, beyond the stairway, is a charming Renaissance work by *Spavento* and *Scarpagnino*. From here there is a fine view of the exterior of the Basilica, with the original brick-work (restored).

**Interior**. The entrance (often moved) is at present in the left-hand corner of the courtyard (behind the Scala dei Giganti). The SCALA D'ORO (1), built in 1558–9, to the design of *Sansovino*, and decorated with gilded stuccoes by *Vittoria*, leads up to the **Primo Piano Nobile** (or second floor). A long gallery leads (right) to the DOGES' PRIVATE APARTMENTS (often closed when exhibitions are being mounted), reconstructed after a fire in 1483.

The first room is the *SALA DEGLI SCARLATTI (2), or Robing Room, with a fine chimneypiece by *Tullio* and *Ant. Lombardo* (c 1501), and, over the door, a *Bas-relief by *P. Lombardo*, doge Leonardo Loredan at the feet of the Virgin. Opposite is a Madonna in coloured stucco (Paduan, early 16C). The gilded ceiling is a fine work by *Biagio* and *Pietro da Faenza* (1506).—The walls of the SALA DELLO SCUDO (3) are covered with maps and charts (1540).—Opposite the entrance is the SALA GRIMANI (4), with a chimneypiece by *T.* and *A. Lombardo* and a ceiling decorated with rosettes. The SALA ERIZZO (5), beyond, has a similar chimneypiece and a good ceiling.—A passage with a Lombardesque ceiling leads to the SALA DEGLI STUCCHI (6), which contains a painting by *Pordenone* (Christ borne by angels), and small works by *Tintoretto, Bonifazio de' Pitati, Bassano,* and *Salviati*. From here there is a good view of the apse of the Basilica. The SALA DEI FILOSOFI (7) housed for a time paintings of philosophers by Tintoretto and Veronese. On the staircase, above the door on the right: *Titian,* St Christopher, a fresco of 1524 (very ruined; light on right).

The Scala d'Oro continues to the **Secondo Piano Nobile**, or third floor. At the top of the stairs is the ATRIO QUADRATO (8), where the fine wooden ceiling has a painting by *Tintoretto* with Justice presenting the Sword and the Scales to doge Girol. Priuli (removed for restoration).—On the right is the *SALA DELLE QUATTRO PORTE (9) by *Ant. da Ponte* (1575), after a plan of *Palladio* and *Rusconi*. This was the waiting-room used by ambassadors. The rich ceiling, by *Palladio*, has frescoes by *Tintoretto*, spoilt by restoration. The fine stucco work is by *Giov. Cambi* (1575). The walls and four doors were decorated for doge Marino Grimani in 1595–1606. On the entrance wall: *Giov. Contarini*, doge Marino Grimani before the Madonna and Saints; *Titian*, with the help of his nephew *Marco Vecellio*, doge Ant. Grimani before the Faith (after its recent restoration, only the figure of St Mark, the helmeted warrior, and the view of the Basin of St Mark's are thought to be by Titian's own hand). On the opposite wall are two paintings by *Carletto* and *Gabriele Caliari*, and *And. Vicentino.* The other end of the room is described after R 12, see below.—The ANTICOLLEGIO (10) has a good ceiling by *Marco del Moro* with a ruined frescoe by *Veronese*. The fireplace by *Scamozzi* has a relief of the Forge of Vulcan, an early work by *Tiziano Aspetti* and *Girol. Campagna*. Opposite the window, *Veronese,* *Rape of Europa; *Jac. Bassano,* Jacob's Return to Canaan; on the end walls (recently restored), *Tintoretto,* *Vulcan's Forge, Mercury and the Graces, *Bacchus and Ariadne, Minerva dismissing Mars.—The SALA DEL COLLEGIO (11; 1577–78; partly in restoration), where the doge and his councillors deliberated and received ambassadors, is a treasure-house of art. The chimneypiece is by Campagna. The *Ceiling, by *Fr. Bello,* the finest in the palace, is doubly precious on account of the wonderful series of paintings (removed for restoration in 1985) by *Veronese* (c 1577), with their superb colouring and skilful design; the most remarkable is that in the centre at the farther end: Justice and Peace offering the Sword, the Scales, and the Olive-branch to triumphant Venice. Other panels bear allegorical figures. Over the entrance, *Tintoretto*, doge And. Gritti before the Virgin; above the throne, *Veronese,* *Doge Seb. Venier offering thanks to Christ for

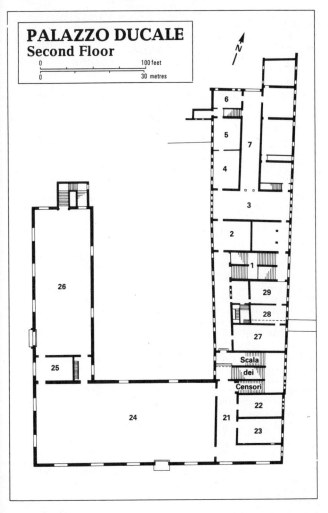

**PALAZZO DUCALE**
**Second Floor**

0 _____ 100 feet
0 _____ 30 metres

the victory of Lépanto. Facing the fireplace, *Tintoretto*, Marriage of St Catherine, doge Nic. da Ponte invoking the Virgin, doge Alvise Mocenigo adoring Christ, three magnificent paintings.

The *SALA DEL SENATO (12), the seat of the doge and his senators, by *Da Ponte*, has another fine ceiling (being restored), by *Cristoforo Sorte* (1581), with Venice exalted among the Gods, by *Tintoretto*, as a centre-piece. Over the throne, *Tintoretto*, *Descent from the Cross—with doges Pietro Lando and Marcantonio Trevisan adoring; on the left wall, *Palma Giovane*, Venice receiving the homage of subject cities presented by doge Fr. Venier, doge Pasquale Cicogna praying, and an Allegory of the League of Cambrai; *Tintoretto*, doge

P. Loredan praying to the Virgin; (on the end wall) *Palma Giovane*, doges Lor. and Girol. Priuli praying to Christ (these last four paintings all removed for restoration).—The door on the left of the throne admits to the CHIESETTA (13; often locked), the doge's private chapel, with a Madonna by *Sansovino*. The ANTICHIESETTA (14; closed) contains *Seb. Ricci's* cartoons for Dal Pozzo's 18C mosaics on the facade of St Mark's.

The door at the end of the Sala del Senato leads back into the Sala delle Quattro Porte (9; comp. above), at this end of which is exhibited (on an easel), *G.B. Tiepolo*'s painting of *Venice receiving the homage of Neptune (it was removed from above the windows where it has been replaced by a photograph). A corridor (with a view of the upper facade of San Zaccaria) leads into the SALA DEL CONSIGLIO DEI DIECI (15), the seat of the Council of Ten. Founded in 1310 as a court which tried political crimes, it became a notoriously severe organ of the government. Judges held office for one year only.—In the right-hand farther corner of the ceiling is an *Old Man in Eastern costume with a Young Woman, by *Veronese*. In the centre of the left-hand side, *Veronese*, Juno offering gifts to Venice, taken by Napoleon to Brussels in 1797 and returned in 1920. The originals of the central subject in this room and the next were taken to Paris in 1797 and did not return. Around the walls, (right) *Fr.* and *Leandro Bassano*, pope Alexander III meeting doge Ziani; (end wall) *Aliense*, Adoration of the Magi; (left wall) *Marco Vecellio*, pope Clement VII and the emperor Charles V.—The SALA DELLA BUSSOLA (16) has a marble chimneypiece and, on the right of the farther door, a 'Bocca di Leone', a box in which secret denunciations were placed. The wall paintings are by *Vecellio* and *Aliense*.—On the right (usually closed) is the SALA DEI TRE CAPI DEL CONSIGLIO DEI DIECI (17). It contains a chimneypiece, and two ceiling-paintings by *Veronese*; on the left is the SALETTA DEI TRE INQUISITORI (18), used by the special commission of the Council of Ten. The original ceiling-paintings by *Tintoretto* have been replaced.

From the landing outside the Sala della Bussola is the approach upstairs (right) to the SALE D'ARMI DEL CONSIGLIO DEI DIECI (19), the Council's private armoury, in which the state arms and armour were stored until the fall of the Republic.

ROOM I. Various suits of armour, including one called Gattamelata's, and one belonging to a page, found on the field of Marignano (1515). In a case: 16–17C helmets (Northern Italian); a unique visored helmet of the 14C, shaped like a bird's beak and made of a single piece; tournament armour (c 1510–20). A long case contains swords (the earliest dating from the 15C), and halberds by G.M. Bergamini (Venice, c 1620–25).—R II (right). In niche, Armour of Henry IV of France, presented by him to the Serenissima in 1603; lances, swords, falchions; suits of armour; Persian arms; horses' frontlets (15–16C).—R III has a superb display of arms and armour. In the centre, two early 'quick-firing' guns, one with 20 barrels, the other with a revolver mechanism. Crossbows and firearms. On the left: fuse-case holding a hundred and six fuses made of perforated and embossed copper, signed by G.A. Comino, and a culverin complete with its carriage and fittings (16C German?).—R IV has a superb view of the basin of St Mark and island of San Giorgio Maggiore. On the walls hang shields. In the cases: 16–17C pistols; muskets and arquebuses; instruments of torture; 16C cuirass.—R V contains a lantern from a dismantled Turkish galleon and painted shields. Beyond R VI (with helmets), steps descend to the Scala dei Censori.

The SCALA DEI CENSORI (20) redescends to the **Primo Piano Nobile**. On the left is the ANDITO DEL MAGGIOR CONSIGLIO (21), with a good 16C ceiling and works by *Dom. Tintoretto*, off which is the SALA DELLA QUARANTIA CIVIL VECCHIA (22), with paintings (right wall) of

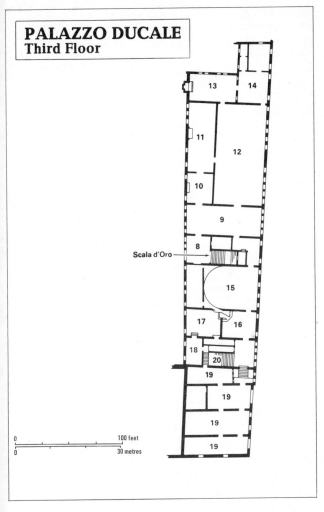

**PALAZZO DUCALE**
**Third Floor**

Scala d'Oro

0           100 feet
0           30 metres

Moses by *And. Celesti*, and (left wall), a painting by *Pietro Malombra*, and a 15C panel of the Virgin and Child. A fragment of mural painting has been revealed behind the panelling. The adjoining SALA DEL GUARIENTO (23) contains the remains of a huge fresco of the *Coronation of the Virgin by *Guariento* (1365–67) which used to adorn the Sala del Maggior Consiglio (see below). This famous work was ruined by the fire of 1577; it was discovered in 1903 beneath Tintoretto's painting. Beyond is the veranda, or 'liagò' used by nobles during intervals in sessions of the Great Council. Here have been placed three statues removed from the Arco Fóscari in the courtyard (comp. p 93): Adam and *Eve by *Ant. Rizzo* (c 1470) and the condottiere Fr. Maria I della Rovere, duke of Urbino by *Giov.*

*Bandini.*—To the right is the *SALA DEL MAGGIOR CONSIGLIO (24), the seat of the governing body of the Republic.

This vast hall, first built on this scale in 1340, was large enough to hold the assembly of Venetian patricians (which reached a maximum of 1700 members). Here laws were ratified and the highest officials of the Republic were elected. The frescoes by leading artists of the time and the magnificent ceiling were all destroyed in the disastrous fire of 1577. The paintings which replaced these in 1578–95, all by Venetian artists, record three important events in the history of the Republic: the Meeting in Venice between Barbarossa and pope Alexander III in 1177; the Fourth Crusade in 1202; and the triumph of doge Contarini after the victory at the Battle of Chioggia in 1379. The hall is 54m long, 25m wide and 15½m high.

On the entrance wall is *Paradise by *Iac.* and *Dom. Tintoretto* (1587–90), the largest oil-painting in the world (7 x 22m). It was removed for much needed restoration in 1982 and is expected back here in 1985. The *Ceiling (recently restored) is divided into 35 compartments of which the most noteworthy are the three central panels: *Veronese,* *Venice surrounded by gods and crowned by Victory, a masterpiece of light and colour (painted just before he died in 1588); *Tintoretto,* Venice surrounded by gods gives an olive-branch to doge Nic. da Ponte; (at the far end) *Palma Giovane,* *Venice welcoming the conquered Nations around her Throne.—The walls are covered with large historical canvases: right wall, episodes from the life of Barbarossa by *Benedetto* and *Carletto Caliari, Leandro* and *Francesco Bassano, Iac. Tintoretto, Paolo dei Franceschi, And. Vicentino, Palma Giovane, Federico Zuccari, Girolamo Gambarato,* and *Giulio del Moro.* On the left wall (with a fine *View from the balcony over the Bacino di San Marco): History of the Fourth Crusade by *Carlo Saraceni, Jean Leclerc, And. Vicentino, Palma Giovane, Dom. Tintoretto,* and *Aliense.* On the end wall, between the windows overlooking the Piazzetta, Triumph of doge And. Contarini after the victory at the Battle of Chioggia by *Paolo Veronese* and assistants. The frieze of the first 76 Doges (from Obelario degli Antenori, c 804, to Fr. Venier, d 1556) begins in the middle of the wall overlooking the Courtyard and runs left to right. It is the work of *Dom. Tintoretto* and assistants; the space blacked in on the wall overlooking the Piazzetta takes the place of the portrait of Marin Falier; an inscription records his execution for treason in 1355.

The last door on the right admits to the *Sala della Quarantia Civil Nuova* (25; sometimes closed), used by a high court of forty magistrates set up in 1492 to act in civil cases for Venetian citizens at home and abroad.—The SALA DELLO SCRUTINIO (26) was used to record the votes of the Great Council for the new doge. The rich ceiling has paintings recording Venetian victories by *And. Vicentino, Fr. Bassano, Aliense,* etc. Above the throne, Last Judgement by *Palma Giovane.* Around the walls are 16C paintings of Venetian battles which start chronologically to the left of the triumphal arch. They are the work of: *And. Vicentino,* the lagoon defended from King Pepin; *Sante Peranda,* Battle of Jaffa, 1123; *Aliense,* Conquest of Tyre; *M. Vecellio,* Defeat of Roger II of Sicily; (opposite wall): *Iac. Tintoretto,* the Venetians at Zara (a late work); *And. Vicentino,* Capture of Cattaro, Battle of Lepanto; *Pietro Bellotti,* Defeat of the Turks in Albania; *Pietro Liberi,* Defeat of the Turks at the Dardanelles.—The huge triumphal arch was erected in honour of Fr. Morosini by *Ant. Gaspari* in 1694; it contains paintings by *Gregorio Lazzarini.* The frieze continues the series of portraits of the doges down to the last one, Lod. Manin; each one was painted by a contemporary artist. There is a view from the window of the courtyard.

A small door to the left of the throne in the Sala del Maggior Consiglio leads out to the Scala d. Censori and a loggia.—On the right are three rooms (not always open) where some paintings from the PINACOTECA (normally in the Doges' Private Apartments; comp. p 94) have been arranged provisionally. In the first room (27): Three winged lions of St Mark by *Jacobello del Fiore, Carpaccio*, and *Donato Veneziano*; copy of the Pietà by Antonello da Messina (in the Museo Correr, comp. p 88).—In the next room (28), *Quentin Metsys*, Mocking of Christ—In the last room (29) are *Works by *Hieronymus Bosch*; and *Giov. Bellini*, *Pietà.

Stairs lead down to the BRIDGE OF SIGHS (by Antonio Contino, 1603) and to the new prisons which replace the old prisons or *Piombi*, so called from their position beneath the leaden roof.

Their miseries are described by Casanova, who escaped from them in 1775. Here also is the entrance to the *Pozzi*, eighteen dark dungeons in the two lowest stories, reserved for the most dangerous criminals. The lowest of them, however, were not below the street level, and they were less terrible than the usual medieval prison.

The Bridge of Sighs is recrossed and the exit is through some rooms of the AVOGARIA, used by a branch of the judiciary formed in 1517. The *Sala dei Censori* has portraits of censors by Domenico Tintoretto, and the *Sala dei Notai* similar portraits of Avogadori and Notaries, by Leandro Bassano, and others.

The *Libreria Sansoviniana (Pl.10;2, *Library of St Mark*), opposite the Ducal Palace, is the masterpiece of *Sansovino* (begun 1537). It was finished by *Scamozzi* (1588–91). Built of Istrian stone, its design is derived from Roman classical architecture, with a Doric ground floor, and an Ionic piano nobile with an elaborate frieze beneath a balustrade crowned by statues, some by *Girol. Campagna*. It was considered by Palladio to be the most beautiful building since the days of antiquity. Beneath the portico are the entrances to the

*The Libreria Sansoviniana and the Piazzetta, by Canaletto*

NATIONAL LIBRARY, the OLD LIBRARY itself, and the ARCHAEOLOGICAL MUSEUM.

The reading rooms of the **Biblioteca Nazionale Marciana** (National Library of St Mark; open to students daily 9–17; Sat 9–13.30) are entered from No. 7, once the approach to the ancient Zecca or Mint (see p 101). Petrarch gave his books to Venice in 1362, but it was not until cardinal Bessarion, a native of Trebizond, presented his fine collection of Greek and Latin MSS in 1468 that the library was formally founded. Cardinal Pietro Bembo was appointed librarian and official historian of the Republic in 1530. Today the library contains about 750,000 volumes and 13,500 MSS (many Greek).

The **Old Library** may only be seen by special permission from the Director. The main entrance at No. 13A (now kept locked) leads to a monumental staircase (with stuccoes by *Vittoria*) which mounts to an anteroom, with a *Fresco of Widsom, by *Titian*, on the ceiling. The Great Hall, restored in 1929, has 21 ceiling-medallions by various artists and ten paintings of Philosophers around the walls by *Tintoretto, Veronese*, and *And. Schiavone*. The exhibition of ancient books is now in a small adjoining room, and includes a late-14C Dante with illuminations, and evangelisteries dating back to the 9C. The precious *Grimani Breviary, illuminated by Flemish artists of c 1500, is rarely shown. A room opening off the stair landing contains *Fra Mauro's Map, a celebrated world-map of 1459 drawn on the island of San Michele (on the right is the bust of the author, perhaps by Bart. Bellano). Also here, the map of Ħadji Mehemed of Tunis (c 1560); Marco Polo's will; portulans; a MS in Petrarch's hand; etc.

At No. 17 in the library portico is the entrance to the **Archaeological Museum** (Pl.10;2; adm see p 65). It was founded in 1523 from a bequest of Greek and Roman sculptures made by Card. Domenico Grimani to the Republic (comp. p 120). It is especially remarkable for its ancient Greek *Sculpture. In R II is a numismatic collection.—R III. 1. Artemis, Roman copy of a Greek archaic work; 10. Triple herm of Hecate (archaistic style of 3C BC); 11. (in centre) *Base of a candelabra (Augustan period).—R IV. In the centre 11. *Abbondanza Grimani, an original of the 5C BC, representing Persephone. The fine series of female statues of 5C and 4C BC, includes (6.) Hera, and (10.) Athena (modelled on the famous Parthenon Athena by Pheidias).—R V contains a series of heads and busts of Athena; funerary reliefs; and a Roman copy of the Apollo Lycius, perhaps after Praxiteles.—R VI. Eros bending the bow of Heracles, after Lysippus; Dionysus and a Satyr, Roman copy of a Greek original; the Grimani altar with Bacchic scenes (1C BC); Heads of Satyrs; Head of an athlete.—R VII (in case: top shelf), 148. Chalcedon cameo (Pergamene art, 3C BC); 150, Female head, thought to be that of Cleopatra, in rock crystal; fragment of a nude warrior in bronze (4C); head of a man in porphyry (Egyptian art of the Roman period); lower shelf: 37. Zulian cameo of Jove (Hellenistic, from Ephesus). Fragment of a female statue with good drapery (2C BC).

Room VIII (closed for restoration). Three *Gallic Warriors, copies of a group presented by Attalus of Pergamum to Athens; 22. Ulysses; Leda and the Swan; 14. Head of a boy (end of 2C BC).—R IX. Among the busts of Roman emperors and others, is one of Trajan.—R X contains more busts including (3.) *Vitellius (?), a particularly fine Roman portrait of the early 2C AD.—R XI. Sarcophagi with reliefs of Niobe and her children, the Rape of Persephone, and a Sea Battle (2C BC). In the centre, Reliquary casket in ivory (Byzantine art of the 5C). A glass case contains Roman ivories and bronzes.—Beyond R XII with fragments representing Venus, R XIII contains reliefs, busts and statues related to Roman religious cults.—R XIV (Loggia). Vintage scenes and Centaurs by Tiziano Aspetti (once thought to be a Roman work).—R XV. Lapidary collection. R XVI. Renaissance copies of Roman busts, and a Romano-Egyptian bust of a priest of Isis. The following rooms contain the Corner collection: R XVIII. Greek and Roman heads and torsos; Black Romano-Egyptian head.—R XIX. Vases and small bronzes.—R XX. Egyptian, Assyrian, and Babylonian antiquities.

At the seaward end of the Piazzetta is the MOLO, on the busy waterfront. Opposite stands the island of San Giorgio Maggiore, divided from the long Giudecca island by a narrow channel. On the

Giudecca can be seen the Palladian facades of the Zitelle and Redentore churches. Nearer at hand is the promontory known as the Punta della Dogana with the church of the Salute. In the other direction (left) the quay extends along Riva degli Schiavoni to the public gardens.—To the right, beyond the end of the Libreria Sansoviniana, is the severe facade of the old **Zecca** (now the Biblioteca Nazionale Marciana, comp. above). This rusticated Doric building was finished in 1547 by Sansovino on the site of the 13C mint. The first golden ducat was issued in 1284, and at the height of the Republic the Venetian 'zecchini' were used as currency throughout the world.—Beyond a small bridge (with a Doric building recently attrib. to Lor. Santi. c 1815) extend the *Giardinetti Reali* (public gardens). These were laid out c 1814 after the demolition of the Republican Granaries. They contain, at the far end, an elaborate neo-classical coffee-house (by Lor. Santi, c 1838). Across the next bridge is the *Capitaneria di Porto* (Port Authority office), once the seat of the Magistrato della Farina. By the San Marco landing-stage is Harry's Bar, founded in the 1920s by Guiseppe Cipriani, which continues to flourish as one of the city's most celebrated restaurants and cocktail bar (entered from Calle Vallaresso).

In the other direction the quay extends in front of the Palazzo Ducale as far as the *Ponte della Paglia*, a bridge of Istrian stone with a pretty balustrade of little columns which crosses Rio di Palazzo. From this bridge may be seen the Renaissance E front of the palace (comp. p 93), and the famous **Bridge of Sighs** or *Ponte dei Sospiri* (Pl.11;1), a flying bridge in Istrian stone by Ant. Contino (c 1600), named from the fact that it was used for the passage of prisoners from the Prigioni to be examined by the Inquisitors of State. The *Prigioni* (prisons; now used for exhibitions by a cultural society) themselves, on the other side of the bridge, are a severe construction begun by G.A. Rusconi (1560), continued by Ant. da Ponte (1589), and completed by Ant. and Tom. Contino (1614).—The Riva degli Schiavoni beyond is described in Rte 3.

# 2   The Grand Canal

The **\*\*Grand Canal** (*Canal Grande*), over 3km long, is the main thoroughfare of Venice. This splendid waterway, winding like an inverted S through the city, is filled with every kind of boat, from waterbuses to motorboats, barges, and gondolas. It is lined on either side with a continuous row of beautiful old buildings, including more than 100 palaces, mostly dating from the 14–18C, though a few date back to the 12C.

It follows the old course of a branch of the Brenta as far as the Rialto, and is 30–70 metres wide, with an average depth of 5 metres. The posts or 'pali' in front of the palaces show the colours of the livery or 'divisa' of their proprietors.

The best way to see the Grand Canal is by gondola (comp. p 60); otherwise the slow vaporetto (water-bus) No. 1 ('accelerato'). In the itinerary which follows the right bank is described from San Marco to the Station, and the opposite bank on the way back from the Station to San Marco.

The landing-stages (*pontili*) on the Grand Canal of the vaporetto No. 1 (comp. Pl.14 & 15) are: *San Zaccaria* (right), *San Marco* (right), *Santa Maria della Salute* (left), *Santa Maria del Giglio* (right), *Accademia* (left), *Ca' Rezzonico* (left), *San*

*Tomà* (Frari; left), *Sant' Angelo* (right), *San Silvestro* (left), *Rialto* (right), *Ca d'Oro* (right), *San Stae* (left), *San Marcuola* (right), *Riva di Biasio* (left), *Ferrovia* (right; railway station), *Piazzale Roma* (left; car park).—Rte 2A is described starting from San Zaccaria landing stage; Rte 2B from Piazzale Roma landing-stage (where the vaporetti begin their journey and it is usually possible to find a seat).

# A. San Marco to the Station: the Right Bank

From Riva degli Schiavoni (SAN ZACCARIA landing-stage) the boat steers out into the Canale di San Marco, passing the Prigioni, the rio crossed by the Bridge of Sighs, Palazzo Ducale, the Piazzetta with the Libreria Sansoviniana, the Zecca, and the Giardinetti. Across Rio della Luna is the low Capitaneria di Porto.—Behind the landing-stage of SAN MARCO (Calle Vallaresso) is the building (with blue awnings) which houses Harry's Bar (comp. p 101). Beyond the Hotel Monaco is the 15C Gothic *Palazzo Giustinian*, with the municipal tourist offices, and the 'Biennale' headquarters. It was a noted hotel in the 19C; Giuseppe Verdi, Théophile Gautier, Ruskin, and Marcel Proust all stayed here.

It is followed by the modern Hotel Baüer Grunwald. Across Rio di San Moisè is the plain classical facade of *Palazzo Treves de Bonfili*, attrib. to Bart. Monopola (17C). *Palazzo Tiepolo* (also 17C) is now occupied by the Europa Hotel. There follow the Hotel Regina, *Palazzo Gaggia* with its tall chimney-pots, and the 15C *Palazzo Contarini* (being restored). Next to it is the tiny *Palazzo Contarini-Fasan* (also covered for restoration), with just three windows on the piano nobile and two on the floor above. The charming 15C decoration includes a balcony with wheel tracery. It is traditionally called the 'House of Desdemona'.—*Palazzo Manolesso-Ferro* (15C Gothic) has been undergoing restoration for years in order to be converted into offices for the Regional administration. *Palazzo Flangini-Fini* is attrib. to Aless. Tremignon (1688). Beyond the rio is the 15C *Palazzo Pisani*, now the Gritti Palace Hotel with a terrace restaurant on the canal. John and Effie Ruskin stayed here in 1851. A gondola ferry operates from Campo Santa Maria del Giglio, at the end of which can just be seen the Baroque facade of the church.

By the landing-stage (SANTA MARIA DEL GIGLIO) is *Palazzo Venier Contarini* (17C), and across the rio, the 17C *Palazzo Barbarigo* adjoins *Palazzo Minotto* (15C Gothic). Next rises the huge *Palazzo Corner* called *Ca' Grande*, a dignified edifice in the full Renaissance style by Sansovino (begun after 1545). Above the rusticated ground floor are the Ionic and Corinthian upper stories. It is now occupied by the Prefecture.—Behind the little garden can be glimpsed the *Casetta delle Rose*, where Canova had his studio, and d'Annunzio lived during the First World War. There follow a series of less distinguished palaces; beyond a narrow rio and two more houses are the two *Palazzi Barbaro*, one 17C, and the other, on Rio dell'Orso, 15C Gothic decorated with marbles and carvings. This is still owned by the Curtis family; in the 19C they here entertained John Singer Sargent, Henry James (who wrote 'The Aspern Papers' during his stay), James Whistler, Robert Browning, and Monet.—Across the rio is *Palazzo Franchetti*, a sumptuous 15C building, arbitrarily restored (and a wing added) in 1896. It is adjoined by a garden, behind which rises the brick campanile of San Vitale.

The wooden **Ponte dell'Accademia** was built in 1932–33 to replace a 19C iron bridge. It has been shored up during restoration, and a temporary bridge built beside it. Beyond *Casa Civran-Badoer* with a small garden, stands *Palazzo Giustiniani-Lolin* (marked by its two pinnacles), an early work by Longhena (1623). It is now owned by the Fondazione Levi, a music study centre. Next comes *Palazzetto Falier* (15C Gothic) with two protruding loggie, rare survivals of the 'liagò' which used to be a characteristic feature of Venetian houses. Across the rio is a palace which incorporates the rusticated corner in Istrian stone of the *Ca' del Duca*, a remarkable building begun by Bart. Bon in the mid-15C, but never completed. It takes its name from Fr. Sforza, Duke of Milan who bought it in 1461 from And. Corner. Steps lead down into the water from the adjoining campo. Beyond is the garden, with statuary, of *Palazzo Cappello Malipiero*, rebuilt in 1622. In the Campo di San Samuele can be seen the 12C campanile of the church (the San Samuele landing-stage is used by water-bus No. 2). The vast *Palazzo Grassi* was begun in 1748 by Giorgio Massari. It is now a cultural centre owned by the Fiat organization, and important exhibitions are held here (comp. p 133). Beyond an alley is the 17C *Palazzo Moro-Lin* with a long balcony above the portico on the water-front. The *Palazzi Da Lezze* and *Erizzo-Nani-Mocenigo*, on the bend of the canal, have been altered from their original Gothic form. *Palazzo Contarini delle Figure* is a graceful Lombardesque building by Scarpagnino (16C) decorated with heraldic trophies and marbles. It is thought to be named after the two figures (difficult to see) beneath the balcony. The four *Palazzi Mocenigo* (with blue and white 'pali' in the water) consist of two palaces on either side of a long double facade. In the first Emmanuel Philibert of Savoy was a guest in 1575, and Giordano Bruno in 1592 (when he was betrayed by his host); in the third (plaque) Byron wrote the beginning of 'Don Juan' (1818) and entertained Thomas Moore. The fourth has blue awnings.—They are adjoined by *Palazzo Corner-Gheltof* (16C). By the San Tomà ferry stands an old low house. Next comes *Palazzo Garzoni* (15C; now owned by Venice University), with two putti high up on the facade.

Beyond a wide rio is the SANT'ANGELO landing-stage next to the modern brick-coloured offices of A.C.T.V. (Azienda del Consorzio Trasporti Veneziano; the Venetian transport headquarters, formerly known as A.C.N.I.L.). *Palazzo Corner-Spinelli*, by Mauro Codussi (1490–1510) is a particularly successful Renaissance palace, with a rusticated ground floor and attractive balconies. Beyond two more rii is the pink *Palazzo Benzon*, which, in the time of the Countess Marina Benzon (c 1818) was the rendezvous of Venetian fashionable society and was visited by Byron, Moore, Canova, etc. Next to the 16C *Palazzo Martinengo*, with two coats-of-arms (the facade once had frescoes by Pordenone), are *Palazzo* and *Palazzetto Tron* (15C restored). On Rio di San Luca stands *Palazzo Corner Contarini dei Cavalli*, an elegant Gothic work of c 1450 with two coats-of-arms and a fine central six-light window. Across the rio rises *Palazzo Grimani*, a masterpiece designed by Sanmicheli before his death in 1559 and built by Giangiacomo dei Grigi. It is now the seat of the Court of Appeal. Next to the rust-coloured facade decorated with marbles of the *Casa Corner Valmarana*, is the *Casa Corner-Martinengo-Ravà*, now the seat of the Azienda Autonoma del Turismo. It was owned by the distinguished Morosini family who were here visited by Paolo Sarpi, Galileo Galilei, Giordano Bruno, etc. In the 19C it was a well-known hotel and James Fenimore Cooper stayed here in 1838.

*Detail from the Miracle of the Cross by Vittore Carpaccio, c 1496, showing the old Rialto bridge*

The Fondamenta del Carbon now skirts the Grand Canal as far as the Rialto bridge. The 13C Veneto-Byzantine *Palazzi Farsetti* and *Loredan* are occupied by the town hall. Palazzo Farsetti, built by doge Enrico Dandolo, was heavily restored in the 19C. Palazzo Loredan (covered for restoration in 1985) has a double row of arches and statues of Venice and Justice beneath Gothic canopies and bears the arms of the distinguished Corner family. Elena Corner Piscopia (1646–84), who lived here, was the first woman to receive a degree (from Padua University in philosophy in 1678).—In the middle of the next group of houses is the tiny Gothic *Palazzetto Dandolo*, with a double row of four-light windows. Just before the bridge across Rio di San Salvador is the large *Palazzo Bembo*, the probable birthplace of Pietro Bembo. Across the rio stánds the white facade of *Palazzo Dolfin-Manin*, by Sansovino, begun in 1538 for a Venetian merchant, Zuanne Dolfin. It is now the office of the Banca d'Italia. The portico on the ground floor extends over the fondamenta.

Beyond the RIALTO landing-stage the boat soon passes beneath **Ponte di Rialto**, a famous Venetian landmark. This replaces a wooden bridge which in turn superseded a bridge of boats which had crossed the Grand Canal at this point since the earliest days of the city's history. Ant. da Ponte won the commission to rebuild the bridge in stone in 1588: other contenders whose designs were rejected included Palladio, Sansovino, and Vignola. Its single arch, 48 metres in span and 7.5 metres high, carries a thoroughfare divided into three lanes by two rows of shops. It bears high reliefs of the Annunciation by Agost. Rubini (16C).—Just beyond the bridge is the **Fóndaco dei Tedeschi**, the most important of the trading centres on the Grand Canal leased by the Venetians to foreign merchants. By the mid-13C the Germans, Austrians, Bohemians, and Hungarians had their warehouses, shops, offices, and lodgings here. The building was reconstructed in 1505 by Spavento and completed by Scarpagnino from the designs of Girolamo Tedesco, and the exterior frescoed by Giorgione and Titian (this has entirely disappeared; fragments survive in the Ca' d'Oro, comp. p 170). It is now the central Post Office.—In the next group of houses are *Palazzo Civran*, with a mask over the door, and the 19C *Palazzo Sernagiotto*, with a columned portico. Beyond the pretty Campiello del Remer (the 13C *Palazzo Lion-Morosini* here has an external staircase), is Rio San Giovanni Grisostomo, followed by three small palaces. Next comes *Ca' da Mosto*, a 13C Veneto-Byzantine building decorated with paterae above the windows. This was the birthplace of Alvise Da Mosto (1432–88), discoverer of the Cape Verde Islands. It later became a famous inn (the Albergo del Leon Bianco). Across Rio dei Santi Apostoli stands *Palazzo Mangilli-Valmarana*, a classical building built on a design by Ant. Visentini for the distinguished English consul Joseph Smith (1682–1779), patron of Canaletto and other Venetian artists. George III acquired Smith's remarkable art collection and library. The palace was completed by 1751.—The name of the adjoining *Palazzo Michiel Dal Brusà* is a reminder of the great fire of 1774 which destroyed the previous Gothic palace on this site. The *Palazzo Michiel dalle Colonne* has a tall columned portico (remodelled by Gaspari in the 17C). Just before the busy ferry station (which serves the Rialto markets), in Campo Santo Sofia, is *Palazzo Foscari* (a fine 15C window has colourful marble columns). On the other side of the campo is the red *Palazzo Morosini-Sagredo* with a pretty balconied Gothic window and a variety of arches on its interesting

*Design for the Ponte di Rialto by Palladio (Francesco Guardi)*

facade. It is adjoined by the brick *Palazzo Pesaro-Rava* (15C Gothic).

Here is the landing-stage for the CA' D'ORO. The *Ca' d'Oro* (comp. p 167) has the most elaborate Gothic facade in Venice (1425–c 1440), famous for its tracery. It was called the 'Golden House' because the sculptural details were originally gilded.—Beyond the green facade of *Palazzo Giusti* (18C, with statues and busts), is *Palazzo Fontana* (16C), the birthplace of Clement XIII (Count Rezzonico, 1693–1769). Across Rio di San Felice is a house with a garden; then *Palazzo Contarini-Pisani*, with a plain 17C facade (above a portico); *Palazzo Boldù*, also 17C (with a rusticated ground floor); and *Palazzo Da Lezze*, with its little garden on the canal. Across the rio stands the handsome *Palazzo Gussoni Grimani della Vida*, attrib. to Sanmicheli (1548–56), formerly decorated with frescoes by Tintoretto. Sir Henry Wotton, the English ambassador lived here in 1614–18. He was a writer and art collector (with a particular interest in drawings by Palladio). James I dismissed him for his contention that an ambassador was an honest man sent to lie abroad for the good of his country. There follow two 17C palaces, and, on Rio della Maddalena, the 16C *Palazzo Barbarigo* which has almost lost its facade frescoes by Cam. Ballini. Across the rio are the 17C *Palazzi Molin* and *Emo* on the bend of the canal, and then *Palazzo Soranzo* with a fine facade probably by Sante Lombardo. *Palazzo Erizzo alla Maddalena* is a 15C Gothic building with a good window. This is adjoined by *Palazzo Marcello* (rebuilt in the 18C), the birthplace of Bened. Marcello (1686–1739), the composer. The imposing edifice in Istrian stone beyond its garden is *Palazzo Loredan Vendramin Calergi*, almost certainly designed by Mauro Codussi, and built in the first decade of the 16C. The facade is a masterpiece of Renaissance architecture with Corinthian columns and pilasters dividing the three stories beneath a classical cornice with a finely carved frieze. Wagner died here on 13 February 1883. It is now the winter home of the Casino, and in summer is often open for art exhibitions—Beyond the rio, *Casa Gatti-Casazza*, with a roof garden (the typical Venetian 'altane'), has been restored in the 18C style.

The landing-stage of SAN MARCUOLA is in front of the unfinished facade of the church. On the other side of a garden is *Palazzo Martinengo Mandelli*, reconstructed in the 18C. There follow several 17C palaces, including *Palazzo Correr-Contarini*. Shortly after the Campiello del Remer, the CANNAREGIO, the second largest canal in Venice, diverges right. *Palazzo Labia* (p 174) can be seen on the canal next to the church of San Geremia. Beyond the church, on the Grand Canal, is the little *Scuola dei Morti* (rebuilt after 1849), and the stone facade of *Palazzo Flangini*, left unfinished by Gius. Sardi. After a group of modern houses, and just before the bridge, is the long *Palazzo Soranzo Calbo Crotta*, a 15C building enlarged and altered. The bridge which serves the Station was built by Eugenio Miozzi in 1932–1934. Just before the FERROVIA landing-stage is the Baroque facade of the church of the *Scalzi* by Gius. Sardi. The railway station was built in 1955. Beyond it rise the huge modern office blocks of the State railways.—The last landing-stage is at PIAZZALE ROMA, the terminus of the road from the mainland.

# B. Piazzale Roma to San Marco; the Right Bank

From PIAZZALE ROMA the boat steers out into the Grand Canal and soon passes the mouth of the *Rio Nuovo*, a canal cut in 1933 as a short route from the Station to Piazza San Marco. Beyond the *Giardino Papadópoli* (public gardens) a bridge crosses Rio della Croce (at the end of which stands the campanile of the church of San Niccolò da Tolentino). The next important edifice on this side of the canal is the 18C church of *San Simeone Piccolo*, with a lofty green dome and Corinthian portico. Just before the Station bridge (comp. above) is *Palazzo Foscari Contarini*, a Renaissance building (covered for restoration in 1985). The boat passes beneath the bridge. Beyond Rio Marin and a pretty garden opens Campo San Simeone Grande with trees and a well. At the far end is a portico along the flank of the church. There follow a group of simple palaces before the landing-stage of RIVA DI BIASIO.

On the corner of the next rio, just beyond a pretty garden, stands the 15C Gothic *Palazzo Giovanelli*. Beyond two more houses is the plain facade of *Casa Correr*, which was the home of Teodoro Correr whose collection forms part of the Museo Correr (p 86). The **Fóndaco dei Turchi** is an impressive Veneto-Byzantine building, unfeelingly restored in the 19C. It was the Turkish warehouse from 1621–1838, and is now a Natural History Museum (see p 154). Beneath the portico are several sarcophagi; one is that of doge Marin Falier, beheaded in 1355.—Across the río is the plain brick facade of the *Granaries* of the Republic. This 15C battlemented edifice bears a relief of the Lion of St Mark (a modern replacement of one destroyed at the downfall of the Republic). The building has recently been restored.—*Palazzo Belloni-Battagià* has two tall obelisks crowning its facade which is decorated with coats-of-arms. It was built by Baldass. Longhena in 1647–63. The fine water-gate is flanked by iron grilles. Across the rio stand *Palazzo Tron* (1590) and *Palazzo Duodo*

(Gothic). Beyond a garden is *Palazzo Priuli Bon*, with 13C Veneto-Byzantine traces on the ground floor.

The SAN STAE landing-stage is next to the church of *San Stae* with a rich Baroque facade (c 1709) by Dom. Rossi. It is adjoined by the pretty little *Scuola dei Battiloro e Tiraoro* (goldsmiths), attrib. to Giac. Gaspari (1711). Next comes *Palazzo Foscarini-Giovanelli* (17C) where doge Marco Foscarini was born in 1695. Across the rio stands the bright clean facade of *\*Palazzo Pésaro*, a grand Baroque palace by Bald. Longhena decorated with grotesque masks. It was completed after Longhena's death in 1682 by Ant. Gaspari, who was responsible for the facade on the rio. It now contains the Gallery of Modern Art and the Oriental Museum (see p 152).—Beyond two smaller palaces rises *Palazzo Corner della Regina*, by Dom. Rossi (1724), now the 'Biennale' archive of contemporary art. It stands on the site of the birthplace of Caterina Cornaro, queen of Cyprus (1454–1510). The lower part of the facade is rusticated and bears masks. A plaque on *Casa Bragadin Favretto* records the studio here of the painter Giacomo Favretto (d 1887). Beyond two more palaces is the gothic *Palazzo Morosini Brandolin*. A bridge connects Fondamenta dell'Olio with the *Pescheria*, a graceful neo-Gothic market hall built in 1907 on the site of the 14C fish-market. Here begin the **Rialto markets** (comp. p 151), the busy wholesale markets of the city, the buildings of which continue right up to the Rialto bridge. The water-front is colourful in the early morning when boats put in laden with fruit and vegetables. A gondola ferry is particularly active here. On the other side of the campo is the long arcaded *Fabbriche Nuove di Rialto*, a serviceable market building which follows the curve of the Grand Canal, begun by Sansovino in 1554. It is now the seat of the Assize Court. Behind the *Erberia*, the fruit and vegetable market, can be seen the *Fabbriche Vecchie di Rialto*, by Scarpagnino. The building at the foot of the Rialto bridge is *Palazzo dei Camerlenghi*, restored by Guglielmo dei Grigi (Il Bergamasco) in 1523–25. The ornate Renaissance facade is curiously angled. This was once the seat of the Lords of the Exchequer; the name of the fondamenta here is a reminder that the ground floor of the palace was conveniently used as a prison.

The boat passes beneath the **Rialto bridge** (comp. p 106). The reliefs of St Mark and St Theodore are by Tiziano Aspetti. At its foot (and partly concealed by it) is *Palazzo dei Dieci Savi*, a building of the early 16C by Scarpagnino. A tondo bears a modern lion, and on the corner stands a figure of Justice (late 16C). This was used by the financial ministers of the Republic. From this point the view down the Grand Canal is closed in the distance by Ca' Foscari and Palazzo Balbi with its prominent obelisks (see below).—Fondamenta del Vin runs in front of a modest row of houses. At the end, behind a garden, is the rust-coloured facade of *Palazzo Ravà*, a successful neo-Gothic building (1906), thought to occupy the site of the palace of the patriarchs of Grado.

Beyond is SAN SILVESTRO landing-stage. *Palazzo Barzizza* bears remarkable reliefs on its facade (12C Veneto-Byzantine). *Palazzo Businello* (formerly *Giustinian*), on the corner of Rio dei Meloni, was rebuilt in the 17C but preserves some Veneto-Byzantine elements. On the opposite corner stands *Palazzo Coccina-Tiepolo Papadopoli*, with its two obelisks. This is a work built in the best Renaissance tradition by Giangiacomo Grigi of Bergamo in the early 1560s. Beyond the garden is *Palazzo Donà*, with a fine 12C–13C window. This is adjoined by the smaller *Palazzo Donà della Madonnetta*, named after a 15C relief of the Madonna and Child set into the facade. It has an interesting arched window with good capitals and paterae. Across the rio stands *Palazzo Bernardo*, with a lovely Gothic facade (c 1442) especially notable for the tracery on the second piano nobile. *Palazzo Grimani* (now *Sorlini*) has an Istrian stone facade decorated with marbles. It is an elegant Lombardesque building of the early 16C. Beyond is the plain facade of *Palazzo Cappello-Layard*, on the corner of Rio San Polo. This was once the residence of the English diplomat Sir Henry Layard (1817–94), the discoverer of Nineveh, whose fine collection of paintings was left to the National Gallery of London in 1916.—Across the rio stands *Palazzo Barbarigo della Terrazza*, named after its balconied terrace on the Grand Canal (now used by the German Institute). Dating from 1568–9 it is attrib. to Bern. Contino. Next comes *Palazzo Pisani della Moretta*, with graceful Gothic tracery of the second half of the 15C. Beyond the 16C *Palazzo Tiepolo* is the smaller *Palazzo Tiepoletto* (15C). There follow two small houses and the rust-coloured *Palazzo Giustinian Persico*, a 16C work.

SAN TOMÀ (FRARI) landing-stage. *Palazzo Civran-Grimani*, on the corner of the rio, dates from the 17C. Just before Rio Nuovo rises the grand *Palazzo Balbi*, probably by Aless. Vittoria (1582–90); this is the seat of the Regional government. Next to it is the plain brick facade of the Fondazione Angelo Masieri for which Frank Lloyd Wright designed a small palace in the 1950's, never built since planning permission was refused. This spot on the Grand Canal is known as the 'Volta del Canal' since it is situated on a sharp bend. The busy Rio Nuovo (comp. p 108) is the short cut to the station. Here stands the beautifully proportioned *Ca' Fóscari* (1428–37), built for Fr. Foscari, doge for 34 years. It has notable tracery, fine marble columns, and a frieze of putti bearing the Foscari arms. It is now the seat of the University Institute of Economics and Commerce.—There follows the double facade of the *Palazzi Giustinian*, begun c 1452 by Bart. Bon. Wagner stayed here in 1858–9 and wrote the second act of 'Tristan'. After two small palaces rises the **Ca' Rezzonico** by Longhena (begun c 1667), with a story added by Giorgio Massari in 1745. It now houses the city's collection of 18C works of art (p 141).

Behind the CA' REZZONICO landing-stage is the 17C Lombardesque *Palazzo Contarini-Michiel*. Next comes the *Palazzetto di Madame Stern*, a modern reproduction of a Venetian Gothic palace, with a garden on the canal. Beyond the plain facade of *Palazzo Moro* stands *Palazzo Loredan dell'Ambasciatore*, so-named because it was the Austrian embassy in the 18C. It is a Gothic building of the 15C with two shield-bearing pages, fine Lombard works from the circle of Ant. Rizzo. Beyond Rio San Trovaso stand the *Palazzi Contarini Corfù* and *Contarini degli Scrigni*. The former is 15C Gothic with vari-coloured marbles, while the second was built in 1609 by Vinc. Scamozzi. Just before the ACCADEMIA landing-stage is the British Vice-Consulate at *Palazzo Querini*. Across the campo can be seen the 18C facade (by Giorgio Massari) of the Scuola della Carità, and the bare flank (with Gothic windows) of the former church of Santa Maria della Carità (both now used by the *Academy of Fine Arts* and the *Accademia Galleries*, comp. p 134).

Beyond the **Accademia bridge** (comp. p 102), is *Palazzo Contarini Dal Zaffo (Polignac)*, a graceful Lombardesque building with fine marble roundels, next to its neglected garden. Next comes *Palazzo Molin Balbi-Valier*, with a handsome ground floor and statues in the portico, followed by *Palazzo Loredan* (now *Cini* ) of the 16C.  Beyond the pretty Campo San Vio, planted with trees, stands *Palazzo Barbarigo*, with a harshly coloured mosaic facade (by Giulio Carlini, d 1887). Next door is *Palazzo Da Mula* (15C Gothic). In the red *Casa Biondetti* Rosalba Carriera (1676–1757) died. *Palazzo Venier dei Leoni* was begun in 1749 and only the ground-floor was completed. The wall on the Canal has a frieze of colossal lions heads at water level, and the building is surrounded by a luxuriant garden. It was owned by Mrs Peggy Guggenheim from 1949 until her death in 1979 and houses her remarkable collection of modern art (comp. p 144).—Beyond is *Palazzo Dario*, a charming Lombardesque building of 1487 in varicoloured marble, with numerous chimney-pots. Its outside walls incline noticeably. Next to it is *Pal. Barbaro* (Wolkoff; 15C). *Palazzo Salviati* was built in 1924 by G. dall'Olivo with a harsh mosaic on its facade. The Salviati glasshouse, founded in 1866, is one of the leading Venetian glass companies. *Palazzo Orio Semitecolo* has fine Gothic windows. A gondola ferry operates from the end of a calle here to Campo Santa Maria del Giglio. The last big palace on this side of the Canal is *Palazzo Genovese*, a successful imitation of the Gothic style built in 1892. Beside it are the low buildings of the ex-abbey of *San Gregorio*, with a delightful water-gate crowned by a large relief of the Saint (which gives on to the cloister; comp. p 145). Behind (on the rio) can be seen the fine apse of San Gregorio.

At the SALUTE landing-stage a marble pavement opens out before the grandiose church of *Santa Maria della Salute* (see p 145), a masterpiece of Baroque architecture by Longhena which dominates this part of the Canal. It is adjoined by the 17C *Seminario Patriarcale*. The *Dogana di Mare*, the customs house, a Doric construction by Gius. Benoni (1676–82) extends to the end of the promontory. The picturesque turret has two telamones who support a golden globe on which is balanced a weathervane of Fortune. The boat re-crosses the Grand Canal (with a fine view of the island of San Giorgio Maggiore) to the SAN MARCO (VALLARESSO) landing-stage.

*The Grand Canal and S. Maria della Salute, by Canaletto*

# 3    Riva degli Schiavoni to San Zaccaria, the Scuola di San Giorgio degli Schiavoni, San Francesco della Vigna, and the Arsenal

At the end of the S facade of Palazzo Ducale, Ponte della Paglia (see p 101) leads across a rio to **Riva degli Schiavoni** (Pl.11;1,2) a wide and busy quay on the basin of St Mark's, with numerous moorings and landing-stages for vaporetti, gondolas, and steamers. It was formerly the mooring-station for the trading vessels from Dalmatia and other Slavonic ports. Beyond the *Prigioni* (p 101) Calle degli Albanesi leads to a small *Aquarium* (adm see p 65) which contains fish from the lagoon as well as the tropics. On the Riva, the *Danieli*, which has been a hotel since 1822, occupies the Gothic Palazzo Dandolo. It numbers among its distinguished visitors George Sand, Alfred de Musset, Charles Dickens, Ruskin, Wagner, and Proust. Its disappointing extension was built in 1948 near the place where doge Vitale Michiel II was killed in 1172. The decree of the same year that no stone building should ever be built on the spot was observed until this century. Across *Ponte del Vin* (with pretty colonnades) towers the Victor Emmanuel Monument by Ettore Ferrari (1887). At a house on the quay here (No. 4161) Henry James finished 'The Portrait of a Lady' in 1881.

Sottoportico San Zaccaria leads under an arch away from the Riva into the peaceful Campo San Zaccaria, with its fine church. Behind the little garden with two elms and architectural fragments is the brick facade of the earlier church which was used as an entrance to the Benedictine convent (with two fine cloisters, now occupied by a police station), and the ancient brick campanile (13C). Along one side of the square the 16C portico of the former cloister is incorporated into the house-fronts. The church of *San Zaccaria (Pl.11;1; open 10–12, 16–18) is built in a remarkably successful mixture of Gothic and Renaissance styles (1444–1515), begin by *Ant. Gambello*, and finished by *Mauro Codussi* (who completed the upper part of the tall facade). Over the doorway is a statue of the patron saint, by *Aless. Vittoria* (in poor condition; the head is missing).

The church is dedicated to Zacharias, the father of St John the Baptist, whose relics are preserved here. It was founded by doge Giustiniano Participazio in the 9C. The famous Benedictine convent was visited annually by the Doge at Easter in gratitude for the gift made to the Signoria in the 12C of part of the convent orchard in order that Piazza San Marco could be enlarged. The ceremony included the presentation to the Doge of the ducal cap (or 'cornu'). Eight doges of the early Republic were buried in the first church.

The elegant INTERIOR (light at W end; fee) has a high aisled nave; the columns on fine raised bases have good capitals. The multiple apse with an ambulatory and coronet of chapels lit by long windows, typical of Northern European Gothic architecture, is unique in Venice.—The aisle walls are entirely covered with 17–18C paintings. The statues of the Baptist and of St Zacharias on the stoups are by *Vittoria*. NORTH AISLE. *Angelo Trevisani*, Visitation; 1st altar, *Gius. Salviati*, The Saviour and Saints; 2nd altar, *Madonna and four Saints, and an angel playing a musical instrument, by *Giov. Bellini*, signed and dated 1505 (light; fee), recently beautifully restored. At the end of the aisle is the tomb of *Aless. Vittoria* (1528–1608), with a bust of the artist by himself (1595).—At the end of the S aisle is an Adoration of the Shepherds by *Ant. Balestra*. A door admits to the CHAPEL OF ST ATHANASIUS (opened by the sacristan; fee), with stalls by *Fr.* and *M. Cozzi.* Over the altar, Birth of St John the Baptist, an early work by *Tintoretto.*—The adjoining CHAPEL OF ST TARASIUS has three fine *Anconas, or altar-paintings by *Ant. Vivarini* and *Giov. d'Alemagna* (1443), with ornate Gothic frames. In the fan vault (the chancel of the previous church) are *Frescoes by *And. del Castagno* and *Fr. da Faenza* (signed and dated 1442; damaged), one of the earliest known works by Tuscan Renaissance painters in Venice. Benèath is a fragment of mosaic pavement, thought to date from the 9C (glass in the floor reveals another fragment).—Steps lead down to the water-logged CRYPT (9C), with low columns.

Opposite the church a calle leads under an arch, the outer face of which is decorated with a large marble relief of the Madonna and Child between St John the Baptist and St Mark, by an unknown sculptor (Tuscan?) of the first half of the 15C. At the end of the little Campo San Provolo (right) a narrow alley leads on to Fondamenta dell'Osmarin. *Palazzo Priuli*, on the corner of the rio opposite, is a fine Venetian Gothic palace, probably dating from the late 14C, with a pretty corner window. The fondamenta ends at Ponte dei Greci, named after the Greek community which settled in this area in the 15C. Venice remained an important centre of Greek culture up until the 19C. The Greeks built the fine group of buildings across the canal in a courtyard behind a decorative wall (by Longhena, 1678). They are approached through a gateway beyond the flank of the Greek *Collegio Flangini* (also by Longhena). Here stand the Scuola di San Nicolò and the church of San Giorgio dei Greci with its 16C leaning campanile.

The church of **San Giorgio dei Greci** (unlocked by the custodian of the Museum, see below) was begun in 1539 on a design by *Sante Lombardo.* The cupola was added in 1571. It contains an iconostasis with late Byzantine figures, a Byzantine Madonna (12–13C), and Christ Pantocrator (early 14C), brought to Venice before the fall of Constantinople. The church was the most important in Europe for the Greek Orthodox rite.

In the **Scuola di San Nicolò dei Greci**, by Baldass. Longhena (1678) is a MUSEUM OF ICONS (adm see p 66) with a good collection (mostly 16–17C), including products from the workshop of the 'madoneri di Rialto', artists from Crete, who, from the 15–18C worked in Venice and combined Byzantine traditions with the local school of painting.

Fondamenta San Lorenzo leads N along the pretty canal. By the bridge, on the corner, is the Gothic Ca' Zorzi. The first bridge leads back across the canal into Calle Lion which ends at another bridge, at the foot of which is the little **Scuola di San Giorgio degli Schiavoni** (Pl.11;2; adm see p 66). This was founded in 1451 by the Dalmations with the aim to protect the Dalmatian community (mainly sailors) in Venice. The facade of 1551 by *Giov. De Zan* bears a relief of St George and the Dragon by *Pietro da Salò*, and a 14C Madonna and Child.

The *INTERIOR is one of the most evocative in the city. The walls of the little room are entirely decorated with a delightful series of *Paintings by *Carpaccio* (1502–08), relating to the lives of the three Dalmatian patron saints, SS. Jerome, Tryphone, and George. On the left wall: St George and the dragon, justly one of his best known paintings; the triumph of St George.—On the end wall: St George baptising the Gentiles; altarpiece of the Madonna and Child attrib. to Benedetto Carpaccio, son of Vittore; the miracle of St Tryphone (the boy Saint is freeing the daughter of the Emperor from a demon, in the form of a basilisk).—On the right wall: Agony in the Garden; Calling of St Matthew; the lion led by St Jerome into the monastery; Funeral of St Jerome; St Augustine in his study having a vision of St Jerome's death.—The room upstairs (from which the Carpaccio paintings were moved after 1551) has 17C decorations, including ceiling paintings attrib. to *And. Vicentino.*—The Treasury of the Guild (including a 15C processional Cross) is kept in the Sacristy.

The fondamenta leads S to the church of *Sant' Antonin* (often closed), rebuilt on a design attrib. to Longhena. It contains a Deposition by Lazzaro Bastiani.

It is necessary to recross the bridge in order to follow the fondamenta N along the canal. Just before a portico an alley diverges left for the church of *San Lorenzo* (open only for exhibitions).

Of ancient foundation the church was damaged in the First World War. Marco Polo (1256–1324) was buried here but his sarcophagus was lost during rebuilding in 1592 by Sim. Sorella. The convent buildings are now used as a hospice. In the area are a number of printing works and carpenters' shops.

Beyond the portico a bridge crosses the rio to Corte Nuova. Here a local chapel forms the unexpected beginning to Calle Zorzi. At the end, Calle del Fontego (left) leads to Campo Santa Giustina. The 18C Palazzo Gradenigo has been abandoned and the church is now used by a school. Fondamenta Santa Giustina leads towards the Fondamente Nuove (the N extremity of the city) which skirt the lagoon (the island of San Michele can be seen in the distance). From here can be reached the octagonal church of *Santa Maria del Pianto* (Pl.7;5) built by Fr. Contini in 1647–59, which, however, is difficult to see behind a high wall. It has been abandoned and closed indefinitely. The first calle on the right, off Fondamenta Santa Giustina, leads to **San Francesco della Vigna** (Pl.7;8). The name recalls the vineyard bequeathed to the Franciscan order for a convent in 1253 by Marco Ziani. On this site, in 1534, doge Andrea Gritti laid the foundation stone of the present church built by his friend *Jac. Sansovino*. The humanist friar Fr. Zorzi was involved in the design of the church. Giov. Grimani paid for the facade to be added in 1568–72 by *Palladio*. It bears two bronze statues of Moses and St Paul by *Tiziano Aspetti*. The tall campanile is by *Bern. Ongarin* (1581).

The dignified INTERIOR (open 7–11.45, 16.45–19) has a broad nave with side chapels between Doric pilasters, and a long chancel (with the monks' choir behind the high altar). On the W wall, Byzantine (13C) relief of the Madonna and Child, and a triptych attrib. to *Ant. Vivarini* (recently restored). The two Stoups bear bronze statuettes signed by *Vittoria.*—SOUTH SIDE. 1st chapel (left wall), Resurrection, a 16C Venetian work of uncertain attribution; 3rd chapel, *Palma Giovane*, Madonna and Child with Saints; 4th chapel, *Paolo Veronese* (attrib.), Resurrection (removed for restoration).—SOUTH TRANSEPT. *Madonna and Child enthroned, a charming large composition by *Ant. da Negroponte* (c 1450). In the CHOIR is the tomb of doge Andrea Gritti (d 1538; comp. above), and, in the pavement in front of the choir, the fine tombstone of Marcantonio Trevisan (d 1554). In front of the high altar, tombstone of And. Bragadin (d 1487). The GIUSTINIANI CHAPEL, on the left, is beautifully decorated with 15C *Sculptures (removed from the earlier church) by *P. Lombardo* and his school. Over the Sacristy door, Monument to doge Trevisan with a 16C statue. In the niche to the right is an alabaster statue of a bishop Saint (16C?). From the NORTH TRANSEPT is the entrance to the CAPPELLA SANTA (light; 100 l.), with a Madonna and Saints recently restored and attrib. to the *School of Giov. Bellini* (1507). From outside the chapel can be seen one of the three surviving 15C cloisters of the convent.—NORTH SIDE. Fifth Chapel, *Veronese*, The Holy Family with SS. John the Baptist, Anthony Abbot, and Catherine. In the 3rd chapel are chiaroscuri by *G.B. Tiepolo* and elaborate 18C sculpted garlands by *Temanza*. The 2nd chapel contains an altar with three statues of Saints, a good work by *Vittoria*. The 1st chapel (the GRIMANI CHAPEL; light, 100 l.) was decorated c 1560 with ceiling paintings by *Battista*

*Franco* and an altarpiece by *Fed. Zuccari*. The bronze statues of Justice and Temperance are by *Tiziano Aspetti* (1592).

From here a number of narrow calli lead SE towards the Arsenal. Beyond a conspicuous neo-classical colonnade (by A. Pigazzi) and the Oratorio di San Pasquale a bridge leads over Rio di San Francesco. A series of calli lead more or less due S, passing Campo delle Gatte where Ugo Foscolo lived in 1792–97. A short way beyond Rio dei Scudi, Calle del Mandolin leads left into the pretty Campiello due Pozzi, with a 14C house. Off Calle Magno, Sottoportico d'Angelo diverges right (the low arch is surmounted by a fine statue of an angel between two hedgehogs in relief). At the end rises the crenellated wall of the Arsenal. The rio is used as a mooring for small boats. This is now followed, along the line of the wall, through a secluded campo across Rio dell' Arsenale into Campo San Martino. The church of **San Martino** (recently restored) was built c 1540 by *Jac. Sansovino* on a Greek cross plan. The earliest church on this site is supposed to have been founded by Paduans in 593. The ceiling has 17C quadratura by *Dom. Bruni*, and St Martin in Glory by *Jac. Guarana*. On the organ, by *Gaetano Callido* (1799) is a Last Supper by *Girol. da Santacroce*. On the right is a 17C monument to doge Fr. Erizzo, who is buried in the centre of the church. In the chapel to the right of the chancel, Risen Christ, by *Girol. da Santacroce*. In the Sacristy, Byzantine Madonna and Child.—The little oratory next door has a 15C relief of St Martin and the Beggar.

At the end of the fondamenta (left) rises the splendid Arsenal Gateway, the land entrance to the **Arsenal** (Pl.12;1,2), beside the two massive towers which protect the entrance from the lagoon. The arsenal remained for centuries the symbol of the economic and military power of the Venetian Republic.

The Arsenal was founded in 1104; it was enlarged from the 14–16C, and now occupies 32 hectares (80 acres). It gave its name (from the Arabic 'darsina 'a', meaning 'workshop') to all subsequent dockyards. Dante visited it in 1306, and again in 1321 when he was sent as emissary to Venice from Ravenna (comp. 'Inferno', xxi; inscribed on a plaque to the left of the gate). At the height of Venetian prosperity it employed 16,000 workmen. It is surrounded by crenellated walls with towers.

The Great GATEWAY, in the form of a triumphal arch, is one of the earliest works of the Renaissance in the city. It was built in 1460 probably by *Gambello* who re-used Greek marble columns with Veneto-Byzantine capitals. The statue of St Justina above is by *Girol. Campagna*. Additions were made in the 16–17C. Beyond the door, is a Madonna and Child signed by *Sansovino*. The doorway is flanked by two colossal lions sent by Fr. Morosini from Piraeus as spoils of war and placed here in 1692. The one sitting upright on the left (which gave the name of Porta Leone to Piraeus) bears a (worn) Runic inscription carved in 1040 by Varangian guards from Byzantium sent to Athens to put down an insurrection; its fellow possibly stood on the road from Athens to Eleusis. The two smaller lions, added in 1718 after the relief of Corfu, may have come originally from the Lion Terrace at Delos.

The interior of the Arsenal (no adm; at present used by the armed forces) can only be seen from vaporetto No. 5 which runs through the main canal of the Arsenale Vecchio (closed to private vessels) on its circular route of the city (comp. p 57). There are long-term plans to convert the Arsenal to civil use when the present military administration comes to an end. An international cultural centre, a naval archaeological museum, and a port for small boats, are among the numerous proposals which have been made for the utilisation of this vast area of the city.

A wooden bridge, which retains the form of previous bridges here

*Ancient Greek lion guarding the Arsenal Gateway*

(which, up until the 18C, were drawbridges) leads across the Canale
dell'Arsenale. The view embraces the oldest part of the Arsenal with
the outlet onto the Fondamente Nuove. Beyond the neo-classical
Guardhouse built in 1829 by Giov. Casoni during the Austrian
occupation, the fondamenta leads back to the quay overlooking the
Bacino di San Marco. Here is the Campo San Biagio with the Museo
Navale (see Rte 13).—Riva Ca' di Dio leads back towards San Marco
past the *Forni Pubblici* (1473) with an ornamental marble frieze.
These were the bakeries of the Republic which supplied the ships as
they set sail from the Arsenal. On the next rio is the *Ca' di Dio*
(restored), a pilgrim hospital founded in the 13C for Crusaders. In
1545 Sansovino added a hospice wing along the rio (seen from the
bridge, with its numerous chimney-stacks). Here begins the Riva
degli Schiavoni (comp. p 112). Some way farther on, just before the
next bridge, Calle del Dose leads into the peaceful Campo Bandiera
e Moro and the church of **San Giovanni in Brágora** (Pl.11;2), rebuilt
in 1475.

INTERIOR. On the W wall, *Palma Giovane*, Christ before Caiaphas. SOUTH
AISLE. Over the side door, in a marble niche, Madonna and Child (late
Byzantine). The 2nd chapel is dedicated to St John the Almsgiver whose relics
were brought from Alexandria in 1247. The front of the sarcophagus (on the
left wall) is carved in wood by *Leonardo Tedesco*. Above the Sacristy door,
Byzantine Madonna and Child in relief. To the right of the door, *Cima da*

*Conegliano,* Constantine and St Helena (1502), with a predella showing the Finding of the True Cross; to the left, *Alvise Vivarini,* The Risen Christ (1498; removed for restoration).—In the SANCTUARY (light on right; fee) a great marble frame encloses the *Baptism of Christ by Cima da Conegliano (1494; poorly restored). On the walls, *Palma Giovane,* Washing of the Feet, and *Paris Bordone,* Last Supper. In the chapel to the left of the apse, Triptych of the Madonna enthroned between St John the Baptist and St Andrea, signed and dated 1478 by *Bart. Vivarini,* and (right) SS. Andrew, Jerome, and Martin, by *Fr. Bissolo.*—NORTH AISLE. *Alvise Vivarini,* Head of the Saviour (removed for restoration), Madonna and Child; 2nd chapel, Madonna and Child in the Byzantine style (on the left wall), and Christ and St Veronica, by the *School of Titian* (in a pretty frame). Just before the last chapel, St Nicholas and scenes from his life (15C). In the lovely 15C font Vivaldi was baptised in 1678.

On the Riva, by the bridge, a plaque on No. 4145 records Petrarch's house. He came to Venice in 1362 to escape the plague in Padua; he lived here with his daughter and her family until 1367. The house was given to him by the Republic in return for his promise to leave his library to the city of Venice (comp. p 100).—Across the bridge is **La Pietà** (recently reopened after restoration), the church of an orphanage for girls founded in 1346 which achieved European fame for its music in the 17–18C. Vivaldi was violin-master in 1704–18 and concert-master in 1735–38, and many of his best compositions were written for the hospital.

The bright *Interior (open Mon., Wed. & Friday 9–12) was sumptuously rebuilt in the present oval plan by *Massari* (1745–60) with galleries for choir and musicians, and an oblong vestibule. The contemporary decorations remain intact, with a fine ceiling fresco of the Triumph of Faith by *G.B. Tiepolo* (1755), and a series of altarpieces: *Fr. Daggiù (Il Cappella),* Madonna and Child with four Saints; *Dom. Maggiotto,* Miracle of St Spiridion; (on the high altar) *G.B. Piazzetta,* Visitation (finished by his pupil *G. Angeli*): *G. Angeli,* St Peter Orseolo; *And. Marinetti (Il Chiozzotto),* Crucifixion. The organ is by *Nacchini* (1759).

Beyond the next bridge is the stretch of the Riva degli Schiavoni already described at the beginning of this Route (p 112) which leads back to San Marco.

# 4    Piazza San Marco to the Galleria Querini-Stampalia, Santa Maria Formosa, and Santi Giovanni e Paolo

From Piazzetta Giovanni XXIII (or 'dei Leoncini', comp. Rte 1), beside the Basilica of San Marco, Calle di Canonica leads along the side of Palazzo Patriarcale (with interesting sculptural fragments in the courtyard) to Rio di Palazzo, across which rises the fine facade of *Palazzo Trevisan-Cappello* (16C; in poor condition), with good marble inlay. From the bridge there is a view right of the Renaissance facade of Palazzo Ducale (comp. p 93), and the Bridge of Sighs. On the other side of the rio, at the end of the short fondamenta, is the entrance (at No. 4312) to the **Museum of Diocesan Art** (Pl.11;1; adm see p 66), and the CLOISTER OF SANT' APOLLONIA.

The tiny CLOISTER, the only Romanesque cloister in the city (early 14C; beautifully restored in 1969) retains its original brick paving. Here are displayed sculptural fragments and inscriptions (some dating from the 9–11C) from the Basilica.—On the far side is the entrance to the DIOCESAN MUSEUM, recently arranged and opened regulárly to the public by volunteers. It contains a collection of sacred art (vestments, missals, church plate, crucifixes, reliquaries, etc) as well as paintings and sculpture from churches either closed permanently or unable to provide safe keeping for their treasures.

At the top of the stairs, in the gallery to the left, 17C lace vestments and embroidered missals from the Scuola di Santa Barbara; pope John XXIII's cardinal's beret; paintings from Sant'Antonin by *Palma il Giovane*, two *Paintings by *Luca Giordano* from Sant'Aponal; *Supper in the House of Simon (1548) by *Moretto da Brescia*, formerly in the church of the Pietà; wood Crucifix of 1300 (being restored) from San Giovanni Nuovo; Redeemer with Saints, a ruined painting by *Tintoretto* from San Gallo.—In the room at the end (right), Allegory of the Scuola del Crocefisso, by *A. Pellegrini*. The huge external and internal organ *Shutters from San Marco signed by *Gentile Bellini* depicting SS. Mark, Theodore, Jerome, and Francis, are temporarily displayed here, and in the adjacent gallery—In the galleries on the other side of the entrance hall: portraits of the 'Primiceri' (head chaplains) of San Marco; silver reliquaries; rock crystal and gilt wood reliquary in the form of a tower and a cupola (17C, from San Martino di Murano); a reliquary with 12C enamels in a 15C setting from Santo Stefano; processional *Crucifix from S Pietro di Castello, with fine half-length figures in the terminals (late 15C); reliquary of St Tryphon, in the form of a leg (late 14C from Santa Maria del Giglio).

The calle in front of the bridge ends in the undistinguished Campo SS. Filippo e Giacomo; at the far end, to the left, a calle (sign-posted 'Querini-Stampalia') leads to the church of SAN GIOVANNI NUOVO (or *San Giovanni in Oleo*), in a stark campo. A church of ancient foundation, it was rebuilt in the 18C by Matteo Lucchesi on a Palladian design (the facade was left half-finished) and it has been closed indefinitely. A passageway leads out onto Rio del Rimedio with interesting water-gates. At the end, a bridge (one of many in this area) crosses into Campiello Querini, with the entrance (across a small canal) to the 16C **Palazzo Querini-Stampalia** (Pl.6;8), the residence of the patriarchs of Venice in 1807–50, now occupied by the Fondazione Querini-Stampalia, the bequest to the city of Count Giovanni Querini (1869). The ground floor was reconstructed in 1961–3 by Carlo Scarpa.

On the first floor is the LIBRARY (open 14.30–23.30; winter 14.30–20, 21–23.30; Sun & fest. 15–19), with over 230,000 vols. and 1100 MSS.—The second floor is occupied by the Pinacoteca (adm see p 66). The pictures are well-labelled and a catalogue of the collection is lent to visitors. On the left of the entrance hall, with its busts, ROOM 1 is filled with charming views of Venetian life in the 18C by *Gabriel Bella*; they provide a valuable documentation of the city at that period.—R 2. *Catarino Veneziano* and *Donato Veneziano*, *Coronation of the Virgin (1372); *15C Venetian School*, Crucifixion.—R 3. Portraits by *Seb. Bombelli* (1635–1719), and *Marco Vecellio*.—R 4 contains paintings by *Palma Giovane* and *Luca Giordano*.—R 5. *And. Schiavone*, Conversion of St Paul (restored in 1981); 16C works.—RR 6 & 7 contain works by *Pietro Liberi*, *Matteo dei Pitocchi*, and others.—R 8. *Lorenzo di Credi*, Adoration of the Virgin; *Giov. Bellini*, *Presentation in the Temple (a copy of a painting by Mantegna now in Berlin); *Palma Vecchio*, Madonna and saints (removed); *Francesco Querini* and *Paola Priuli Querini*, two unfinished portraits (1528).—The ceiling of R 9 bears an Allegory by *Seb. Ricci* (removed for restoration). Here are displayed: *Francesco da Santacroce*, Adoration of the Magi; *Palma Vecchio*, Madonna and saints (removed); (on an easel), *Vincenzo Catena*, *Judith.—RR 11–13. Genre paintings by *Pietro* and *Aless. Longhi*; beyond a corridor, R 15 (left), the BEDROOM, has tapestries of 16C Flemish workmanship.—RR 16, 17. RED AND GREEN DRAWING-ROOMS; in R 17 are four fine large portraits of officials of the Republic, including *Giov. Dolfin by *G.B. Tiepolo* (removed), and the Procurator Francesco Querini, by *Pietro Liberi*; Louis XVII mirrors.—Beyond R 18, with stucco decoration, R 20,

*St Barbara by Palma Vecchio (in S. M. Formosa)*

the DINING ROOM, has a case of Sèvres porcelain (late 18C), and a collection of biscuit ware on consoles.

CAMPO SANTA MARIA FORMOSA (Pl.6;8), approached from behind its church, is one of the most lively near San Marco. It has a small daily market and lies in an area abounding in canals. At the end bordered by a canal with four small bridges is *Ca' Malipiero Trevisan* (No. 5250), attrib. to Sante Lombardo. Just out of the campo, reached by Ruga Giuffa and Ramo Grimani is the monumental entrance to the huge *Palazzo Grimani*, attrib. to Sanmicheli (being restored), with three antique busts. Here was housed the famous Grimani collection, left to the Republic and now forming the nucleus of the Archaeological Museum (comp. p 100).—In the campo, *Palazzo Vitturi* (No. 5246) has Veneto-Byzantine decorations. A small house (No. 6129) was the home of Sebastiano Venier, victor of Lépanto (plaque). *Palazzo Donà*

*The Colleoni monument by Verrocchio (Campo Santi Giovanni e Paolo)*

(No. 6125–26) has a pretty doorway and good windows. At the end, *Palazzo Priuli* is a classical work by Bart. Monopola (c 1580). The church of **Santa Maria Formosa** (Pl.7;7), rebuilt by *Mauro Codussi* in 1492 with a dome, has been restored since 1916. The name is derived from the tradition that the Madonna appeared to its founder San Magno in the 7C in the form of a buxom matron.

Of the two facades, that towards the campo, crowned by five 17C statues, dates from 1604; the other (1542), at the main W entrance, overlooks a canal. The Baroque campanile has a grotesque mask at its foot.

INTERIOR. The Greek-cross plan of the primitive church, derived from Byzantine models, was preserved by *Codussi* when he gave the interior its beautiful Renaissance form in the 15C. The chapels are divided by double open arches. SOUTH AISLE. Over the Baptistery, Tondo of the Circumcision, attrib. to *Vinc. Catena*. 1st chapel, *Bart. Vivarini*, Triptych of the Madonna of the Misericordia (1473; light on left), and (over the door) *L. Bastiani* (attrib.), Holy Father and four Angels.—In the SOUTH TRANSEPT (with a Last Supper by *Leandro Bassano*) is the CHAPEL OF THE BOMBARDIERI. Here is the composite *Altarpiece by *Palma Vecchio* (1522–24), notable especially for the colourful and majestic figure of St Barbara in the centre, typical of the Giorgionesque style of Venetian beauty. On the right wall of the CHAPEL OF THE SACRAMENT (in the N transept) is a Circumcision (much darkened) by a follower of *Cima da Conegliano*.—The ORATORY (opened on request) contains works by *Sassoferrato* and *Pietro de Saliba*.

In front of the earlier facade of the church, Fondamenta dei Preti runs along the canal across a bridge (note the Roman aedicula with a Latin inscription, set in to the corner of a house here) to Ponte del Paradiso. Here the calle has a fine overhead arch with a 14C relief of the Madonna and donor and coats-of-arms of the Foscari and Mocenigo families. The calle preserves its wooden eaves for the whole of its length.

Calle Larga Santa Maria Formosa leads out of the campo. The narrow Calle Trevisan (sign-posted 'Santi Giovanni e Paolo') soon diverges left; beyond a rio it emerges in CAMPO SANTI GIOVANNI E PAOLO (*San Zanipolo*; Pl.7;5), historically one of the most important campi in the city. Its simple houses are dominated by the huge Dominican church. On a fine pedestal rises the superb equestrian *Statue of Bartolomeo Colleoni, the famous condottiere, begun by *Verrocchio* in 1481.

Colleoni (c 1400–75), who had served Venice as a general, left a legacy to the Republic on condition that an equestrian monument was erected in his honour in Piazza San Marco. In 1479 the Signoria ordered that it should be erected instead in the campo in front of the Scuola di San Marco. This splendid monument, a masterpiece of the Renaissance, was finished after Verrocchio's death, with the pedestal, by *Aless. Leopardi* (1488–96) who was also responsible for the casting of the entire monument. During the First World War it accompanied the Horses of St Mark to Rome.

The church of *Santi Giovanni e Paolo** (*San Zanipolo*; Pl.7;5) disputes with the Frari the first place among the huge Gothic brick churches of Venice. It was founded by the Dominicans in 1246, though the present church was begun in 1333 and not consecrated until 1430. It was restored in 1921–26. It is the burial place of twenty-five doges, and after the 15C the funerals of all doges were held here. The fine FACADE was never finished; against it are the tombs of three doges including (second on the left) the donor of the site, Iacopo Tiepolo. The *DOORWAY, recently attrib. to *Bart. Bon* (with good carving) incorporates six Greek marble columns from Torcello. It is flanked by Byzantine reliefs of the Madonna and Angel Gabriel. On the corner facing the campo is an interesting early relief of Daniel in the lion's den.—From the campo, beyond the fine 16C well-head decorated with garlanded putti, can be seen the Gothic exterior of the Chapel of the Addolorata (the brick pavement of the campo has been revealed here below ground level), and the huge stained glass window of the S transept. The exterior of the Gothic apse (seen from the calle behind; restored in the 19C) is particularly noteworthy. (The numbers in the text refer to the Plan on p 123.)

The vast solemn INTERIOR (open 7–12.30, 15.30–19.30; 101m long; 46m across the transepts), has lofty aisles separated from the nave by ten columns of Istrian stone blocks, and is notable for the slenderness of its arches and its beautiful luminous choir. Wooden tie-beams help to stabilize the structure of the edifice (an architectural feature of several Venetian churches). Among the impressive series of funerary monuments to doges and heroes of the Republic are some masterpieces of Gothic and Renaissance sculpture. The Dominican friars are well informed about their church.—WEST WALL. Around the doorway is the colossal tomb of doge Alvise Mocenigo (d 1577) and his wife. In niches below are two Saints by *Pietro Lombardo*. To the right is the Monument (1) to doge Giovanni Mocenigo (d 1485), by *Tullio Lombardo*, and to the left, the *Monument (2; recently cleaned) to doge Pietro Mocenigo, a masterpiece by *Pietro Lombardo*, with the help of his two sons, *Tullio* and *Antonio* (1476–81).

Inside a triumphal arch flanked with niches containing statues of warriors, the Doge as a General stands on his sarcophagus borne by three warriors depicting the three Ages of Man. The sarcophagus bears reliefs of his most famous victories and the inscription is a reminder that the monument was set up at the expense of his enemies. The religious element (introduced at the top of the monument with a relief of the Maries at the sepulchre) takes second place to the explicit intention to glorify the Doge as a hero of the Republic.

SOUTH AISLE. Sarcophagus (3; with Christ enthroned in glory and two Angels) of doge Ranier Zeno (d 1268). 1st altar (4), Madonna and Saints, attrib. to an artist of the early 16C (*Fr. Bissolo?*); Monument (5) to Marcantonio Bragadin, the defender of Famagusta (1571) flayed alive by the Turks (his bust surmounts an urn behind which a niche contains his skin). 2nd altar (6), *Giovanni Bellini*, *Polyptych of St Vincent Ferrer, with a Pietà and Annunciation above (light on left; fee). In its original frame, this is a beautiful early work; the figure of St Christopher crossing a river is particularly remarkable.—In the pavement in front of the next chapel, Tombstone of Ludovico Diedo (d. 1466), a masterpiece of niello work. The CHAPEL OF THE ADDOLORATA (7) was given its Baroque decoration c 1639. The richly ornamented ceiling contains paintings by *G.B. Lorenzetti*.—Beneath the huge Baroque monument (1708, by *And. Tirali*, with the help of *Ant. Tarsia*, *Giov. Bonazza*, and *Marino Gropelli*) to two Valier doges is the entrance to the CHAPEL OF THE MADONNA DELLA PACE (8), with a Byzantine Madonna brought to Venice in 1349, and (right wall) a Flagellation by *Aliense*. The CHAPEL OF ST DOMINIC (9) has bronze reliefs by *Gius. Mazza* (1715–20) and a ceiling painting of the *Saint in Glory by *G.B. Piazzetta* (1727).

SOUTH TRANSEPT. *Alvise Vivarini*, Christ bearing the Cross (1474); *Giov. Martini da Udine*, or *Cima da Conegliano*, Coronation of the Virgin. The monument (10) above to Nic. Orsini (d 1509), Count of Pitigliano, Prince of Nola, defender of Padua in 1588, has an ungainly equestrian statue in gilded wood. The stained *Glass (restored in 1983) in the great window was made in Murano from cartoons by *Bart. Vivarini* and *Girol. Mocetto* (1473), and possibly also *Cima da*

1. predella good (?)

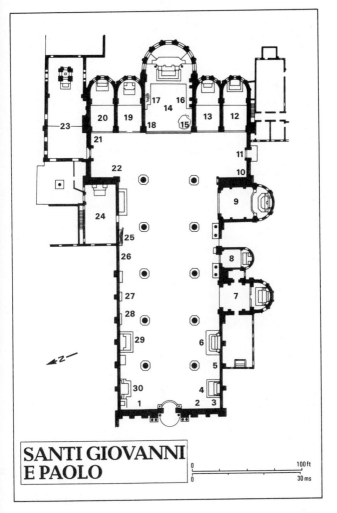

# SANTI GIOVANNI E PAOLO

| 0 | | | | 100 ft |
| 0 | | | | 30 ms |

*Conegliano.* On the altars below: *Lorenzo Lotto*, St Antonine (1542; removed for restoration), and *Rocco Marconi*, Christ between SS. Peter and Andrew (one of his best works). Surrounding the door, Monument (11) to the condottiere Brisighella (d 1510).

CHOIR CHAPELS. 1st chapel (12). On the black marble altar are two bronze statues from a Crucifixion group by *Aless. Vittoria*. On the right, Tomb of Sir Edward Windsor (d 1574) attrib. to *Vittoria*, and on the left, Sarcophagus with the figure of a warrior thought to be Paolo Loredan.—2nd Chapel (13). High up in the fan vault are frescoes attrib. to *Palma Giovane*. The Lombardesque altar bears a statue of St Mary Magdalen by *Bart. di Francesco da Bergamo* (1524).

On the right wall is a modern reconstruction of the Monument to Vettor Pisani (d 1380), which incorporates the original framework, the statue, and the inscription. Pisani was the popular victor over the Genoese at the battle of Chioggia, decisive to the survival of the Republic. To the left the hanging sarcophagus of Marco Giustiniani della Bragora (d 1346) is supported by curious heads.—The CHOIR (14) is closed by a polygonal apse, lit by fine Gothic windows. The Baroque high altar, begun in 1619 (and attrib. to *Longhena*) blends surprisingly well into the Gothic setting. On the right wall is the Gothic *Tomb (15) of doge Michele Morosini (d 1382), highly approved by Ruskin. It takes the form of an elaborate tabernacle with statuettes in niches flanking the effigy of the doge. The mosaic of the Crucifixion is attrib. to 15C Tuscan artists. The carving is attrib. to the *Dalle Masegne* school. Beyond is the Renaissance tomb (16) of doge Leonardo Loredan (d 1520; wrongly dated) by *Grapiglia*, with a statue by *Campagna* and allegorical figures by *Danese Cattaneo*.—On the left wall, monumental *Tomb (17) of doge Andrea Vendramin (d 1478), a masterpiece of the Renaissance designed by *Tullio Lombardo*, with the help of *Antonio*. The architectural design of the monument takes the form of a Roman triumphal arch (with a relief of the Madonna enthroned in the lunette) above the effigy of the doge surrounded by allegorical figures and warriors, all beautifully carved, some from classical models, others in the late-Gothic style.—To the right are traces of 14C frescoes. The Gothic tomb (18) of doge Marco Corner (d 1368) was moved in the 19C to make room for the Vendramin monument. The *Madonna is signed by *Nino Pisano*.—The 3rd Choir Chapel (19) has paintings by *Leandro Bassano*.—4th Choir Chapel (20), two hanging sarcophagi, of Iac. Cavalli (d 1384), with an effigy by *Paolo Dalle Masegne*, and of doge Giovanni Dolfin (d 1361).

NORTH TRANSEPT. The bronze statue (21) of doge Sebastiano Venier (d 1578), who commanded the fleet at Lépanto, is by *Ant. Dal Zotto* (1907). Above the door of the Chapel of the Rosary is the tomb of doge Antonio Venier (d 1400), and, left, the monument to his wife and daughter, Agnese and Orsola Venier (d 1411), both sumptuous works after the *Dalle Masegne*. The tomb (22) of Leonardo Prato (d 1511) bears a wooden equestrian statue attrib. to *Lor. Bregno*.

The CHAPEL OF THE ROSARY (23; light essential; fee), erected in memory of the battle of Lépanto at the end of the 16C from the designs of *Vittoria*, was gutted in 1867 by a fire. All its paintings perished, as well as Titian's St Peter Martyr and a Madonna and saints by Giov. Bellini, which had been placed here temporarily. It underwent restoration after 1913 and was finally re-opened in 1959. The ceiling *Paintings by *Paolo Veronese* of the Annunciation, Assumption, and Adoration of the Shepherds, were brought here from the ex-church of the Umiltà. The wooden benches are finely carved by *Giac. Piazzetta* (1698). In the choir the altar tabernacle is attrib. to *Aless. Vittoria* or *Girol. Campagna*; it encloses a terracotta Madonna and Child by *Carlo Lorenzetti*. On the walls are statues of Prophets and Sibyls by *Aless. Vittoria*, and fine 18C marble reliefs by *G.M. Morleiter*, *Giov.* and *Ant. Bonazza*, and *Alvise* and *Carlo Tagliapietra*. The ceiling-painting of the Adoration of the Magi is another good work by *Paolo Veronese*.

NORTH AISLE. *Bart. Vivarini*, Three Saints (fragments of a polyptych). The fine 18C organ is by *Gaetano Callido*. Over the Sacristy door, the busts of Titian and of the elder and younger Palma form the funerary monument designed by *Palma Giovane* (d 1628) for himself. He was one of the most prolific of the Venetian painters, and his

*Interior of SS. Giovanni e Paolo, with the tombs of doge Andrea Vendramin and doge Marco Corner*

works are to be found in almost every church in the city. The 16C SACRISTY (24) has an interesting interior with good carved benches.—The rest of the N aisle is crowded with funerary monuments. The *Monument (25) to doge Pasquale Malipiero (d 1462) by *Pietro Lombardo* is one of the earliest Renaissance monuments in Venice. It is a masterpiece of delicate carving. The monument (26) to Senator Gianbattista Bonzi (d 1508), attrib. to *Giov. Maria Mosca*, is placed above two blind arches with statues, and the effigies of Alvise Trevisan, the scholar (d 1528), and doge Michele Steno (d 1413). Beyond the classical monument with an equestrian statue of the Condottiere Pompeo Giustiniani (d 1616) is the *Tomb (27) of doge Tommaso Mocenigo (d 1423) in a transitional style by *Piero di Niccolò Lamberti*, and *Giovanni di Martino*.—The *Monument (28) to doge Nicolò Marcello (d 1474), by *Pietro Lombardo*, is a fine Renaissance work. Beyond the altar (29) with an old copy of Titian's St Peter Martyr (comp. p 124, Chapel of the Rosary) is the equestrian monument of General Baglioni (d 1617). The last altar (30) is a Renaissance work by *Gugl. dei Grigi Bergamasco*. Here is a statue of St Jerome signed by *Aless. Vittoria.*

Beside the facade of the church is the **Scuola Grande di San Marco** (Pl.7;5), one of the six great philanthropic confraternities of the Republic. The sumptuous *Facade by *P. Lombardo* and *Giov. Buora* (1487–90?), was finished by *Mauro Codussi* (1495). It is an original work of great charm with unusual trompe l'oeil panels (on the lower part), by *Tullio* and *Ant. Lombardo*, and St Mark with the Brethren of the School, ascribed to *Bart. Bon*, in the lunette over the doorway (recently restored). The interior is now occupied by the civic hospital of Venice which extends to the lagoon. The door leads into the hall, its architecture typical of the lower halls of the other Scuole.

The INTERIOR (adm sometimes on request, 9–12) incorporates the church of *San Lazzaro dei Mendicanti* (1601–31), by Vinc. Scamozzi, now the hospital chapel (with a good early work, St Ursula, by Tintoretto, and a Crucifixion with the Madonna and St John by *Veronese*). The hospital *Library* has a fine coffered ceiling by Pietro and Biagio da Faenza.—The Fondamenta dei Mendicanti leads N past the facade of San Lazzaro (by Gius. Sardi, 1673) to the Fondamente Nuove (view in the distance towards the cemetery island of San Michele with its dark cypresses).

Beyond the S flank of Santi Giovanni e Paolo the salizzada continues to the heavy Baroque facade of the church of the OSPEDALETTO (or *Santa Maria dei Derelitti*), rebuilt by *Longhena* (1674).

The good interior (entered by the side door through the hospital next door) contains the organ above the high altar, flanked by the Birth of the Virgin, the Visitation, and small paintings of the Annunciation, attrib. to *Ant. Molinari*. The fine paintings high up above the arches along the walls include (4th from the door on the S side) a Sacrifice of Isaac, by *G.B. Tiepolo*. In the nearby hospital, founded for orphans in 1527, is an elegant MUSIC ROOM (adm only with permission from the director), by Matteo Lucchesi (with frescoes by *Guarana*). The Institute had a high musical reputation.

In front of the Ospedaletto, Calle dell'Ospedale (sign-posted 'San Marco') leads S across two canals (interesting views) to Fondamenta della Tetta. From here it is a short way back (sign-post; right) to Santa Maria Formosa (comp. p 121) and the direct route which returns to San Marco. However San Marco can also be reached by the slightly longer but more interesting route through a secluded part of the town described below.—Across the bridge (left) Calle della Madonnetta leads past Ramo I° della Madonnetta. Here is a garden wall overhung by trees opposite a palace with an outside staircase. Farther along the calle is a quaint old corner shop (No. 5142; disused). In Largo San Lorenzo (with a view left of the church of San Lorenzo, comp. p 114) the Gothic *Palazzo Dolfin* (No. 5123) has a handsome doorway. In the other direction the calle leads out on to Rio San Severo with several fine (if dilapidated) palaces and their water-gates. The house on the corner (No. 5136) incorporates two ancient columns into its facade. Across the rio is the classical facade of the huge 16C *Palazzo Grimani* (comp. p 120), with its monumental water-gate. On the left opens Borgoloco San Lorenzo with two pretty well-heads. On the other side of the canal, before Ponte San Severo, are the two *Zorzi* palaces: the Gothic *Palazzo Zorzi-Bon*, with two water-gates, and *Palazzo Zorzi*, by Mauro Codussi (c 1480), with three water-gates. At the end of the fondamenta, in Campo San Severo, another Gothic palace has a tall doorway. The bridge crosses the canal beside Palazzo Zorzi, which has an entrance on the salizzada beneath a long balcony. Beyond the tiny Campo del Tagliapietro, with a fine well-head, Calle della Corona, a local shopping centre, continues across Rio di San Provolo, from which Calle della Sagrestia diverges right for San Giovanni Nuovo (comp. p 118). From here it is a short way back to Piazza San Marco.

# 5    San Marco to the Rialto via the Merceria

The narrow **Merceria** (Pl.10;2 and Pl.6;8) is the shortest route from Piazza San Marco to the Rialto. It is the busiest thoroughfare of the city and always crowded. It contains many well-stocked shops, a lot of which cater for the tourist trade. On the way to the Rialto it changes name five times: Merceria dell'Orologio, Merceria di San Zulian, Merceria del Capitello, Merceria di San Salvador, and Merceria 2 Aprile.

It leaves Piazza San Marco under the Torre dell'Orologio (comp. p 86). Just beyond the arch of the clock tower, above the Sottoportego del Cappello (left), a relief of an old woman is a reminder of Bajamonte Tiepolo's conspiracy against doge Pietro Gradenigo in 1310 which was foiled when his standard-bearer was killed by a mortar which an old lady let fall from the window-sill here. At the first bend (right) in the Merceria stands the church of **San Giuliano** (*San Zulian*; Pl.10;2), a church rebuilt in 1553 by *Jac. Sansovino* (and completed after his death by *Aless. Vittoria*). The facade, well-suited to this unusually cramped site, bears a seated •Statue by *Sansovino* of Tommaso Rangone, the wealthy scholar from Ravenna, who paid for the rebuilding of the church, and is buried in the chancel.

The dark INTERIOR (light; fee) has a simple rectangular plan with two side chapels flanking the sanctuary. By the right window, *Sante Peranda*, St Roch curing the plague-stricken in a lazzaretto. The fine ceiling (1585) has a painting of St Julian in glory by *Palma Giovane* and assistants. Above the side entrance, Coronation of the Virgin and three Saints, by *Girol. da Santacroce*. On the Sanctuary walls hang two huge paintings by *Ant. Zanchi.* The chapel to the left of the Sanctuary has a good stucco vault and statues of St Catherine and Daniel, all by *Vittoria.* The marble relief of the Pietà is by *Girol. Campagna.* Over the 1st S altar, Pietà above three Saints, by *Paolo Veronese,* and over the 1st N altar, Madonna enthroned with Saints, by *Boccaccio Boccaccino.*

The Merceria continues (sign-posted for the Rialto) across the wide Rio dei Barettari. To the right beneath the portico (No. 4939) is the former entrance to the famous *Ridotto Venier,* the meeting place of elegant society in 18C Venice. Farther on, the apse and flank of the church are skirted before emerging in Campo San Salvatore. The rebuilding of the church of **San Salvatore** (Pl.6;7) was begun by *Giorgio Spavento* in 1508, and, after his death, continued by *Tullio Lombardo.* It was finished by *Jac. Sansovino.* The Baroque facade, to a design of *Guis. Sardi,* was added in 1663.

The plan of the •INTERIOR with its domes and barrel vaults is one of the best examples in Venice of the way in which the problems of light and construction were solved at the height of the Renaissance. SOUTH AISLE. Between the first two altars, Monument to And. Dolfin by *Giulio Del Moro* (1602) with two busts by *Campagna*, between the next ·two, Monument to doge Fr. Venier (d 1556), with statues of Charity and *Hope, sculpted by *Sansovino* when nearly 80 years old (the second altar has a sculpted Madonna and Child by *Campagna*); over the 3rd altar (by *Sansovino*) is *Titian*'s splendid *Annunciation, painted in 1566 (light; fee).—In the SOUTH TRANSEPT, Tomb of Caterina Cornaro (Cornèr), queen of Cyprus (d 1510), by *Bern. Contino*, with good reliefs. Over the high altar a Transfiguration by *Titian* (c 1560) screens a silver reredos, a chef d'oeuvre of Venetian goldsmith's work (14C). Titian's painting is lowered mechanically (on request by the sacristan) to reveal the altarpiece (the original silver gilt panels folded up for easy transportation; the upper and lower rows of sculpture are later additions). In the floor in front of the altar, the unusual tomb of a merchant has recently been discovered: very worn frescoes attrib. to *Fr. Vercellio* can be seen through a glass roundel. In the chapel to the N, Supper at Emmaus by the *School of Giov. Bellini* (light in sanctuary; fee).—NORTH AISLE. The 3rd altar is designed by *Aless. Vittoria*, with statues of St Roch and St Sebastian. In a niche by the side door, statuette of St Jerome by *Danese Cattaneo* (1530). The organ, designed by *Jac. Sansovino* has doors painted by *Fr. Vecellio*. Between the 2nd and 1st altars is the dark classical monument of doge Lorenzo and Gerol. Priuli by *Cesare Franco* (1567). The Sacristy has a fine Renaissance interior.

The column outside the church commemorates Manin's defence of Venice in 1848–49. The *ex-Scuola di San Teodoro* has a facade by *Gius. Sardi* (1655). Merceria 2 Aprile (right) leads into CAMPO SAN BARTOLOMEO (Pl.6;8), the crowded business centre of Venice. It is at the cross-roads of the city. The spirited statue of Goldoni, the dramatist of Venetian life, is by Ant. Dal Zotto (1883; restored in 1985).—Off Salizzada Pio X (which leads to the steps of the Rialto bridge) is the inconspicuous entrance (in the calle to the left) to the church of SAN BARTOLOMEO (rebuilt in 1723; closed indefinitely). This was formerly the church of the German community in Venice, and Dürer painted his famous Madonna of the Rosary (now in Prague) for the church when he was in the city in 1506. The organ paintings by *Sebastiano del Piombo* of SS. Louis of Toulouse and Sinibaldus have been restored and are at present exhibited at the Accademia (comp. p 136); the other two, of SS. Bartholomew and Sebastion, are being restored in 1985. At the foot of the campanile is an amusing grotesque mask.—From the Campo (behind the statue) Sottoportego della Bissa leads across a wide bridge to the church of **San Lio** (Pl.6;8; often closed), dedicated to pope Leo IX (1049–54).

In the rectangular INTERIOR the organ (above the W door) bears paintings by the 18C Venetian school. Right wall: 1st altar, an ancient and much venerated Madonna and Child; at the end of this wall (difficult to see), Pietà, attrib. to *Liberale da Verona*, in an elaborate sculpted frame. The domed GUSSONI CHAPEL (right of the high altar) has lovely sculptural details by *P.* and *T. Lombardo*, and a marble relief of the Pietà. On the left wall of the sanctuary is a large Crucifixion by *Pietro Muttoni*, an ex voto for the plague of 1630. By the 1st left altar is a painting of St James Major by *Titian* (temporarily displayed since its restoration in the Museo Diocesano d'Arte Sacra). The ceiling (restored in 1982) contains a painting by *Gian Dom. Tiepolo*.

Calle della Fava leads S to the church of **Santa Maria della Fava** (or *Santa Maria della Consolazione*; Pl.6;8), begun in 1705 by *Ant. Gaspari*, and completed by *Massari*. The nave is decorated with statues in niches by *Torretto*, Canova's master. On the S wall (1st altar), *G.B. Tiepolo*, Education of the Virgin (an early work); N wall (2nd altar) *G.B. Piazzetta*, *Madonna and St Philip Neri.—From the bridge over Rio della Fava can be seen (left) the gothic facade of *Palazzo Giustinian-Faccanon*, which faces *Palazzo Gussoni*, a Lombardesque building. Calle dei Stagnieri leads directly back to Campo San Bartolomeo and the Rialto (comp. p 128).

# 6    San Marco to the Rialto via Santo Stefano

Beyond the colonnade at the end of Piazza San Marco beneath the Ala Napoleonica (comp. p 86) is the wide Calle dell'Ascension with a post office. At the extreme end on the right Calle Salvadego leads to the Bacino Orseolo, a pool usually filled with moored gondolas. The Hotel Cavalletto here is on the site of the Ospizio delle Orsoline, founded as a hospice for pilgrims in 977 by doge Pietro Orseolo.—To the left of the post office, Calle Seconda dell'Ascension (sign-posted for the Accademia) continues past Calle Vallaresso which leads down to the San Marco landing-stage on the Grand Canal. At No. 1332 a theatre and restaurant occupy the *Ridotto*, a famous gambling house set up here by Marco Dandolo in 1638, and closed by order of the Republic in 1774. It has tall windows on the piano nobile. Beyond (right) the Frezzeria, a busy shopping street, Calle del Ridotto opens on the left. It leads to Ca' Giustinian (the municipal tourist office and the 'Biennale' headquarters). The flank of the church is skirted to reach the campo in front of the church of **San Moisè** (Pl.10;4), by *Aless. Tremignon* (1668). Its over-elaborate Baroque facade has good relief sculpture. Its brick campanile is seen to the right.

The INTERIOR (open to visitors 15.30–19) contains some good 17–18C paintings, including (right and left of the organ by *Gaetano Callido*, 1801), Crucifixion by *Girol. Brusaferro*, and Stoning of St Stephen, by *Sante Piatti*. South side: 1st altar, *Gius. Diamantini*, Adoration of the Magi; 2nd altar, *Pietro Liberi*, Invention of the True Cross. The SACRISTY contains a remarkable bronze altar frontal of the Deposition, by *Nic.* and *Sebastiano Roccatagliata* (1633). The prettily framed small paintings (all labelled) include works by *Morleiter, Gius. Angeli, G.B. Canal* and *Vinc. Guarana*.—An extraordinary sculpted altarpiece fills the apse. Inside the entrance an inscription in the pavement marks the grave of John Law (1671–1729), originator of the 'Mississippi Scheme', transferred from San Geminiano in 1808.

The pretty Rio San Moisè is used as a mooring for gondolas. To the left can be seen the side facade of Palazzo Trevès de'Bonfili (p 102), and, across the Grand Canal, the low Dogana building. Beyond is the broad Calle Larga 22 Marzo (22 March 1848, the date of Manin's rebellion), enlarged in 1880 (a number of banks have their head offices here). Half-way along, Calle del Sartor da Veste diverges right. It crosses a canal before reaching Campo San Fantin, crowded with monumental buildings, including the Fenice theatre. Almost filling the campo is the charming Renaissance church of SAN FANTIN, probably by *Scarpagnino* (1507–49). It is notable for its beautiful domed sanctuary and apse, attrib. to *Sansovino* (1549–63). Nearby is the SCUOLA DI SAN FANTIN (now the seat of the ATENEO VENETO), with an Istrian stone facade (recently restored) by collaborators of Aless. Vittoria. Adm is sometimes granted to visitors (ring at the entrance in the calle to the left). It contains paintings by *Paolo Veronese* and his school, and a bronze portrait bust of Tommaso Rangone by *Vittoria*. **La Fenice** (Pl.10;1) is one of the most important opera-houses in Italy.

The fine neo-classical building is by *G.A. Selva* (1792). After a fire in 1836 it was rebuilt on the same lines by *G.B. Meduna*. In this famous opera house Rossini's 'Tancredi' was first performed in 1813, and many of Verdi's operas had their opening nights (including 'Rigoletto' in 1851, and, disastrously, 'La Traviata' in 1853). In this century it was the première of Stravinsky's 'The Rake's Progress' (1951) and Benjamin Britten's 'The Turn of the Screw'. It became the centre of the political life of the city after the fall of the Republic.—When rehearsals are not in progress adm to the charming interior is granted on request.

In the campiello to the left is the 15C *Casa Molin*, with an outside staircase (restored) and Veneto-Byzantine fragments. Calle della Fenice now skirts the huge building; it emerges beneath a portico near the water-gate. Several calli continue round the theatre to Calle Gritti (or 'del Piovan'). This leads down to Campo Santa Maria Zobenigo which opens on to the Grand Canal (with a gondola ferry). Here stands the church of **Santa Maria del Giglio** (or *Santa Maria Zobenigo*; Pl.10;3). The fine Baroque facade was built by *Gius. Sardi* in 1680–83. The church was rebuilt at the cost of the Barbaro family; the facade bears portraits of them, and plans of Zara, Crete, Padua, Rome, Corfu, and Spálato recording the victories of various members of the family in the service of the Republic.

INTERIOR. The 17–18C paintings above the cornice of the nave are by *G.B. Volpato* and *Ant. Zanchi*. The 18C Stations of the Cross include paintings by *Fr. Fontebasso, G.B. Crosato, Giac. Marieschi, Gasp. Diziani*, and *Dom. Maggiotto*. The 17C ceiling paintings are by *Ant. Zanchi*. The 16C paintings on the W wall include a Last Supper by *Giulio Dal Moro*, and Four Sibyls by *Gius. Salviati*.—SOUTH SIDE. 1st altar. *J.K. Loth*, Virgin and St Anthony of Padua and the Martyrdom of St Eugene. The CAPPELLA MOLIN (restored in 1975) displays the contents of the Treasury, and a Madonna and Child with the young St John, attrib. to *Rubens*. Other paintings here include works attrib. to *Fr. Fontebasso* and *Dom. Tintoretto*.—SOUTH SIDE. 2nd chapel. *G.M. Morleiter*, St Gregorio Barbarigo; 3rd chapel, *Palma Giovane*, Visitation. The SACRISTY (light; fee) is a fine 17C room, with, above the lavabo, a head of the young St John the Baptist by a Tuscan artist. Beneath the organ in the SANCTUARY are two paintings of the Evangelists by *Iac. Tintoretto*. The high altar is a fine 18C work, with sculptures of the Annunciation by *Meyring*.—NORTH SIDE. 2nd chapel. *G.M. Morleiter*, Immaculate Conception. 3rd chapel, *Tintoretto*, Christ with two Saints (damaged by restoration).

The calle continues (signposted 'Accademia') across two more bridges (view from the second to the right of a pretty wrought-iron parapet, and to the left of the side facade of Palazzo Corner, now the Prefecture, comp. p 102) to Campo San Maurizio. On the left (No. 2667) is the Gothic *Palazzo Zaguri* (now a school), and on the right the church of SAN MAURIZIO, begun in 1806 by G.A. Selva and Ant. Diedo. There is a fine tabernacle on the altar. The leaning brick campanile which can be seen behind belongs to Santo Stefano (see below).—Calle del Piovan leads on past (No. 2762) the little *ex-Scuola degli Albanesi* (1531) with Lombardesque reliefs on the facade. This was the meeting-place of the Albanian community who were established in this area by the end of the 15C. Beyond the next bridge (view right of the Rio Santissima, so named because it runs beneath the E end of Santo Stefano, comp. below), the calle soon emerges into the huge

CAMPO SANTO STEFANO (or *Morosini*; Pl.10;1), one of the pleasantest in the city.

Here is the statue of Nicolo Tommaseo (1802–74), an eminent man of letters. On the left (No. 2802–3) is the 17C *Palazzo Morosini*, home of doge Francesco Morosini (1688–94). On the opposite side of the campo is the long *Palazzo Loredan* (No. 1945). The Gothic structure was remodelled after 1536 by Lo Scarpagnino (the fine door-knocker with Neptune is by Aless. Vittoria). The Palladian facade on the N end was added by Giovanni Grapiglia. It is now occupied by the Istituto Veneto of Science, Letters, and Arts. The corner of the campo is filled by the imposing *Palazzo Pisani*, now the Conservatory of Music. This remarkable building, one of the largest private palaces in Venice, was begun by Bart. Monopola (1614) and continued by Girol. Frigimelica (1728). The two interior courtyards are divided by a huge open-arched loggia.—The other end of the campo is occupied by the early Gothic church of *Santo Stefano (Pl.10;1), rebuilt in the 14C and altered in the 15C. The fine brick facade bears a portal in the florid Gothic style (restored).

The Gothic INTERIOR with three apses has tall pillars alternately of Greek and red Veronese marble. The fine wood tricuspid *Roof in the form of a ship's keel, is thought to have been built by the same architect, *Fra. Giovanni degli Eremitani*, who built the church of the Eremitani in Padua.—SOUTH SIDE. 1st altar, Birth of the Virgin, by *Nicoló Bambini* (1709); 2nd altar, two marble statuettes by the Lombardesque school; 3rd altar, Immaculate Conception, by *Jac. Marieschi* (1752–5). Near the entrance to the Sacristy, bronze relief, also attrib. to a Lombardesque master. In the SACRISTY (light; 100 l.) are three paintings (right wall) by *Iac. Tintoretto* (the Last Supper, Washing of the Feet, and Prayer in the Garden), and (left wall) *Bonifazio Veronese*, Madonna and Child with Saints; above the door, Adoration of the Magi, Flight into Egypt, and Massacre of the Innocents, by *G. Diziani* (1733). Above the door into the small Sacristy the sculptural fragments include a Head of St Sebastian, by *Tullio Lombardo*. The small Sacristy has an alabaster Madonna and Child above the door (Tuscan, early 15C).—On the walls of the SANCTUARY are two 15C marble screens, and, in the choir in the apse are elaborate wooden stalls (seen through glass) by *Leon. Scalamanzo* and *Marco* and *Fr. Cozzi* (1488). NORTH SIDE. Above the door of the Baptistery, St Nicholas of Tolentino, a Lombardesque work. Inside the Baptistery (sometimes locked) is the funeral stele of Giovanni Falier, by *Canova*, c 1808. Outside can be seen the cloister of 1532 with the tomb of doge And. Contarini (d 1382). The tomb of Giac. Surian (1493) on the W wall of the church, is a graceful Renaissance composition. The sepulchral seal of Fr. Morosini, in the pavement of the nave, was cast by *Fil. Parodi* in 1694.

At the other end of the campo stands the monumental facade of SAN VITALE (deconsecrated; an exhibition centre). It contains (over the high altar) a painting of San Vitale by *Carpaccio* and an Immaculate Conception by *Seb. Ricci*. The characteristic campanile incorporates an antique Roman inscription. Campo San Vitale ends on the Grand Canal at the foot of the Accademia bridge (comp. p 102). The area across the bridge is described in Rte 7. To the right of the facade, from Campiello Loredan a bridge leads across to Calle del Frutarol. Beyond a school, Rame Calle del Teatro diverges left to Corte del Duca Sforza, with a tree and an archway on the Grand Canal (view left to the Accademia, and right to Ca' Rezzonico). Palazzo del Duca has a private museum of 18C porcelain—A series of narrow calli continue more or less straight on (signposted 'Palazzo Grassi') to emerge (by a house with a plaque recording Giac. Casanova's birth in this calle in 1725) at CAMPO SAN SAMUELE (Pl.9;2). The campo, with a quaint 12C campanile, opens on to the Grand Canal (and has

*Interior of Santo Stefano*

a landing-stage and a gondola ferry). Opposite stands Ca' Rezzonico (p 141). The ancient church of *San Samuele* (sometimes used for exhibitions) contains frescoes by the 15C Paduan school. **Palazzo Grassi** (18C; comp. p 103) was acquired by the Fiat organisation in 1984. It is to continue to be used as a cultural centre and as the seat of important exhibitions. The interior (being restored in 1985) contains a staircase frescoed with carnival scenes attrib to Aless. Longhi. The small theatre in the garden is also being restored.

Calle delle Carozze leads up to Salizzada San Samuele, with the house (plaque) where Paolo Veronese died in 1588. Calle Corner is surmounted by a high Gothic arch. Ramo di Piscina continues to the curiously shaped Piscina San Samuele. At the end (left) Calle del Traghetto leads down to the gondola ferry across the Grand Canal to San Tomà. Beyond two bridges Calle del Pestrin leads back past the raised Campiello Nuovo to Santo Stefano (comp. above). To the left the pretty CAMPO SANT' ANGELO (Pl.10;1) is soon reached beside the former convent of Santo Stefano which fills one side of the campo. Its door is surmounted by a lunette with a relief of St Augustine and monks (15C Paduan school). Here there is a view of the fine tower of Santo Stefano, the most oblique of the many leaning towers of Venice. The little *Oratory* contains a large wooden Crucifix (16C) and an Annunciation by Palma Giovane. Among the fine palaces here is the Gothic *Palazzo Duodo* (No. 3584), once the Tre Stelle inn, in which the composer Dom. Cimarosa died in 1801. It faces *Palazzo Gritti* (No. 3832), another Gothic building.

Calle del Spezier (sign-posted 'Rialto'), a busy shopping street, leads out of the campo. The first turning on the left (signposted for Palazzo Fortuny) leads along Rio terrà della Mandorla; beneath the arch (by the entrance to a hotel) at the end (right) is the grand 15C *Palazzo Pesaro degli Orfei*, now the **Museo Fortuny** (Pl.10;1). This was the home of the Spanish painter Mariano Fortuny (1871–1949) who here designed the famous Fortuny silks. The house (adm see p 66), with a fine old wooden staircase and loggia in the courtyard, has a remarkable 'fin de siècle' atmosphere, and is filled with curios and the artist's own works. Exhibitions are held on the second floor, and a collection of paintings by Virgilio Guidi (1892–1983), donated to the Museum, are exhibited on the top floor. The splendid main facade of the palace gives on to the small Campo San Benedetto. The church of SAN BENEDETTO is open only in the afternoon.

INTERIOR. South side, 2nd altar. *Bernardo Strozzi*, St Sebastian tended by the Holy Women. Over the main altar, Virgin with SS. Dominic and Michael, by *Carlo Maratta*; over the doors on either side, *Seb. Mazzoni*, a Priest recommended to the Virgin by St Benedict, and St Benedict with St John the Baptist and the Virtues (1649). North side, 1st altar, *G.B. Tiepolo*, San Francesco di Paola.

Salizzada della Chiesa leads towards the high bare wall of the Rossini theatre; just before it, Calle Sant'Andrea diverges left via Sottoportico delle Muneghe for Rio San Luca. From the bridge the view towards the Grand Canal includes the back and side of Palazzo Grimani (now the Court of Appeal, comp. p 103). Inside the church of *San Luca* is a damaged high altarpiece by Veronese. Pietro Aretino (d 1556) was buried here.—Behind the church is Campiello San Luca where Palazzo Magno (No. 4038) has a fine brick doorway (13C). From here Ramo della Salizzada leads on to CAMPO MANIN (Pl.10;1), with a 19C monument to the patriot Daniele Manin (by Luigi Borro), and the

Cassa di Risparmio building by Pier Luigi Nervi and Angelo Scattolin (1964). Calle della Vida (sign-posted) leads towards *Palazzo Contarini del Bovolo* (Pl.10;2), celebrated for its graceful spiral *Staircase and loggia by Giov. Candi (c 1499) in an open courtyard (with a collection of well-heads).—From here the Grand Canal is soon reached via Campo Manin: off Salizzada San Luca long narrow alleys run down to Riva del Carbon (comp. p 103) which skirts the Grand Canal as far as the Rialto bridge.

# 7    Dorsoduro: the Gallerie dell'Accademia, the Carmini, and Ca'Rezzonico

At the foot of the Accademia bridge (Pl.9;4; comp. p 102) Campo della Carità is dominated by the flank of the former church of Santa Maria della Carità. This, the ex-convent (with its Gothic doorway surrounded by large reliefs dating from 1377), and the Scuola della Carità (founded in 1343; the Baroque facade is by Giorgio Massari) are now occupied by the ACADEMY OF FINE ARTS and the ACADEMY PICTURE GALLERY. The **\*\*Gallerie dell'Accademia** (Pl.9;4) contains by far the most important collection of Venetian paintings in existence. The works cover all periods from the 14C, and the 15C art of Giovanni Bellini, through the wonderful era of Titian, Tintoretto, and Veronese, down to Tiepolo and the 18C. Admission see p 65.

Since the paintings are well labelled and all the works are of the highest quality, only a selection of the paintings is given below, and asterisks have been used sparingly.—The Academy of Fine Arts was founded in 1750, and G.B. Piazzetta was the first director; he was succeeded by G.B. Tiepolo.

Stairs mount to ROOM 1, the former chapter house of the Scuola della Carità, with a superb gilded wooden *Ceiling, ascribed to *Marco Cozzi* (1461–84) with carved cherubs and paintings by *Alvise Vivarini* (Holy Father) and *Dom. Campagnola* (four Prophets). At the top of the stairs, 15. *Iacobello del Fiore*, Justice between the archangels Michael and Gabriel.—In the centre, *21. *Paolo Veneziano*, Coronation of the Virgin, and stories from the life of Christ and St Francis; (on the other side of the screen) 5, 5a. *Lor. Veneziano*, SS. Peter and Mark.—To the right, 786. *Paolo Veneziano*, Madonna enthroned with angels; *Lor. Veneziano*, 9. Annunciation and four Saints; 650. Marriage of St Catherine and Saints; (in case), 25. *Iacobello Alberegno*, Triptych with Crucifixion and Saints; 100. *Stef. Veneziano*, Polyptych of the Apocalypse; (on the wall), 1. *Iacobello del Fiore*, Coronation of the Virgin in Paradise.—At the end of the room, *10 *Lor. Veneziano*, large Polyptych with the Annunciation, Saints, and Prophets.—Left wall: 33. *Mich. Giambono*, Coronation of the Virgin in Paradise; 14. *Venetian school (14C)*, Triptych with the Madonna of Humility; 19. *Nicolò di Pietro*, Madonna and Child (signed and dated 1394); 1236. *Ant. Vivarini*, Madonna and Child; 13. *Iacobello del Fiore*, Madonna of the Misericordia; 3. *Michele Giambono*, St James the Greater between other Saints. On the wall: 24. *Michele di Matteo*, Polyptych of St Helena and stories of the

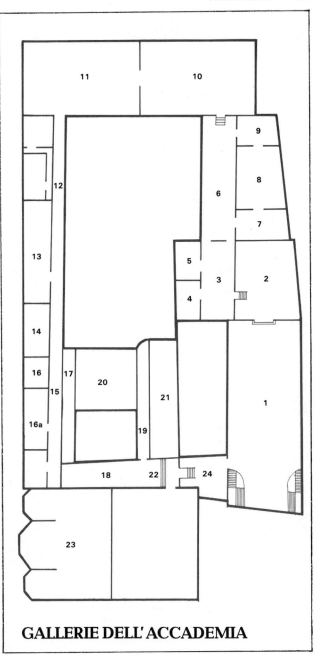

GALLERIE DELL' ACCADEMIA

Cross; (over the stairs), 1328. *Venetian School (late 14C)*, Madonna.—In the centre of the room: *18. Cross of St Theodore, 15C Venetian goldsmiths' work.—On the back of the screen on the entrance to R 2, 11. *Jacopo Moranzone*, Polyptych of the Assunta.

ROOM 2 contains a superb group of large altarpieces. 89. *Carpaccio*, The ten thousand martyrs of Mount Ararat (1510); 69. *Marco Basaiti*, The Prayer in the Garden (temporarily removed for restoration); *38. *Giov. Bellini*, Sacred Conversation: Madonna enthroned with Saints (the 'Pala of San Giobbe'); *39. *Marco Basaiti*, Calling of the sons of Zebedee (1510); 815. *Cima da Conegliano*, Madonna 'of the Orange tree', between SS. Jerome and Stephen; 44. *Carpaccio*, Presentation of Christ in the Temple (1510); 611. *Cima*, Incredulity of St Thomas; 166. *Giov. Bellini* (and his School), Pietà; 36. *Cima*, Madonna enthroned with Saints.—ROOM 3. 592. *Cima da Conegliano*, Archangel Raphael and Tobias and two saints; 82. *Benedetto Diana*, Madonna and Child with Saints; 603. *Cima*, Madonna between SS. John the Baptist and Paul; *Seb. del Piombo*, St Sinibaldus and St Louis of Toulouse, the interior organ shutters from the church of San Bartolomeo a Rialto, which have been exhibited here since their restoration and while the church is closed; 604. *Cima*, Deposition; (on easel) 70. *Follower of Giorgione (Seb. del Piombo?)*, Sacred Conversation; 602. *Giov. Buonconsiglio*, Three Saints; 80. *Bart. Montagna*, Madonna with SS. Sebastian and Jerome.

ROOM 4 contains a group of exquisite small paintings: *610. *Giov. Bellini*, Madonna and Child between SS. Paul and George; 586. *Hans Memling*, Portrait of a young man; *Giov. Bellini*, *613. Madonna and Child between SS. Catherine and Mary Magdalene; *591. Madonna and Child; 628. *Cosmè Tura*, Madonna and Child; *835. *Jac. Bellini*, Madonna and Child; *47. *Piero della Francesca*, St Jerome in the desert; *588. *And. Mantegna*, St George; *583. *Giov. Bellini*, Madonna and Child blessing (removed in 1985).—ROOM 5. 87. *Giov. Bellini*, Head of the Redeemer (fragment); *Giorgione*, *272. Old Woman (c 1508–9; the frame is probably original); *915. 'La Tempesta', a famous painting of uncertain subject-matter. It is one of the few paintings attrib. with certainty to Giorgione. *Giov. Bellini*, 595. Five allegories, *594. Madonna and Child, *596. Madonna 'degli Alberetti', *612. Madonna 'dei cherubini rossi', 883. Pietà, in a landscape, 881. Madonna and Child between St John the Baptist and a female Saint.

ROOM 6. *320 *Paris Bordone*, The fisherman presenting St Mark's ring to the Doge (fine architectural background); 205. *Bernardino Licinio*, Portrait of a lady; 210. *Iac. Tintoretto*, Madonna 'dei Camerlenghi', the treasurers of the Republic; 314. *Titian*, St John the Baptist, an uncharacteristic work; *291. *Bonifazio*, Dives and Lazarus the beggar; *Palma Vecchio*, St Peter enthroned with Saints.—R 7. 303. *Bernardo Licinio*, Portrait of a lady; 299. *Giov. Cariani* (attrib.), Portrait; 912. *Lor. Lotto*, Gentleman in his study.—R 8 contains paintings by *Bonifazio* and his school, including (1305.) Madonna dei Sartori (Madonna of the Tailors), with SS. Omobono and Barbara, the only work known to be signed and dated by *Bonifazio*. 95. *Venetian School*, Visitation; 640 *And. Previtali*, Crucifixion; 737. *Gerol. Romanino*, Entombment; 639. *And. Previtali*, Christ-child in the manger; 1306. *Rocco Marconi*, Christ and the Adulteress; *147 *Palma Vecchio*, Holy Family and two Saints.—R 9. *Sante Zago* (?), Tobias and the angel; 1035. *Titian*, Symbols of the Evangelists; 917. *Bonifazio*, God the Father, with the Piazza below.

*Madonna and Child by Giovanni Bellini (Accademia Gallery)*

ROOM 10. *203. *Paolo Veronese*, Christ in the House of Levi (1573), a splendid Venetian banquet-scene framed in a Palladian loggia; the figure in the foreground against the pillar on the left is the painter himself. The secular character of this painting brought Veronese into conflict with the Holy Office, and the name was changed from 'The Last Supper' to 'Christ in the House of Levi' before it was hung in the refectory of San Zanipolo. *Tintoretto*, *831. Transport of the body of St Mark, *42. Miracle of St Mark; 283. St Mark rescuing a Saracen; 875. (with *Dom. Tintoretto*) Dream of St Mark; 245. *Titian*, Portrait of the Procurator Iacopo Soranzo; 213. *Tintoretto*, Crucifixion; *400. *Titian*, Pietà (recently restored).—ROOM 11. 252. *Leandro Bassano*, Resurrection of Lazzarus; (above) 45. *Paolo Veronese*, *Allegory of Venice (a ceiling painting); *Tintoretto*, 41. Cain and Abel, 900. Creation of the animals, 43. Adam and Eve; 777. *Bernardo Strozzi*, Dinner in the house of the Pharisee; *G.B. Tiepolo*, 343. Frieze with the miracle of the bronze serpent (very ruined), Discovery of the True Cross by St Helena (in the tondo above); 751. *Luca Giordano*, Crucifixion of St Peter; *Veronese*, 37. Madonna enthroned with Saints, 260. Annunciation, 1324. Marriage of St Catherine. (On screen) 212. *Veronese*, Allegory of the Battle of Lépanto, painted shortly after the battle.

CORRIDOR (12), Landscapes, bacchanals and hunting-scenes by *Fr. Zuccarelli, Gius. Zais*, and *Marco Ricci*.—R 13 is devoted to *Tintoretto, Andrea Schiavone*, and the *Bassano* family. Especially interesting are the portraits by *Tintoretto*: *234. The Procurator And. Cappello, 233. Doge Alvise Mocenigo, 230, 237, 896, and 1012.—R 14. 544. *Tiberio Tinelli*, Luigi Molin; 829. *Bern. Strozzi*, Doge Fr. Erizzo; 914. *Jan Lys*, Sacrifice of Isaac; and paintings by *Dom. Fetti*. R 16 has amusing mythological scenes by *G.B. Tiepolo*, and (1315.) Head of an Old Woman by *Gius. Nogari*. ROOM 16a. 453. *Dom. Pellegrini*, Bartolozzi the engraver; 478. *Aless. Longhi*, Tommaso Temanza; *483. *G.B. Piazzetta*, Fortune-teller; 778. *Vittore Ghislandi (Fra Galgario)*, Count Vailetti; 493. *Aless. Longhi*, Allegory.—R 17 (closed for restoration in 1985), has a number of Venetian scenes, including works by *Canaletto* and *Guardi* (709. Isola di San Giorgio). Farther on, works by *G.B. Pittoni, Seb. Ricci* and *G.B. Tiepolo*, portraits by *Rosalba Carriera* and interiors by *Pietro Longhi*.—R 18, contains architectural scenes by *Moretti, Gaspari* and *Joli*; 906. *Mengs*, Archaeologist; on the right, statuettes by Canova.

Off this corridor is an entrance (not always open) to the upper part of the large church of the Carità (1441–52) with a wood roof and three polygonal apses (R 23). 103, 103a. *Carlo Crivelli*, SS. Jerome, Augustine, Peter and Paul.—In the apse: 621–621c. *Giov. Bellini and bottega*, four early triptychs painted for this church: St Laurence, the Nativity, St Sebastian, and the Madonna. The four kneeling sculptured angels date from the 15C.—In the left apse, *570. *Gentile Bellini*, Blessed Lorenzo Giustiniani (a ruined painting); 105. *Carlo Crivelli* (?), SS. Roch and Sebastian, and two other Saints.—Carved gilded wood 15C ancona by *Bart. Giolfino*; *Bart. Vivarini*, *581. Polyptych of the Nativity and Saints, 585, 584. SS. Barbara and Mary Magdalen, 825. St Ambrose enthroned and Saints; *615. Madonna and Child with SS. Andrew, John the Baptist, Domenic, and Peter.—*Alvise Vivarini*, 618, 619, 607. Madonna and Child with St Anne and Saints; *617. *Gentile Bellini* (attrib.), Madonna enthroned with four Saints.—*Girol. da Treviso*, 886. Madonna and four Saints, 96. *Transfiguration; *Lazzaro Bastiani*, *823. Funeral of St Jerome,

824. Communion of St Jerome; 28. *And. da Murano*, Triptych with SS. Sebastian, Vincent, Roch and Peter Martyr; in the lunette, Madonna della Misericordia.—The other half of the room is used for exhibitions.

ROOM 19. 600. *Boccaccio Boccaccino*, Marriage of St Catherine; *Marco Basaiti*, 68, 68a. SS. James and Anthony Abbot; 76. *Marco Marziale*, Supper at Emmaus; 90. *Carpaccio*, Meeting of SS. Anne and Joachim; 1343. *Bart. Montagna*, St Peter and a donor; *Marco Basaiti*, 645. Portrait, 108. Dead Christ, 107. St Jerome; 589. *Antonello de Saliba*, Christ at the column; 599. *Agost. da Lodi*, The Washing of the feet.—On the left is R 20, with charming paintings from the Scuola di San Giovanni Evangelista (end of 15C and beginning of 16C), relating especially to the miracles of the relic of the Cross given in 1369 to the school by Filippo de'Masseri on his return from Jerusalem.

\*566. *Carpaccio*, Cure of a lunatic by the Patriarch of Grado (interesting costumes and view of the old wooden Rialto bridge); 562. *Giov. Mansueti*, Healing of a sick child (interesting details of a Venetian interior); *Gentile Bellini*, 568. Recovery of the relic from the Canal of San Lorenzo (the first of the ladies on the left is Caterina Cornaro); 563. Healing of Pietro de'Ludovici by touching a candle in contact with the relic; \*567. Procession of the relic, showing the Piazza as it was in 1496; 565. *Benedetto Diana*, A child fallen from a ladder is miraculously saved; 561. *Lazzaro Bastiani*, Filippo de'Masseri offers the relic to the Chief Guardian of the Scuola di San Giovanni Evangelista; 564. *Giov. Mansueti*, The brothers fail in their attempt to carry the relic inside the church of San Lio, at the funeral of a companion who had disparaged it.

Beyond the corridor is R 21 (closed in 1985), which contains \*572–580. *Carpaccio*, Legend of St Ursula (1490–96; restored in 1985), painted for the Scuola di Sant'Orsola. The series is almost contemporary with Memling's delicate miniature-like works at Bruges (1489), with which it is interesting to make a comparison.

576. Glory of St Ursula and her 11,000 Virgins; 572. The ambassadors of England demand the hand of Ursula, daughter of King Maurus of Brittany, for Hereus, son of their King Conon; on the right, Ursula's answer; 573. Dictating the conditions of the marriage (a delay of 3 years for Ursula to make a pilgrimage to Rome and the conversion of Hereus to Christianity); 574. Departure of the ambassadors to England and the reading of the conditions to Conon; 575. Hereus meets Ursula and Ursula leaves from Rome; \*578. Dream of Ursula; an angel foretells her martyrdom; 577. Ursula, with Hereus and the 11,000 meets Pope Cyriac at Rome (view of Castel Sant'Angelo); 579. The pilgrims and the Pope reach Cologne; 580. The Huns, besieging Cologne, massacre the pilgrims; funeral of St Ursula.

The last room is ROOM 24, the former 'albergo' of the Scuola della Carità (with benches and a fine 15C ceiling): \*626. *Titian*. Presentation of the Virgin (1538; recently restored), painted for its present position. The solitary figure of the infant St Mary is charmingly graceful and the distant view of the mountains is a reminder of the artist's alpine home. \*625. *Ant. Vivarini* and *Giov. d'Alemagna*, large Triptych (1446), also painted for this room; 606–608. *Montagnana*, Annunciation. The Reliquary of Cardinal Bessarion is 14–15C Byzantine workmanship.

Outside the Accademia a calle (on the line of the facade) leads W to the Campiello Gambara; beyond, the pretty Rio di San Trovaso is soon reached. The first bridge leads across to the Calle and Fondamenta della Toletta which traverse a local shopping area (No.

1169 has a wood roof-top 'altane', a characteristic Venetian balcony). Beyond the next bridge a passageway with two arches leads on to the campo in front of the church of SAN BARNABA (Pl.9;3; open in the morning), by Lorenzo Boschetti (1749–76), with a 14C campanile (seen to the left). The ceiling fresco is by Costantino Cedini. On the 2nd S altar, Three Saints, attrib. to Fr. Beccaruzzi; 2nd N altar, Two Saints and the Pietà, attrib. to Giov. and Bern. d'Asola; 3rd N altar, Veronese (attrib.), Holy Family.—A fondamenta leads down the peaceful Rio di San Barnaba (with a greengrocer's barge moored alongside). The first bridge, Ponte dei Pugni has white marble foot-marks which recall the traditional fights which took place in the 14–18C on the bridge (formerly without a parapet) between rival factions of the city. At the end of the canal the 17C campanile of the church of the Carmini (comp. below) is conspicuous. On the opposite side of the canal is the house where Ermanno Wolf-Ferrari (1876–1948), the composer, was born (plaque). The bridge leads across to a calle which follows the wall of the church past a fine Romanesque porch decorated with Byzantine reliefs to the campo in front of the **Cármini** (Pl.9;1; *Santa Maria del Carmelo*). The 16C facade is the work of *Seb. Mariani da Lugano*. The church is being restored in 1985 and the nave is covered with scaffolding.

The most striking feature of the spacious basilican INTERIOR is the gilded wooden sculptural decoration in the nave beneath a frieze of 17–18C paintings. On the W wall is a monument to Iac. Foscarini (d 1602) by the school of Sansovino.—SOUTH AISLE, 2nd altar, *Nativity, by *Cima da Conegliano* (c 1509; light on altar). The vault above the 2nd and 3rd altars is frescoed by *Seb. Ricci*. 3rd altar, *Ant. Corradini*, Virginity (1721), and on the balustrade, two bronze angels by *Girol. Campagna*; 4th altar, *Polidoro da Lanciano* (attrib.), Circumcision.—In the chapel to the right of the main altar, a small bronze plaque with a *Relief of the Deposition is ascribed to *Fr. di Giorgio Martini*; it includes portraits (right) of Federico da Montefeltro and Battista Sforza (c 1474). The grandiose singing-galleries are decorated with paintings by *And. Schiavone*, and others. The chancel walls are covered with four large paintings by *Palma Giovane, Gaspare Diziani*, and *Marco Vicentino*. Above the high altar hangs a 14C gilded wood Crucifix.—NORTH AISLE, 2nd altar, *Lor. Lotto*, SS. Nicholas, John the Baptist and Lucy (1529; light on altar), with a remarkable landscape beneath. On the wall near the W door is a vast canvas by *Padovanino*.—The 16C cloister now belongs to the adjoining School of Applied Art.

From the campo in front of the church a fondamenta leads along the rio past the huge *Palazzo Zenobio*, now an Armenian college (adm sometimes granted on request). Built at the end of the 17C on a design by Ant. Gaspari, it contains a fine ballroom.

The **Scuola Grande dei Carmini**, beside the church, is attrib. to *Baldass. Longhena* (1668). In the INTERIOR (adm see p 66) the 18C decoration of the ground floor hall includes monochrome paintings by *Nic. Bambini* and an altarpiece by *Sante Piatti*. An elaborate staircase with stucco decoration leads up to the Salone with fine ceiling paintings by *G.B. Tiepolo* (1739–44), including the *Virgin in Glory. The paintings on the walls are by *Ant. Zanchi* and *Greg. Lazzarini*. Outside the adjoining room, Judith and Holofernes, by *G.B. Piazzetta*. The second room contains an Assumption by *Padovanino*.

Beyond the Scuola opens the huge CAMPO DI SANTA MARGHERITA (Pl.9;1) surrounded by simple low houses, some of them dating from the 14–15C. At the end, beyond the market stalls, the domed campanile of San Pantalon (see below) and the square tower of the

Frari (comp. p 157) can be seen in the distance. The isolated building is the *Scuola dei Varotari* (tanners), which bears a worn relief of the Virgin amidst the brothers of the School (1501). At the far end of the campo, an old house and the stump of a campanile bear interesting sculptural fragments (including a statue of the titular saint) from the former church of St Margaret whose decayed facade is just out of the campo, next to the campanile. Beyond it, a bridge leads over the busy Rio Nuovo (comp. p 108) to the campo in front of the bare unfinished facade of the church of **San Pantalon** (Pl.9;1; closed 11.30–16.30).

The INTERIOR is illuminated on request by the sacristan (offering). The nave roof is covered by a huge *Painting (1680–1704) on canvas in remarkable perspective by *Gian. Ant. Fumiani*, who was buried in the church; he was killed in a fall from the scaffolding at the end of the work. It describes events in the life of the titular saint, and his martyrdom under Diocletian. In the 3rd chapel on the S side the altarpiece and the painting on the left wall (both of San Bernardino) are by *Veronese* (and pupils). In the 2nd chapel, San Pantaleone healing a child, commissioned from *Veronese* for the high altar of the church by the parish priest in 1587. In the chapel to the left of the high altar (seen through a grille) are an elaborately carved Gothic tabernacle, and the Coronation of the Virgin by *Giov. d'Alemagna* and *Ant. Vivarini* (1444).—In front of the church (right) the Campiello de Ca'Angaran has a remarkable large sculpted roundel of a Byzantine Emperor (late 12C).

Calle San Pantalon leads to the busy Crosera (a short way farther N, via Calle della Scuola, is the church of the Frari and the Scuola Grande di San Rocco, comp. pp 157, 162); some way along the Crosera to the right Corte Foscari opens out by the fire-station.

At the end across the bridge over Rio Nuovo is the crenellated brick wall of *Ca' Foscari*, with the main entrance gate to the University which occupies the palace (its main facade on the Grand Canal is described on p 110). On the right is *Palazzo Dolfin*, also owned by the university (permission is sometimes granted to see the Ballroom with its interesting frescoes). Beyond is Campiello dei Squellini with its clump of plane trees. From here Calle del Capeler and its continuation, Calle delle Botteghe lead south, roughly parallel to the Grand Canal. At the foot of the bridge which leads over to Campo San Barnaba (comp. p 140), the fondamenta leads along the canal left to the **Ca' Rezzonico** (Pl.9;2). It was begun by *Longhena* (c 1667) and completed by *Massari* (1756); its grandiose facade is seen from the Grand Canal (comp. p 110).

The palace was the last home of Robert Browning and he died in 1889 in the small apartment on the first floor (usually kept locked). Whistler also occupied a room here in 1879–80. The palace contains the **Museo del Settecento Veneziano** (adm see p 66); the city's collection of 18C art, displayed in rooms decorated in the most sumptuous 18C style with superb views over the Grand Canal.

From the fine courtyard and atrium the grand STAIRCASE (by *Massari*) mounts to the **First Floor**. One of the putti ('Winter') on the banister is signed by *Juste Le Court*.—The Ballroom (1) has a fine ceiling fresco by *G.B. Crosato*. The remarkable set of furniture is elaborately carved by *And. Brustolon* (1662–1732). The 18C chandeliers are also noteworthy.—The door on the right leads into R 2 with a ceiling fresco depicting an allegory of the marriage of Ludovico Rezzonico by *G.B. Tiepolo*, and a prettily stuccoed alcove (3). Stairs lead down from here to another series of rooms including Browning's apartment (comp. above); these have been closed indefinitely.—R 4 contains pastels and miniatures by *Rosalba Carriera*, and a portrait of an old Lady with a fan, attrib. to *Lor. Tiepolo*.—In R 5 are displayed 17C tapestries of Flemish manufacture.

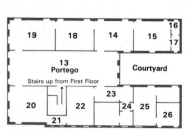

**Second Floor**

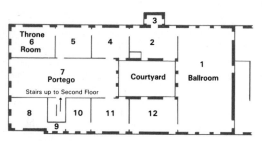

**First Floor**

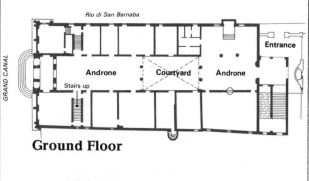

**Ground Floor**

# CA' REZZONICO

On the ceiling, Allegory of Virtue by *Jac. Guarana*. The lacquer-work door dates from the 18C.—The sumptuous THRONE ROOM (6) overlooks the Grand Canal. The ceiling fresco of the Allegory of Merit is by *G.B. Tiepolo*. An elaborate frame surrounds the portrait of Pietro Barbarigo by *Bern. Castelli*.— The PORTEGO (7), with a balcony on the Grand Canal, has two statues of atlantes by *Aless. Vittoria*.—R 8 (closed for restoration) has another fine ceiling fresco ('Strength and Wisdom') by *G.B. Tiepolo* (removed for restoration). Also here: *Gian Domenico Tiepolo*, Four heads of old men (also in restoration); *Aless. Longhi*, Portrait of Bart. Ferracina. The furniture is by *Brustolon*.—Beyond a passage, 9, the LIBRARY (10; closed for restoration) has ceiling paintings by *Fr. Maffei*. The 18C books on display were published in Venice. The chandelier was made in Murano. A passage, 11, with three paintings by *Gregorio Lazzarini* leads into R 12 with more elaborate furniture by *Brustolon* and a ceiling by *Fr. Maffei*. The paintings include: *Gregorio Lazzarini*, Rape of Europa; *Jacopo Amigoni*, Judith and Holofernes, Jael killing Sisera.

From the Portego (see above) stairs continue up to the **Second Floor**. Here the PORTEGO (13) is arranged as a picture gallery which contains (right) *Gius. Zais*, Four rustic scenes; *Dom. Tiepolo*, Saint; *Giov. Lys*, Judith and Holofernes; *G.A. Pellegrini*, Muzias in Porsenna's camp; *G.B. Piazzetta*, Death of Darius.—In the room (14) to the right ahead, are three detached frescoes by *Fr. Guardi*.—ROOM 15 is a charming bedroom with the bed in an alcove. The adjoining closet (16) has an oval ceiling fresco of a hawk in flight by *Gian Dom. Tiepolo*.—R 17, the BOUDOIR, has graceful stucco decoration.—From R 14 (comp. above) there is access to the GREEN DRAWING ROOM (18) with fine lacquer furniture, views of Venice, and a ceiling fresco attrib. to *Fr. Guardi*.—ROOM 19, the LONGHI ROOM, has another fine ceiling by *G.B. Tiepolo*, and an interesting series of 34 small genre paintings by *Pietro Longhi* with contemporary scenes of Venetian life (one with a rhinoceros). To the right of the door into the next room, the 'Painter's Studio' (removed for restoration) shows Longhi in his studio. The life-size portrait of Fr. Guardi is also by Longhi. On the other side of the Portego, R 20 has two paintings by *Fr. and Gian Ant. Guardi*: the 'Sala del Ridotto' and the 'Parlatorio delle monache' (convent scene). A passageway (21), with a rosary-maker's signboard by *Fr. Guardi*, leads down to ROOM 22, with an 18C spinet. There follow a charming series of rooms (23–26) reconstructed from the Villa di Zianigo, the Tiepolo villa near Mira and decorated with *Frescoes by *Gian Dom. Tiepolo*, including 'The New World' (1791) and delightful carnival scenes with clowns, and satyrs.—The THIRD FLOOR, which has been closed for years, has a puppet theatre, an 18C pharmacy, costumes, etc.

From Campo San Barnaba, the landing-stage of 'Ca' Rezzonico' on the Grand Canal is reached via Calle del Traghetto, or it is a short walk back to the Accademia (comp. p 134).

# 8  Dorsoduro: from the Accademia to Santa Maria della Salute, the Zattere, and San Sebastiano

At the foot of the Accademia bridge, and to the left of the Academy buildings (comp. Pl.9;4), the wide Rio terrà di Sant'Agnese leads away from the Grand Canal towards the Giudecca canal (which can just be seen in the distance, beyond a clump of trees). Calle Nova a Sant'Agnese (a shopping street) diverges left to cross the pretty Rio di San Vio. In *Palazzo Cini* (No. 864; left) on the canal the **Vittorio Cini Collection** (Pl.9;4) of Tuscan paintings and decorative arts was opened to the public in 1984 (adm see p 65). This was the home of Vittorio Cini (1884–1977), patron of the arts, collector, philanthropist, and politician. The collection now belongs to the Giorgio Cini Foundation.

The paintings are arranged on the FIRST FLOOR (lift). In the entrance hall, 18C Neapolitan sedan chair. ROOM I. (in case) *Giunta Pisano*, Processional Cross; *Taddeo Gaddi*, two small predella scenes from the life of St John the Evangelist; *Guariénto*, Ascension; ivories from the 15C bottega of *Baldassare degli Embriachi* in Venice. *Maestro di Badia a Isola*, *Maestà (c 1315). The Tuscan dower chest has relief decoration dating from 1340–60. *Bernardo Daddi*, Crucifixion; *Master of the Horne Triptych*, *Madonna enthroned and two Saints.—In the main hall: *Lor. di Niccolò*, Polyptych; *Sassetta*, Madonna of Humility; *Maestro dell'Osservanza*, Redeemer; *Vecchietta*, St Peter Martyr; *Maestro Francesco dell'Orcagna* (second ñalf of the 14C), St Paul enthroned with Saints. In a stuccoed alcove is displayed a set of Venetian porcelain by the Cozzi manufactury (1785–95).—ROOM III. *Botticelli* and pupils, *Judgment of Paris; *Piero di Cosimo*, *Madonna and Child with two angels, a beautiful composition, perhaps the painter's masterpiece; *Piero della Francesca* (attrib.), *Madonna and Child.—R IV. *Pontormo* *Double portrait of two friends; *Filippo Lippi*, Madonna and Child with Saints, angels, and a donor, a small painting in an interesting setting.—A spiral staircase leads up to the second floor, where a selection of the Cini collection of illuminated MSS, miniatures, books, Venetian and Bolognese drawings, prints, etc. is displayed.

On the other side of the bridge, Campiello San Vio opens on to the Grand Canal. Here a little votive chapel incorporates reliefs from the church of San Vio (demolished in 1813). The Anglican church of ST GEORGE was given to the English community in Venice in 1892 by Sir Henry Layard. It is normally open for services on Sunday, and contains the tombstone of consul Joseph Smith (1682–1770), art collector and diplomat, removed here from the cemetery on the Lido in 1974.—The narrow Calle della Chiesa continues to a bend in the Rio delle Torreselle. Here the fondamenta on the left side of the canal continues to Calle San Cristoforo which continues to the entrance of *Palazzo Venier dei Leoni* (comp. 111). Here the *Peggy Guggenheim Collection (adm see p 65) provides one of the most representative displays of modern art (after 1910) in Europe. During the winter months the palace is adapted for temporary exhibitions.

The palace was the home of Mrs Peggy Guggenheim from 1949 until her death in 1979. It is now owned by The Solomon R. Guggenheim Foundation. In the sculpture garden there is a Byzantine-style bishop's throne, and sculptu.es by *Arp, Moore, Jacometti, Paolozzi*, and others.

The entrance hall of the palazzo leads on to the terrace fronting the Grand Canal with *Marino Marini*'s equestrian statue, Angel of the Citadel. To the l. of the entrance hall is the DINING ROOM (R1) with Cubist works, including: *Picasso*, The Poet; *Léger*, Men in the City, and paintings by *Braque, Delaunay, Gris, Metzinger*, and sculptures by *Archipenko, Laurens*, and *Lipchitz.—Room 2 contains De Stijl and Constructivist works (*Mondrian, Van Doesburg, Vantongerloo; Lissitzky, Malevich*, and *Pevsner*).—Beyond *Chagall*'s Rain, at the end of the corridor, is the entrance to RR 3 and 4 overlooking the Canal. Paintings here include: *Kandinsky*, Landscape with Church; *Severini*, Sea = Dancer, and works by *Balla, Braque, Picasso*, and *Villon*. There are also sculptures by *Arp, Lipchitz*, and *Pevsner*, as well as *Brancusi*'s, Maiastra. The corridor leading to the E. wing displays works on paper (*Klee, Kupka*), a relief by *Picabia*, collages by *Schwitters*, and five box constructions by *Cornell.—Room 5 houses several paintings by *Ernst, Magritte*, Empire of Light; *Dali*, Birth of Liquid Desires; and other Surrealist paintings by *Tanguy* and *Delvaux*. There are also three sculptures by *Giacometti* including, Headless Woman.—ROOM 6 contains works by *De Chirico, Miró; Picasso*, Baignade; and sculptures by *Brancusi* and *Gonzalez.—Off R 6 is the BEDROOM with *Calder*'s large mobile

*Palazzo Venier dei Leoni, begun in 1749, which houses the Peggy Guggenheim Collection of Modern Art*

and silver bedhead, and a number of paintings by Peggy Guggenheim's daughter, Pegeen.

At the end of the corridor there are paintings by *Baziotes, de Kooning, Motherwell, Rothko,* and *Tobey.* From here stairs lead down to the 'BARCHESSA.' The wall looking on to the garden is lined with sculptures including works by *Pomodoro, Lassaw,* and *Hare.* The Barchessa houses post-war European and American art: *Pollock,* Moon Woman, and Alchemy, etc; *Bacon,* Study for a Chimpanzee; and works by *Gorky, Still, Sutherland, Dubuffet, Jorn, Alechinsky,* and others.

The calle ends in the attractive little Campiello Barbaro with four trees and a fountain. From here Calle and Ramo Barbaro continue (with a view from the first bend of the garden of the cupola of Santa Maria della Salute) across Rio della Fornace (with double fondamenta) between the Grand Canal and the canal of the Giudecca. Its name recalls the brick ovens which were formerly here. Beyond several glass-blowing works (visitors are admitted) and a passageway which leads to the gondola ferry on the Grand Canal for Campo Santa Maria del Giglio, Campo San Gregorio is dominated by the Gothic facade of the church (now used as a restoration centre). The calle tunnels beneath the former monastic buildings (with the entrance at No. 172 to the charming cloister on the left, now part of a private house) to emerge beside (right) the fine triple apse (1342) of San Gregorio. A wooden bridge leads across to the campo on the Grand Canal.

\*Santa Maria della Salute (Pl.10;4; open 8–12, 15–17.30) was built in 1631–81) in thanksgiving for the deliverance of Venice from the plague of 1630–31 (which had left 46,000 dead, some 30 per cent of the population of Venice). It is a beautiful octagonal church built partly of Istrian stone and partly of 'marmorino' (brick covered with marble dust), the masterpiece of *Baldass. Longhena.* A unique building, and particularly well adapted to its impressive site at the entrance to the city, it dominates the view of the Grand Canal from the lagoon. The water is reflected on its bright surface.

EXTERIOR. It has a central plan with six lateral facades; the entrance is approached by a monumental flight of steps. Huge volutes surmounted by statues support the drum of the fine dome crowned by a lantern; a smaller cupola covers the east end. The sculptural decoration is attributed to *Fr. Cavrioli, Michele Ongaro, Tommaso Ruer, Juste Le Court, Fr. Cabianca,* and *Bernardino Falcone.*

INTERIOR. The high dome with its drum pierced by large windows sheds a beautiful light on the central area of the church with its circular aisle (enhanced when the central door is open on to the Grand Canal). The polychrome marble is extremely fine. The large Sanctuary, with the high altar beneath a second dome is, in contrast, dimly lit. In the chapels to the right are three fine altarpieces of the Life of the Virgin by *Luca Giordano*. On the left side, the 1st altar has an Annunciation by *Pietro Liberi*, and on the 3rd altar is the Descent of the Holy Spirit, by *Titian*, recently restored. The High Altar, designed by *Longhena*, bears good sculptures, including the *Virgin casting out the plague, by *Juste Le Court* (restored in 1984). In the centre is a 12–13C Byzantine Madonna and Child brought from Crete by Francesco Morosini in 1669. The bronze Paschal *Candalabrum is by *And. Bresciano* (1570), friend of Vittoria. The altar is flanked by four columns from the Roman theatre at Pola. The roundels in the ceiling behind the altar were painted by *G. Salviati.*

The GREAT SACRISTY (opened by the sacristan; fee) contains, over the altar *St Mark enthroned between SS. Cosma and Damian, and SS. Roch and Sebastian, a votive painting for the liberation of Venice from the plague, an early work by *Titian*. It has recently been returned after restoration. The 15C tapestry which forms the altar frontal is of exquisite workmanship (note the charming landscapes). The tabernacle formerly contained a mosaic Madonna, a rare Byzantine work made for Santa Sophia in Constantinople in 1115; this has been removed for safety. On either side of the altar are eight roundels of the Evangelists and Doctors of the church, by *Titian*. To the right of the altar is another votive painting, the Madonna between angels with a model of the Salute, by *Il Padovanino*. On the wall opposite the entrance, *Tintoretto*, *Marriage at Cana (restored in 1984), *Marco Basaiti* (attrib.), St Sebastian. On the wall to the right of the entrance, *Girolamo da Treviso*, St Roch between SS. Sebastian and Jerome. In the ceiling are three *Canvases (Cain and Abel, Sacrifice of Isaac, David and Goliath), fine works in remarkable perspective by *Titian*.—The SMALL SACRISTY (sometimes opened on request) contains a kneeling figure of doge Agostino Barbarigo, from the family tomb in the church of the Carità, attrib. to *Ant. Rizzo*; and a frieze of patriarchs by the school of *Carpaccio.*

The Doge visited the church annually on 21 November in a procession across a pontoon of boats from San Marco. This anniversary is still celebrated (comp. p 64), and for the occasion a Madonna and Child attrib. to Gentile Bellini is exhibited behind the high altar.

From the campo, with its fine pavement in front of the church, there is a splendid view: directly opposite the landing-stage is the tiny Gothic facade (being restored) of Palazzo Contarini-Fasan (p 102), and, to the left towards the Accademia bridge seen in the distance, rises Palazzo Corner (p 102). In the other direction, the tip of the campanile of San Marco can be seen near the half-hidden facade of Palazzo Ducale, and, in the far distance, the tall campanile and dome of San Pietro di Castello.—In the campo by the church is the entrance to the **Seminario Patriarcale** (Pl.10;4; adm willingly granted by previous appointment). The CLOISTER contains tombs and inscriptions, and a collection of sculpture, and the ORATORY has a Lombardesque altar. The GRAND STAIRCASE by *Longhena* (with a ceiling painting by *Antonio Zanchi*) overlooks a garden on the Giudecca canal with

*The Riva della Salute in 1897 (the wooden 'felze' were used on gondolas in bad weather)*

some fine old trees. In the REFECTORY is a Last Supper by *Giov. Laudis*, and two paintings by *Aliense*. In the corridor, Portrait of Benedict XIV by *Subyleras*.

The **Manfrediniana Picture Gallery** was left to the Seminary by Fed. Manfredini of Rovigo (1743–1829). The ENTRANCE HALL contains sculpture by the *Dalle Masegne*, and *Pietro Lombardo* (Nativity), and a Greek bust of a poet (1C AD).—ROOM I. Triptych by *Temporello* (one of the few works known by this artist, a follower of Giovanni Bellini); Madonna and Child, St Joseph, and one of the Magi, a sculptural group of c 1250 (recently restored); (above) painted frieze of six bishops of Olivolo (fragment); *Holy Family, by a follower of Leonardo (*Boltraffio?*); *Ant. Vivarini*, SS. Nicholas and Ambrose; '*Maestro Pfenning*' (attrib.), Death of the Virgin; *Filippino Lippi*, panels of Christ and the woman of Samaria, and Christ and Mary Magdalen. In the centre, *Gerard David*, Kerchief of St Veronica; *Cima da Conegliano*, Madonna and Child; *Catalan school of 14C*, Madonna and Child crowning Santa Eularia.—ROOM II contains five terracotta *Busts by *Aless. Vittoria* (recently restored): they are portraits of Girolamo Grimani, Apollonio Massa, a famous doctor, Nicolò da Ponte, Pietro Zen, and a condottiere. The detached *Fresco above is by *Paolo Veronese*. The paintings include: *Titian*, Apollo and Daphne; *Bachiacca*, Deposition; *Beccafumi*, Penelope. The busts of Card. Agostino and Card. Pietro Valier are early works by *Gian Lorenzo Bernini*.—ROOM III. *Canova*, Bust of Gian Matteo Amadei; *Pittoni*, Two monochrome sketches; and a collection of small paintings of the Dutch and Italian schools.—The LIBRARY has a central ceiling painting by *Seb. Ricci*. Outside are two alabaster roundels with reliefs of galleons (second half of the 16C).

The narrow fondamenta continues past the DOGANA DI MARE, the customs house, with a low Doric facade by Gius. Benoni (1676–82) on the canal. At the extreme end of the promontory stands a little turret surmounted by a golden ball with a weathervane supported by two telamones. The superb *View embraces the whole Basin of St Mark's: the campanile of San Marco, the domes of the Basilica, the Mint, the end of Sansovino's Library, and the Palazzo Ducale; then the long Riva degli Schiavoni as far as the Giardini Pubblici. Opposite lies the island of San Giorgio Maggiore with its Palladian church. The beginning of the Giudecca island is marked by the grey patrol boats moored outside the customs office; standing out from the long line of house-fronts which follow are the facades of the churches of the Zitelle and the Redentore.

The FONDAMENTA DELLE ZATTERE (Pl.10;6,5 and Pl.9;6,5) skirts the wide Giudecca canal, busy with shipping including the large ocean-going vessels bound for the industrial port and oil refinery of Marghera, and with the car ferries which ply to and from the Lido.—Beyond the Dogana and the garden wall of the Seminary (comp. above), and a short way beyond the first bridge, Rio terrà dei Catecumeni opens out onto a characteristic Venetian court with a single row of trees and two houses above a low portico. The school here succeeds an Institution founded in 1571 for the conversion of slaves and prisoners of war to Christianity.—Next come the huge MAGAZZINI DEL SALE (salt warehouse; now used partly as boat-houses). In the 11–15C one of the richest resources of the Republic was the salt monopoly. The exterior was reconstructed in a neo-classical style by G. Alvise Pigazzi (c 1835–40). The splended 15C interior is sometimes opened for exhibitions in connection with the 'Biennale' (comp. p 63). From here there is a good view of the Palladian facade of the church of the Redentore across the Giudecca canal (comp. p 185). Across Rio della Fornace (which extends to the Grand Canal) is the SPIRITO SANTO (open 15–18, Sun 9–11), a church founded in 1483 with a Renaissance facade. The interior, remodelled in the 18C contains a painting of the Redeemer and Saints (1st S altar; restored in 1983) by *Giov. Buonconsiglio*, and (3rd N altar), Marriage of the Virgin by *Palma Giovane*. The upper nuns' chapel (opened on request) contains an 18C cycle of paintings of the Mysteries of the Rosary, including an Assumption by *Fr. Fontebasso*.—On either side of the church are the former Scuola del Spirito Santo, founded in 1506, with a facade by *Aless. Tremignon* (1680; now a private house), and a disappointing building of 1958. From here there is a distant view, beyond a huge 19C factory (the 'Mulino Stucky'), of the industrial port of Marghera. The huge classical building by Ant. da Ponte (with a fine colossal stone head on either end of the facade) of the INCURABILI (now an Institute for children), was once one of the four main hospitals of the city.

It was founded in 1522 by Gaetano Thiene, and in 1537 Ignatius Loyola was a visitor here. At the end of the 16C the orphanage attached to the hospital became famous for its girls choir; Jac. Sansovino designed an oval church in 1567 in the courtyard, particularly adapted to these concerts (c c molished in 1831).

Beyond the Rio San Vio, the Zattere becomes more animated. On the corner is a house (now a hotel) where John Ruskin stayed in 1877 (plaque). Beyond a mooring for barges, is the church of the **Gesuati** (Pl.9;6; *Santa Maria del Rosario*; adm 8–12, 17–19), a fine building by *Giorgio Massari* (1726–43).

The interior has a remarkably successful design, with the dark high altar lit
from behind. The good ceiling (Story of St Dominic) is frescoed by *G.B. Tiepolo*,
who also painted (1st altar on the right) the *Virgin in Glory with SS. Rosa,
Catherine of Siena, and Agnes of Montepulciano. 1st altar, opposite, Three
Saints, by *Seb. Ricci*; 3rd N altar, Crucifixion, by *Tintoretto* (c 1570); 3rd S Altar,
Three Saints, by *G.B. Piazzetta*. The elaborate high altar is encased in lapis
lazuli and has precious marble columns.—The church of *Sant'Agnese*, in the
campo behind the Gesuati, was founded in the 12–13C (rebuilt).

On the Zattere is the Renaissance church of SANTA MARIA DELLA
VISITAZIONE (1493–1524) with a good Lombardesque facade and
portal. The interior (entered from the institute on the right) contains
a charming wood roof (recently restored) filled with painted panels
by the 16C Umbrian school.—The next bridge crosses Rio San
Trovaso, which has a picturesque old boat-building yard ('squero')
with a wooden balcony, where gondolas are repaired and built. The
quay of the Zattere, lined with trees, provides a mooring for large
ships; here are the offices of several shipping companies. It continues
as far as the Maritime Station (comp. p 150); while Sottoportico
Fioravante leads away from the water-front along a narrow alley and
over a bridge into Campo San Trovaso, with a raised cistern around
its well-head. The church of **San Trovaso** (Pl.9;3; *Santi Gervasio e
Protasio*; open 7.30–11, 17–19; winter 8–11, 16–18; the church is
poorly lit and should be visited in daylight) was rebuilt at the end of
the 16C with two facades (the second one is in the campo at the
side).

INTERIOR. 3rd N Altar, *Palma Giovane*, Birth of the Virgin and Deposition; N
Transept, *Iac. Tintoretto*, Last Supper (restored in 1979), and (in the chapel to
the left of the high altar), Temptation of St Anthony. On either side of the choir
are the last works (Adoration of the Magi and Expulsion from the Temple) by
*Iac. Tintoretto*, completed by his son *Domenico* and others. In the chapel to the
left of the S door, is a charming painting of *St Chrysogonus on horseback, by
*Mich. Giambono* (on the wall facing the window). In the chapel opposite, the
altar bears a lovely marble bas-relief attrib. to the '*Maestro di San Trovaso*',
one of the most interesting products of the Venetian Renaissance. Over the S
door is a Last Supper by *And. Vicentino*.

Across Rio San Trovaso can be seen *Palazzo Nani* (15C). A house in
the campo bears a Byzantine relief of St Peter. Fondamenta Bonlini
continues along Rio di Ognissanti; opposite rises *Ca' Michiel*, with
its two protruding wings, famous for its garden in the 16C. Across
the next bridge the fondamenta passes the hospital and church of
*Ognissanti* and (No. 1461) a house with reliefs and lions' heads. An
old boat-yard faces Rio della Avogaria. The calle ends at Rio di San
Basilio on which (by the next bridge, right) is the church of *San
Sebastiano** (Pl.8;4), rebuilt after 1506 by *Scarpagnino*, and decorated
in 1555–70 by *Paolo Veronese* who lived in the neighbouring salizzada
and is buried in the church. It has been well restored and is open to
visitors 10–12, 16–19 (winter, 15–17) exc. Sun.

INTERIOR. There are three sets of lights (200 l. each) in the corridor off the left
aisle on the way to the sacristy to illuminate the ceiling, the sanctuary and the
side altars. In the panels of the beautiful CEILING is the *Story of Esther
(1555–56) by *Veronese*, and Prophets, Apostles, and Evangelists, with charming
decoration by his brother *Benedetto Caliari*. At the beginning of the S side,
over the altar beneath the gallery, St Nicholas, by *Titian* (1563; a late work). In
the church proper: SOUTH SIDE, 2nd altar, *Tommaso Lombardo*, Madonna and

To add: classical interior + Tintoretto style.     square table etc

Child with the young St John, a marble group; beyond the 3rd altar, the huge Tomb of Abp. Podocattaro of Cyprus (d 1555), by *Sansovino*.—In the CHOIR are more *Paintings by *Veronese*; over the altar, also designed by *Veronese*, Madonna and Child with St Sebastian (c 1570); left wall, St Sebastian encourages SS. Mark and Marcellian to martyrdom (c 1565); right wall, Second martyrdom of St Sebastian. The chapel to the N of the choir has a majolica pavement of 1510, and in the floor in front is the tomb of Paolo Veronese (d 1588) and of his brother Benedetto Caliari (d 1598); on the wall is a bust of Paolo. The organ, by *Fr. Fiorentino* and *Dom. da Treviso* (1558), was designed by *Veronese* who painted the panels. Beneath it a door admits to the SACRISTY, with a panelled and painted ceiling, one of the earliest of Veronese's works in Venice (1555). The fine series of paintings (including a Resurrection) are by *Brusasorci* and *Bonifazio*. The NUNS' CHOIR, with frescoes of the trial and martyrdom of St Sebastian by *Veronese* and his brother and the Gallery from which the ceiling of the main church can be seen well, have been closed for some two years since the staircase is in need of repair.—Over the 3rd N altar, *Veronese*, Madonna, St Catherine, and a friar, said to be among his earliest works. The chapel also contains fine sculpture by *Aless. Vittorio* (busts of Marcantonio Grimani, St Mark, and St Anthony Abbot).

A short way farther N, across two campi, is the church of the ANGELO RAFFAELE. Over the main door is a sculptured Tobias, angel and dog attrib. to *Seb. Mariani da Lugano*. The entrance is by the side door next to the campanile. In the dark interior, designed on a Greek-cross plan in 1618, by *Fr. Contino*, the organ bears paintings of Tobias and the angel by *Fr.* or *Giov. Ant. Guardi*.

Behind the church, in Campo dell'Angelo Raffaele is a well-head in Istrian stone dated 1349. A merchant called Marco Arian left funds in his will for its erection to provide fresh water for the district. He died in 1348 of the plague, believing that the outbreak of the epidemic could have been caused by contaminated water.—In front of the church, across the rio, Fondamenta Briati leads to the Gothic Palazzo Arian (No. 2376; now a school), opposite the end of Rio San Sebastiano. The remarkable six-light window has fine tracery and two plutei.

Fondamenta Barbarigo, on the other side of the rio, leads through an area traditionally inhabited by fishermen and sailors. Beyond Corte Maggiore (which opens onto another canal), near the Stazione Marittima, is the church of **San Nicolò dei Mendicoli** (Pl.8;3; open 7–12, 15.30–19.30; winter 7–12, 16–19). Founded in the 7C, it was subsequently rebuilt and restored many times (most recently in 1977). It has a detached campanile and a little 15C porch (entrance on N side). The charming interior has interesting wood sculptures, and paintings by *Alvise Dal Friso* and other pupils of Paolo Veronese in the nave. In the apse is a wooden statue of the titular Saint, by the school of *Bon*. In the ceiling is a tondo of St Nicholas in glory by *Montemezzano*, and, on either side, Miracles of St Nicholas, by *Leonardo Corona*.

To leave this remote part of the city it is necessary to return to San Sebastiano (comp. p 149), from where the water-front of the Zattere is regained near the Maritime Station and landing-stage of vaporetto No. 5 (for San Marco; comp. p 59). On foot, the Zattere may be followed back to Rio San Trovaso; from here it is a short walk to the Accademia bridge.

# 9    From the Rialto to the Station via Palazzo Pésaro and San Giacomo dell'Orio

The **Rialto** bridge (Pl.6;7; comp. p 106) stands at the topographical centre of the city. A bridge has existed at this point since earliest times, and it remained the only bridge across the Grand Canal throughout the Republic. The area known as the Rialto ('Rivo-alto', 'high bank') is thought to have been one of the first places to be settled by the earliest inhabitants of the lagoon because it was one of the highest points and the best protected. Since the beginning of the Republic it has been the commercial and economic centre of Venice. The markets, established here as early as 1097, were reconstructed by Scarpagnino along the lines of the medieval buildings, after a disastrous fire in 1514.

The walkways of the Rialto bridge descend past the 16C Palazzo dei Camerlenghi (comp. p 109) and the E end of San Giacomo (comp. below), with a 12C inscription exhorting merchants to honesty. The busy Ruga degli Orefici leads through the colourful market in front of the porticoed *Fabbriche Vecchie*, by Scarpagnino. These buildings also extend around the Campo San Giacomo which opens out on the right. Here, amidst the stalls and barrows, is the little church of **San Giacomo di Rialto** (*San Giacometto*; Pl.6;7; open 10–12), traditionally thought to have been founded in AD 421, and considered the oldest church in Venice. It was restored in 1071. It is preceded by a Gothic entrance portico; above is a large clock of 1410. The domed Greek-cross plan on a tiny scale, derived from Byzantine models, was faithfully preserved in the rebuilding of 1601. The interior retains its six ancient Greek marble columns with finely carved 11C Corinthian capitals. Over the high altar, St James and angels by Aless. Vittoria (1602), and on the right, Annunciation, by Marco Vecellio.—Across the campo is the *Gobbo di Rialto* by Pietro da Salò (16C), a crouching figure which supports a flight of steps leading to a rostrum of Egyptian granite from which the laws of the Republic were proclaimed. Behind the Fabbriche Vecchie, the Erberia, the wholesale market for fruit and vegetables, opens on to the Grand Canal, adjoined by Sansovino's Fabbriche Nuove (p 109) and the markets which extend along the canal to the fish market (comp. below).

At the end of Ruga degli Orefici, in the broad Ruga Vecchia San Giovanni (left), an archway forms the entrance to **San Giovanni Elemosinario** (Pl.6;7; closed for restoration), a church rebuilt by *Scarpagnino* in 1527–29, but preserving its campanile of 1398–1410.

INTERIOR, on a Greek-cross plan. The frescoes on the cupola by *Pordenone* were discovered under a thin layer of plaster in 1985. The high altarpiece of the patron saint distributing alms was painted for the church by *Titian* (c 1545). In the chapel to the right of the main chapel, *Pordenone*, SS. Catherine, Sebastian, and Roch; on the left wall of the church, *Marco Vecellio*, doge Leonardo Donà receiving the Holy Water from the parish priest of the church. The church also contains various works by *Leon. Corona* and *Palma Giovane* (including a lunette of St Roch healing the plague-stricken).

Ruga dei Spezieri continues the line of Ruga degli Orefici into Campo delle Becarie with the arcaded hall of the *Pescheria* (fish market, comp. p 109). From here, across a bridge set at an angle, and beneath a covered passage-way, the wide Calle dei Bottari is soon reached and the market area left behind. To the left (signposted for the Station and Piazzale Roma) Calle dei Cristi continues to Campo San Cassiano. Here the church of **San Cassiano** (Pl.6;5; open to visitors 10–12, 16.30–19) is an early foundation, rebuilt except for the 13C campanile in the 17C.

INTERIOR. In the SANCTUARY are three remarkable paintings (light; fee) by *Tintoretto*; the *Crucifixion, the Resurrection, and Descent into Limbo. The altar front was carved by *Enrico Meyring* in 1696. SOUTH AISLE, 1st altar, *Rocco Marconi* (attrib.; also attrib. to Palma Vecchio), Christ between Saints (removed since 1966 for restoration). In the chapel to the right of the high altar, *Leandro Bassano*, Visitation, Annunciation to St Zacharias, and Birth of St John. Next to the Sacristy is a chapel decorated in 1746, with an altarpiece (Madonna and Child with St Charles Borromeo and St Philip Neri) signed by *G.B. Pittoni* (1763), and Christ in the Garden by *Leandro Bassano*.—The 1st altarpiece in the NORTH AISLE is by *Matteo Ponzone* (Crucifix with four Saints).

A bridge leads over to Calle dei Morti, at the end of which Calle della Regina continues right (at the end can be seen part of the huge *Palazzo Corner della Regina*, now the 'Biennale' archives; the main facade on the Grand Canal is described on p 109). Calle del Ravano continues across Rio delle Due Torri (with a view right of the side facade of Palazzo Pésaro, see below). Across the next bridge is the fine *Palazzo Agnusdio*, with a relief of three angels over the Gothic door, and a patera with the mystic lamb over the water-gate. Its window has good Gothic sculptures of the Annunciation and the four Symbols of the Evangelists. The fondamenta here leads down to the courtyard of **Palazzo Pésaro** (Pl.5;6; closed for restoration since 1981). The great Renaissance palace (comp. p 109) contains the *Galleria Internazionale d'Arte Moderna* (1st and 2nd floors) and the *Museo Orientale* (2nd floor); some of the rooms have fine views over the Grand Canal. The elaborate Renaissance well-head from the Zecca has an Apollo by Danese Cattaneo. The contents are being rearranged during restoration work and therefore the description below may not be accurate when the palace is reopened.

The **Gallery of Modern Art** (adm see p 65), contains a large collection of paintings and sculptures, mostly purchased at the 'Biennale' art exhibitions. Rearrangements are frequent, but the works are all labelled, and the most important exhibits are usually on the top floor. Among the artists whose work is represented may be mentioned: *Ippolito Caffi, Medardo Rosso, Arturo Martini, Pio Semeghini, Guglielmo Ciardi, Fr. Messina, Emilio Greco, Fr. Hayez, Telemaco Signorini, Giov. Fattori, De Chirico, Carlo Carrà, Fil. de Pisis, Felice Casorati, Fed. Zandomeneghi, Giac. Favretto, Gius. De Nittis, Lor. Viani* and *Felice Carena.—Rodin* (casts of the Thinker and the Burghers of Calais), *Kandinsky, Paul Klee, Max Ernst, Gustave Klimt, Matisse, Mirò, Bonnard, Corot, Rouault, Dufy*, and *Marc Chagall*.

The **Museum of Oriental Art** (adm see p 66), the bulk of whose collections were presented by Prince Henry of Bourbon-Parma, Count of Bardi, is devoted principally to Japanese and Chinese art, with specimens of Siamese and Javanese work. The museum was reopened after restoration in 1985. The Japanese paintings are especially interesting, and the lacquer-work and bronzes are of high quality. Notable also is the fine Khmer figure of Buddha (Cambodia; 12C).

At the end of Calle Pesaro, an iron bridge (right) leads to the little Campo San Stae which opens on to the Grand Canal (with a vaporetto landing-stage). Across the Canal (left) stands the 16C Palazzo Vendramin (p 107) and, on this side just by the landing-stage, is Palazzo Priuli Bon with Veneto-Byzantine details. The church of **San**

**Stae** (*San Eustachio*; Pl.5;6) presents a splendid Baroque facade to the waterfront. The work of *Dom. Rossi*, it was financed by doge Alvise II Mocenigo in 1710. Both it and the bright white and grey interior have recently been restored.

The INTERIOR (open 9.30–12.30, 15–18) has an interesting collection of 18C paintings. RIGHT SIDE, 1st chapel, *Nic. Bambini*, Madonna in glory and Saints. The SANCTUARY has an early work by *Seb. Ricci* on the ceiling and a series of good small paintings: right wall, lower row: *G.B. Tiepolo*, Martyrdom of St Bartholomew; *Greg. Lazzarini*, St Paul; *G. A. Pellegrini*, Martyrdom of St Andrew; (middle) *Gius. Angeli*, Fall of Manna; (upper row) *Pietro Uberti*, Martyrdom of St Philip; *Nic. Bambini*, Communion of St Jacob; *Angelo Trevisani*, Martyrdom of St Thomas. On the left wall (lower row); *G.B. Piazzetta*, *Martyrdom of St Jacob; *Seb. Ricci*, *St Peter freed from prison; *Ant. Balestra*; Martyrdom of St John the Evangelist; (middle) *Gius. Angeli*, Sacrifice of Melchizedek; (upper row) *Silvestro Maniago*, St Mark the Evangelist; *G.B. Pittoni*, St Simeon; *G.B. Mariotti*, St Taddeo.—SACRISTY. Over the altar, Crucifix by *Maffeo Verona* and the Dead Christ by *Pietro Muttoni*. The two paintings with stories from the life of Trajan are by *Giustino Menescardi* and *G.B. Pittoni*.—Left Side of nave. Sculpted Crucifix by *Gius. Torretto*, and funerary monuments of the Foscarini family by *Torretto*, *Ant. Tarsia*, *P. Baratta*, and *P. Groppelli*. 2nd chapel, *Fr. Migliori*, Assumption; 1st chapel, *Jac. Amigoni*, SS. Andrew and Catherine. The organ above the W door is by *Gaetano Callido* (1772).

Beside the church is the charming little *Scuola dei Battiloro e Tiraoro* (Goldsmiths), built in 1711.—The salizzada leads away from the Grand Canal past the brick campanile with a 13C stone angel at its base. Calle Tron diverges right for *Palazzo Tron* (now owned by the University) which contains frescoes by Guarana (adm sometimes granted). Farther on in the salizzada are several fine (but dilapidated) palaces, including (No. 1920) a 13C building and (No. 1992), the 17C *Palazzo Mocenigo* (sometimes open for organized tours in winter). Beyond, Ramo di Rioda diverges left across two canals for the church of **Santa Maria Mater Domini** (Pl.5;6; it has been closed for years for restoration), a Renaissance building probably after a design by *Giov. Buora* (1502–40), with an Istrian stone facade.

The pretty INTERIOR is in very poor condition; all the paintings have been removed for restoration. They include: *Vinc. Catena*, Martyrdom of St Christina (1520); *Fr. Bissolo*, Transfiguration; *Bonifazio*, Last Supper; and *Tintoretto*, *Invention of the Cross.—In the 1st S chapel the fine altar bears three marble figures of saints by *Lor. Bregno* (1524) and *Ant. Minello*; over the main altar, high relief of the Madonna and Child (Florentine school). In the chapel to the left of the high altar, SS. Mark and John, statuettes by *Lor. Bregno*; in the chapel to the right of the high altar is a carved altar also attrib. to *Lor. Bregno*. On the left wall, Madonna in prayer, marble bas-relief (13C Byzantine).
   The campo, with a fine well-head, has several good palaces. At the end (No. 2120) *Palazzetto Viaro* has a distinguished row of tall trefoil windows (14C) and a relief of a lion (almost obliterated). No. 2173 has ogee windows with, above, a frieze of Byzantine crosses and paterae. Opposite, No. 2177 has a quatrefoil decoration (almost completely ruined).

It is now necessary to return to Salizzada San Stae (comp. above). Just to the left Calle del Tentor continues roughly parallel to the Grand Canal, across two bridges. From the second, Ponte del Megio, there is a view left of Campo San Giacomo dell'Orio (see below). The fondamenta continues right to Ramo del Megio and (left) a salizzada which returns to the Grand Canal and the **Fóndaco dei Turchi** (Pl.5;4), from 1621–1838 the warehouse of the Turkish merchants. Once the most characteristic Veneto-Byzantine palaces (12–13C) in the city, it was virtually rebuilt after 1858.

In 1381 it was given to the Dukes of Ferrara, and here, as their guests stayed
John Palaeologus, the Byzantine Emperor in 1438, and Tasso in 1562. It now
contains a NATURAL HISTORY MUSEUM (adm see p66) where the exhibits
include an Ouranosaurus over 3.5m high and 7m long and a giant crocodile
nearly 12m long, both found in the Sahara in 1973. There is also a lapidary
collection. The material from the Venetian lagoon includes an ancient boat.

On the other side of the Grand Canal rises the church of San Marcuola

*Capitals of the Fóndaco dei Turchi sketched by John Ruskin for
'The Stones of Venice' (1853), when he found the palace 'a ghastly
ruin'*

and (right) Palazzo Vendramin. From the salizzada, Calle dei Preti leads right along the side of the church of SAN GIOVANNI DECOLLATO (Pl.5;5; *San Zan Degolá*). Deconsecrated in the 19C, the building is now used as a concert hall (sometimes unlocked on request at the convent in Calle dei Preti). The basilican interior has Greek marble columns and Byzantine capitals and a ship's keel roof. The left apse chapel has interesting 13C frescoes recently discovered.—From the campo Calle del Capitello zig-zags back to Calle Larga (right) which leads into the large Campo San Giacomo dell' Orio, with its plane trees and the tall 13C campanile of the church of **San Giacomo dell' Orio** (Pl.5;5; open 7.30–12, 17–20.30). Of ancient foundation, it was rebuilt in 1225, and altered in 1532.

The INTERIOR contains massive low Byzantine columns (12–13C), one (in the S transept) of verde antico, and one (behind the pulpit) with a fine flowered capital. There is a beautiful 14C wooden 'ship's keel' *Roof. Around the W door (beneath the organ) are paintings attrib. to *And. Schiavone*, including two Prophets flanking the door. The huge Stoup in Greek marble, was probably used as a font.—SOUTH AISLE. 1st altar, Madonna and Child, Tuscan wooden statue. In the SOUTH TRANSEPT the old wall of the church has been exposed with interesting fragments embedded in it.—In the NEW SACRISTY (unlocked by the sacristan) is a ceiling painting of the Allegory of Faith, by *Veronese* (recently restored) and four Doctors of the Church. The interesting paintings include: *Fr. Bassano*, Madonna in glory with SS. John and Nicholas; (opposite, above a fine carved fragment) St John the Baptist preaching. It incorporates portraits of Bassano's family and of Titian (on the extreme left wearing a red hat). Beneath is a small Crucifixion by *Palma Giovane*; *Bonifazio Veronese* (attrib.), Supper at Emmaus.—In the pretty domed chapel to the right of the high altar are paintings by *Padovanino*, *Del Moro*, and *Palma Giovane*. SANCTUARY. *Lor. Lotto*. Madonna and four Saints (1546); Crucifix by *Lor. Veneziano*. On the walls are two large marble crosses, fine Lombardesque works. On the left pier, the statuette of the Virgin annunciate was formerly over the door of Santa Maria Mater Domini. A charming Byzantine work, it shows the Virgin with a spindle in her hand. The chapel to the left of the high altar contains two detached Byzantine fresco fragments (13C) from San Giovanni Decollato, including an Annunciation.—The OLD SACRISTY, with finely carved wood furniture, is entirely decorated with paintings by *Palma Giovane* (1575). Over the door is a 14C bas-relief of the Madonna and Child with donor. To the left of the door, *Buonconsiglio*, Three Saints (recently restored).—NORTH TRANSEPT. *Veronese*, SS. Lawrence, Jerome, and Prosper (much restored), and two good early works by *Palma Giovane* with stories from the life of St Laurence. The N porch contains a wood crucifix (13C?).

To the S of the church (across a bridge), the name of Corte dell'Anatomia recalls the site of an anatomical theatre built here in 1671.—The area N of the church, reached by Ramo dell'Isola, has boat-building yards and large warehouses which, until recently, were surrounded on four sides by canals (now filled in except for Rio di San Zan Degolà).

Across the rio, Ruga Bella leads (left) to Campo Sauro; Calle Larga dei Bari continues right to the church of **San Simeone Grande** (*San Simeone Profeta*; Pl.5;5).

The low INTERIOR has a wide nave with antique columns and statues above the arcade. On the N wall, near the main door, is a Last Supper by *Tintoretto*. Over the high altar, *Palma Giovane*, Presentation in the Temple. In a niche in the S aisle is a carved figure of St Valentine (Lombardesque) and, on the end wall, above an arch, 14C carved angel. In the chapel to the left of the main chapel is an *Effigy of St Simeon (c 1317–18), by *Marco Romano*.—In the Sacristy is a painting of the Trinity attrib. to *Giov. Mansueti*.—The flank of the church faces its campo on the Grand Canal. Beneath the portico is an interesting 14C relief of a Saint.

A bridge leads across Rio Marin and the calle (right) leads down to the Grand Canal in front of the Station bridge. Just to the left is the church of **San Simeone Piccolo** (Pl.4;6), on a stylobate with an interesting pronaos with Corinthian columns and a high green dome. It is the best work of *Giov. Scalfarotto* who built it in 1718–23 on a plan derived from the Pantheon in Rome. The interior is open only for concerts.—From the landing-stages in front of the Station vaporetti return down the Grand Canal (or the shorter Rio Nuovo) towards San Marco.

# 10  From the Rialto to the Station via the Frari and the Scuola Grande di San Rocco

From the foot of the Rialto bridge (comp. Rte 9) Fondamenta del Vin (Pl.6;7) skirts the Grand Canal as far as Rio terrà San Silvestro which leads away from the water-front. It passes a column with an 11C capital (set in to the wall of a house) before reaching (left) the church of **San Silvestro** (Pl.6;7).

The neo-classical INTERIOR is by *Lor. Santi*. The apse (with the organ on the E wall) is divided from the nave by Corinthian columns. RIGHT SIDE: 1st altar. *Tintoretto*, Baptism of Christ; 2nd altar. *Johann Karl Loth*, Holy Family,—LEFT SIDE: 1st altar, *Girol. da Santacroce*, St Thomas Becket enthroned (interesting for its iconography). On the left wall is a Gothic polyptych in an elaborate 14C frame.

Opposite the church is *Palazzo Valier* (No. 1022), with a Doric doorway, where Giorgione died in 1510. In the peaceful Campo San Silvestro the fine brick campanile has a stone bas-relief. Calle del Luganegher leads from here to the busy Campo Sant'Aponal with eight calli leading into it. Here is the deconsecrated church of SANT'APONAL (*Sant'Apollinare*; Pl.6;7). Founded in the 11C, it was rebuilt in the 15C. On the Gothic facade, above a round window, is a badly worn relief of the Crucifix (14C); below, in a tabernacle, is the Crucifixion and episodes from the life of Christ (1294). The interior is used as an archive.—To the left, in Calle del Campaniel, is the Romanesque campanile (a 13C relief of the Lion of St Mark has been removed from its base and put in store at the Correr Museum).

Calle del Ponte Storto leads to the bridge of the same name; on the right (No. 1280) is the birthplace of Bianca Cappello (c 1560–87), the 'daughter of the Republic' and wife of Fr. Medici. Across the canal the sottoportico continues past an unusually narrow calle to the next bridge which recrosses the canal. Calle Cavalli soon diverges right to emerge, across another bridge, in CAMPO SAN POLO (Pl.5;8), one of the largest and most attractive in the city. Its shape makes it a favourite playground for children. Among the interesting palaces which follow the curved side of the campo (once bordered by a canal) are (No. 1957) the well-proportioned Baroque *Palazzo Tiepolo*, attrib. to Giorgio Massari, and (No. 2169) *Palazzo Soranzo*, with its marble facing and good capitals. The church of **San Polo** (Pl.5;8) bears interesting reliefs (the earliest dating from the 13C) on the exterior of the E end. It is entered by the S doorway, a fine Gothic work attrib. to *Bart. Bon* with two angels holding an inscription and crowned by the half-figure of St Paul.

The INTERIOR, with a 'ship's keel' roof, was altered in 1804 by *Davide Rossi* and given a neo-classical arcade. On the left of the W door, Last Supper, by *Iac. Tintoretto* (light; fee). At either side of the S entrance door are interesting sculptural fragments. On the high altar, Crucifix (Venetian, early 15C). In the left apse chapel, *Veronese*, Marriage of the Virgin (light; fee).—Left side: 3rd altar, *P. Piazza*, Preaching of St Paul; 2nd altar, *G.B. Tiepolo*, Virgin appearing to a Saint.—At the W end is the entrance to the ORATORY OF THE CRUCIFIX (light essential; fee). It contains the *Stations of the Cross by *Gian Dom. Tiepolo* (1749), incorporating remarkable portraits of Venetian 18C society. On the ceiling have been hung a Glory of Angels and *Resurrection, also by Tiepolo. Three of the paintings were removed for restoration in 1984.

From the N side of the Campo, Rio Terrà S Antonio and Calle Bernardo lead towards Rio Terrà Secondo (Pl.5;6), where, at No. 2311, a small Gothic palace is the traditional site of the Aldine Press set up by the Roman scholar Aldus Manutius in 1490 and famous for its publication of the Greek classics.

Outside San Polo the isolated Campanile (1362) has two fine Romanesque lions carved at its base. From Ponte San Polo the main facade, by Sanmicheli, of *Palazzo Corner Mocenigo* (begun after 1545; at present covered for restoration) can be seen on the canal (right). Frederick Rolfe (Baron Corvo) lived in an apartment here in 1909–10. Calle dei Saoneri continues to Rio terrà dei Nomboli. Here the dark Ramo Pisani diverges towards the Grand Canal and *Palazzo Pisani della Moretta* (now used by the Monteverdi Society; adm by previous appointment). The fine 18C interior has been beautifully restored. Beyond is *Palazzo Barbarigo della Terrazza* (with the German Institute) on the Grand Canal.—Calle dei Nomboli continues to (No. 2793) *Palazzo Centani* (15C), the birthplace of Carlo Goldoni (1707–93), the playwright. Known as the CASA GOLDONI it has a picturesque Gothic courtyard with a splendid staircase and a pretty well-head. The interior (adm see p65) contains Goldoni relics and an Institute of Theatrical Studies (with a Library).—Beyond Ponte and Campiello San Tomà (with a relief of the Madonna of the Misericordia) CAMPO DI SAN TOMÀ (Pl.5;7) is soon reached. The church has been closed for years for restoration. Calle del Traghetto leads down to the gondola ferry which crosses the Grand Canal diagonally to the calle near Santo Stefano (comp. p133). In Campo San Tomà the 15C *Scuola dei Caleghexi* (i.e. shoemakers; being restored in 1985) bears a charming relief of St Mark healing the cobbler Ananias from the East, by Pietro Lombardo (1478), and a Madonna of the Misericordia. Behind the little building, Calle Larga leads up to the *Frari* (Pl.5;7), properly the church of *Santa Maria Gloriosa dei Frari*, and dedicated to the Assumption. Its size rivals that of San Giovanni e Paolo, and it contains remarkable sculptures and paintings. It is open to visitors from 9 or 9.30–12, 14.30 or 15–18; fest. 14.30–18 (an entrance fee is charged to cover the expense of the lighting).

The original Franciscan church was founded c 1250. The present church, built of brick in the Italian Gothic style, was begun c 1330 but not finished until after 1443. The majestic campanile (the tallest in the city after St Mark's) dates from the second half of the 14C. On the severe W front the Gothic doorway has sculptures attrib. to *Aless. Vittoria* (the Risen Christ), and the workshop of *Bart. Bon*. The usual entrance is on the N side near a doorway with a statue of St Peter; another door on this side has a fine relief of the Madonna and Child with angels attrib. to a Tuscan master of the first half of the 15C. The church faces SW, but is here described as though it had the altar at the E end.

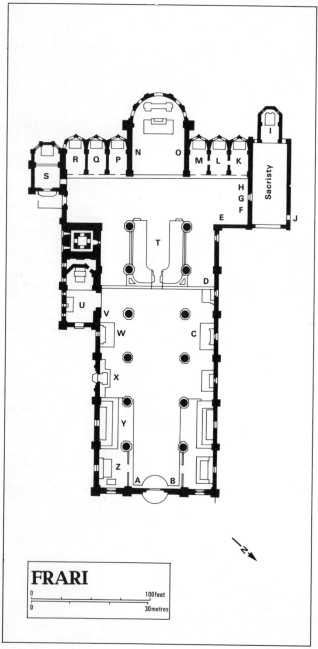

FRARI

0 _____ 100 feet
0 _____ 30 metres

The imposing *INTERIOR, 90m long, is cruciform with an aisled nave of 8 bays joined by wooden tie-beams. In the centre is the Monks' Choir, the arch of which frames Titian's magnificent Assumption in the apse. Many of the most interesting monuments in the church are high up and difficult to see. (The letters in the text refer to the Plan on p158).—On the right of the main door, Tomb (A) of Pietro Bernardo (d 1538), thought to be a late work by _Tullio Lombardo_; to the left of the door, Tomb (B) of the Procurator Alvise Pasqualino (d 1528), attrib. to _Lor. Bregno_.—SOUTH AISLE. Near the 1st column, Stoup with a bronze statuette of St Agnes by _Girol. Campagna_, forming a pair with the one opposite bearing a statuette of St Anthony of Padua (1609). Above the place where the great painter is believed to be buried, is the ungainly Mausoleum of Titian, by _L._ and _P. Zandomeneghi_ (1838–52). 2nd altar, Purification of the Virgin and Saints, by _G. Salviati_ (1548); on the 3rd altar (C), *Statue of St Jerome by _Vittoria_. Beyond the 4th altar (with a Martyrdom of St Catherine, by _Palma Giovane_), and up a few steps, is a Monument (D) to Bp. Marco Zen, of Torcello (d 1641).—In the SOUTH TRANSEPT is the unusual *Monument (E) to Iac. Marcello (d 1484), recently attrib. to _Giovanni Buora_, with a fresco high up after _Dom. Morone_. On the right of the sacristy door is the sarcophagus (F) of Beato Pacifico, beneath an elaborate canopy, ascribed to _Nanni di Bartolo_ and _Michele da Firenze_, in florid Gothic style of 1437; over the door is the fine tomb (G) by _Lor. Bregno_ of Bened. Pésaro, the Venetian general who died in Corfu in 1503 (with interesting reliefs of battle-ships and fortresses). The statue of Mars is by _Baccio da Montelupo_. On the left is the Gothic tomb (H; c 1406) of Paolo Savelli, the first in Venice to include an equestrian statue. The statues of the Madonna and Child and the Annunciation have been attrib. to _Jac. della Quercia_.

In the apse of the SACRISTY is a *Triptych (I) of the Madonna and Child between SS. Nicholas of Bari, Peter, Mark, and Benedict, by _Giovanni Bellini_ (1488), a perfect expression of the religious sentiment of this great and typical Venetian. The splendid frame is by _Jacopo da Faenza_. Also displayed here: a Lombardesque lavabo; Deposition by _Nic. Frangipane_; and a marble tabernacle by _Tullio Lombardo_.—A few steps lead down to the CHAPTER HOUSE (J) which looks out onto the Palladian Cloister with its elaborate well-head. Here is the sarcophagus of doge Fr. Dandolo (d 1339), with a lunette above by _Paolo Veneziano_ showing the Doge and Dogaressa presented to the Virgin by SS. Francis and Elizabeth (thought to be the earliest ducal portrait drawn from life to have survived). Part of the Treasury is displayed here, and a 17C clock signed by _Fr. Pianta il Giovane_.

SOUTH CHOIR CHAPELS: 3rd chapel (K), Altarpiece by _Bart Vivarini_ (1482) in its magnificent original frame; 2nd chapel (L), Two Gothic funerary monuments, including that of Duccio degli Uberti (d 1336, recently attrib. to _Andriolo de'Santi_.) The 1st chapel (M) contains the Altar of the Florentines erected in 1436. The wooden statue of *St John the Baptist by _Donatello_ (1438; recently restored) is the first documented work in the Veneto by this artist.—The apse of the SANCTUARY is lit by windows and is filled with _Titian's_ huge *Assumption (1518; recently restored), celebrated among his masterpieces for its dramatic movement and its amazing colouring. The high altar dates from 1516. On the N wall is the *Tomb (N) of doge Nic. Tron (d 1473), by _Ant. Rizzo_, one of the most sublime examples of Renaissance funerary art in Venice. Opposite is the fine

Tomb (O) of Fr. Fóscari, who died in 1457 after 34 years as doge. The late Gothic mausoleum is traditionally attrib. to *Ant.* and *Paolo Bregno.*—NORTH CHOIR CHAPELS: 1st chapel (P), *Bern. Licinio,* Madonna and saints; 2nd chapel (Q), on the right wall, Tomb of Melchiorre Trevisan (d 1500), by *Lor. Bregno* (?); 3rd chapel, (R), St Ambrose and eight other saints, begun by *Alvise Vivarini* (1503) and finished by *Marco Basaiti;* on the floor a plain slab marks the grave of Claudio Monteverdi (date of birth incorrect; 1567–1643); 4th chapel (S; usually locked, but partly visible through the grille), Tomb of Fed. Corner, an unusual but graceful work (of Tuscan provenance) with an angel in a niche holding an inscription. The font bears a statue of St John, exquisitely carved in marble by *Sansovino* (1554). On the altar, *St Mark enthroned and four other saints, by *Bart. Vivarini* (1474; in a fine frame).—The NORTH TRANSEPT contains a delicately carved bench-back attrib. to *Lor.* and *Crist. Canozzi da Lendinara* (15C). The pretty circular monument to Genorosa degli Orsini and San Maffeo Zen is by the Lombardesque school.

The RITUAL CHOIR (T), which extends into the nave (an unusual arrangement in Italy), contains three tiers of *Stalls carved by *Marco Cozzi* (1468), with intarsia decoration by *Lor.* and *Crist. Canozzi.* The Choir Screen by *Bart. Bon* and *Pietro Lombardo* is faced with marble and decorated with figures of Saints and Prophets in relief; above are ten Apostles and a Crucifixion between the Virgin and St John the Evangelist, with Angels as lecterns.—In the NORTH AISLE is the CAPPELLA EMILIANI (U) containing a marble altarpiece with ten statues in niches by the school of *Jacobello Dalle Masegne* (15C), and the tomb of Bp. Miani, with five similar statues. Next comes the monument (V) to Bp. Iac. Pésaro (d 1547), with a fine effigy. Over the Pésaro altar (W) is the *Madonna di Ca' Pésaro, by *Titian* (completed in 1526; recently restored), a marvel of composition and colour. Commissioned by Bp. Pésaro in 1519, it shows the Madonna and Child with Saints before members of the Pésaro family (Bp. Pésaro is to the left, and his brother to the right, both kneeling). The mausoleum (X) of doge Giov. Pésaro (d 1659), a bizarre Baroque work, is attrib. to Longhena, with sculptures by *Barthel.* The Mausoleum (Y) of Canova (1827), by his pupils, including *Bart. Ferrari,* and *Luigi Zandomeneghi,* reproduces Canova's design for a monument to Titian. The altar of the Crucifix (Z), designed by *Longhena,* has sculptures by *Juste Le Court.*

The adjoining conventual buildings, with the Palladian cloister (comp. above) and another in the style of Sansovino, contain the **State Archives**, re-structured c 1815–20 by L. Santi. Among the most famous in the world, they fill some 300 rooms. They provide a remarkable documentation of the Venetian Republic.

Beyond the interesting apse of the Frari is **San Rocco** (Pl.5;7), a church designed by *Bart. Bon the Younger* (1489) but almost entirely rebuilt in 1725 (facade of 1765–71).

INTERIOR. Flanking the W door are two statues (David with the head of Goliath, and St Cecilia) by *Giov. Marchiori* (1743). To the left and right, Annunciation and St Roch, by *Iac. Tintoretto.*—SOUTH SIDE. 1st altar, *Seb. Ricci,* Miracle of San Francesco di Paola. Between the 1st and 2nd altars, two large paintings: (above) St Roch taken to prison, attrib. to *Iac. Tintoretto,* and (below) Pool of Bethesda, by *Iac. Tintoretto.* In the Sanctuary the altar has two marble statues of St Sebastian and St Pantaleone by *Giov. Maria Mosca;* on either side are putti frescoed by *Pordenone.* The carved dossals are attrib. to *Giov. Marchiori.* On the walls (difficult to see well): (right) *Iac. Tintoretto,* *St Roch cures the plague victims, the first Venetian painting to show the Saint inside a hospital

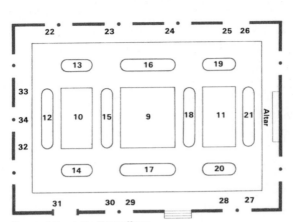

Key to paintings in the Chapter House

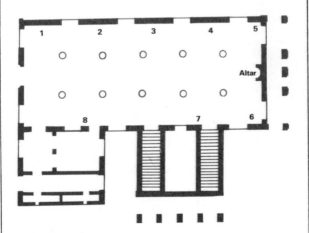

**Ground Floor**

# SCUOLA DI SAN ROCCO

(1549; restored in 1979), and (left) St Roch comforted by an angel; above (right),
St Roch in solitude, and (left) St Roch healing the animals.—NORTH SIDE. 2nd
altar, *Fr. Solimena*, Annunciation and God the Father with angels. Between the
1st and 2nd altars (high up) St Martin and St Christopher by *Pordenone*. 1st
altar, *Seb. Ricci*, St Helena and the Discovery of the True Cross.

Beside the church is the *Scuola Grande di San Rocco (adm see p
66), begun for the important Confraternity of St Roch (founded in
1478) by *Bart. Bon the Younger* (1515), and finished by *Scarpagnino*
(1549), who added the extravagant main facade. The less imposing
canal facade is also by *Scarpagnino*. The interior is famous for its
works by *Tintoretto*, who here, in over fifty **Paintings produced
one of the most remarkable pictorial cycles in existence.

In 1564 a competition was held for the decoration of Scarpagnino's recently
completed building. Tintoretto was the winner, having entered a finished work
(rather than a preparatory sketch) of St Roch in Glory, already in place in the
Sala dell'Albergo. A year later he was elected a Brother of the Confraternity,
and spent the next twenty-three years working on the paintings (without the
help of collaborators). In return he received a modest pension from the
Brotherhood. When Ruskin visited the Scuola in 1845 he commented 'As for
*painting*, I think I didn't know what it was until today' and his visit inspired
him to pursue his study of the city and her art. Since restoration in 1969–74 the
full splendour of the colours used by Tintoretto can again be appreciated.

The columned GROUND FLOOR HALL, where religious ceremonies
were held, was the last to be painted in the Scuola by *Tintoretto*
(1582–87). The superb cycle of paintings illustrating the Life of the
Virgin Mary begins on the left wall near the entrance: Annunciation
(1); Adoration of the Magi (2); Flight into Egypt (3); with a splendid
landscape); Massacre of the Innocents (4); and (5) Mary Magdalen
reading in a charming twilight landscape. Opposite, on the right wall
(6), the matching panel represents St Mary of Egypt, also reading in
a landscape. The Circumcision (7) appears to have been painted
partly by the bottega of Tintoretto and by his son *Domenico*. The last
painting, the Assumption (8), has suffered from poor restorations in
the past.—The statue of St Roch on the altar is by *Girol. Campagna*
(1587). A selection of objects from the rich Treasury of the Confraternity is also exhibited here: 14C reliquaries, a 15C portable altar,
paxes, pastoral crosses, a fine 16C chalice, etc.

The *GRAND STAIRCASE, by *Scarpagnino* (1544–46) has two huge
paintings commemorating the end of the plague of 1630, the one on
the right by *Ant. Zanchi* (1666), and the one opposite by *Pietro Negri*
(1673).—The huge CHAPTER HOUSE is a splendid hall by *Scarpagnino*.
The paintings here by *Tintoretto* (1576–81) represent (on the ceiling)
Old Testament subjects, and (on the walls) New Testament subjects,
chosen in a careful iconographical scheme related to the teaching of
St Roch and his efforts to relieve thirst, hunger, and sickness. The
huge central painting (9) shows Moses erecting the brazen serpent
to save those bitten by fiery serpents sent by God as a punishment.
The subjects of the other remarkable paintings are as follows: 10.
Moses striking water from the rock to quench the people's thirst; 11.
The miraculous fall of Manna from Heaven; 12. Adam and Eve (the
Fall of Man); 13. God the Father appearing to Moses; 14. Moses led
into the desert by the Pillar of Fire; 15. Jonah issuing from the belly
of the whale; 16. Vision of Ezekiel of the Resurrection; 17. Jacob's
ladder; 18. Sacrifice of Isaac; 19. Elisha's miracle of the loaves of
bread (restored by *Gius. Angeli* in 1777); 20. Elijah fed by an angel;
21. The Jewish Passover.—The eight smaller panels in chiaroscuro

*Moses striking water from the rock, Tintoretto (detail of the Chapter House ceiling in the Scuola Grande di San Rocco)*

are replacements by *Gius. Angeli* (1777) of works by Tintoretto.—The paintings on the walls represent New Testament subjects: 22. Adoration of the Shepherds; 23. Baptism of Christ; 24. Resurrection of Christ; 25. Agony in the Garden; 26. The Last Supper; 27. Miracle of the Loaves and Fishes; 28. Resurrection of Lazarus; 29. Ascension; 30. Miracle of Christ at the pool of Bethesda (damaged by poor restorations); 31. Temptation of Christ.—On the end walls: (32.) and (33.) SS. Roch and Sebastian; and, on the altar, 34. Vision of St Roch (with the help of his son *Domenico*). The two statues on the altar of St John the Baptist and St Sebastian are late works by *Gerol. Campagna*.—Here also are exhibited some easel paintings: *Titian*, Annunciation (acquired by the Scuola in 1555); *Tintoretto*, Visitation; *G.B. Tiepolo*, Hagar and Ishmael comforted by an angel, and Abraham visited by an angel, both acquired by the Scuola in 1785. The walls of the presbytery have carved wooden reliefs of the life of St Roch by *Giov. Marchiori*.—The late 17C carved wood benches around the great hall by *Fr. Pianta il Giovane* incorporate bizarre figures including, near the altar, a caricature of Tintoretto and a self-portrait. The processional lanterns ('fanaloni') date from the 18C. Beneath the Temptation of Christ (on the right of the door into the Sala dell'Albergo), is hung the portrait of a man by Tintoretto, once considered to be a self-portrait.

The SALA DELL' ALBERGO was the first to be decorated by *Tintoretto* (1564–67). On the carved and gilded ceiling, St Roch in Glory (comp. above) and twenty smaller panels with heads of putti, the four seasons, allegories of the Scuole Grande of Venice, and the Cardinal Virtues. The vast Crucifixion is generally considered to be his masterpiece. On the opposite wall, Christ before Pilate, Crowning of Thorns, and the Way to Calvary.—Here also are displayed: the fragment of a frieze from the ceiling of three apples, showing Tintoretto's remarkable painting technique; Christ carrying the Cross, a greatly venerated painting by *Titian* which hung in the church of San Rocco from c 1510 until 1955; and Christ in Pietà, now generally attrib. to the circle of *Giorgione*.

It is now necessary to return round the Frari to reach the bridge in front of the facade of the church. Across the rio, Fondamenta dei Frari leads left to another bridge and (left) Rio terrà San Tomà (in front of the Archivio di Stato, comp. above). Calle del Magazzen and its continuation soon reach the fine courtyard (left) in front of the **Scuola di San Giovanni Evangelista** (Pl.5;7), one of the six chief confraternities, founded in 1261. The first court has a beautiful marble screen and portal by *Pietro Lombardo* (1481). In the second court is the flank of the Scuola (right) dating from 1454 with a relief of Brothers of the Scuola kneeling in front of St John the Evangelist (1349) and Gothic windows; ahead is the entrance (1512) to the Scuola, with double windows above. To the left is the church, or oratory, with its campanile.

The INTERIOR of the Scuola (ring for adm at the offices of an international restoration committee; see p 66) has a collection of sculptural fragments on the ground floor, including a relief of the Resurrection of Christ, by the workshop of *Rizzo*. The double *STAIRCASE, a work of great skill and elegance, by *Mauro Codussi* (1498) leads up to the SALONE, transformed by *Giorgio Massari* (c 1727). On the walls is a 16C cycle of paintings with scenes from the life of St John the Evangelist: *Dom. Tintoretto*, St John at the Temple of Ephesus; *Sante Peranda*, Martyrdom of St John; *Dom. Tintoretto*, Transfiguration. On the opposite wall: *And. Vicentino*, St John and the philosopher Craten; *G.B. Cignaroli* (18C), Adoration of the Magi; *Dom. Tintoretto*, St John revives two dead men; *Cignaroli*, Adoration of the Shepherds; *Vicentino*, St John revives Drusiana.—The ceiling (1760) has scenes from the Apocalypse by *Gius. Angeli*, *Gasp. Diziani*, *Jac. Marieschi*, *Jac. Guarana*, and *Gian Dom. Tiepolo*. On the altar, statue of St John attrib. to *G.M. Morleiter*.—The adjoining ORATORIO DELLA CROCE (seen through a grille) contains a precious Reliquary of the Cross (1379) brought from Cyprus.

A long dark calle, by the former entrance to the Scuola, continues past modern buildings, to emerge on Rio delle Muneghette. Fondamenta delle Sacchere leads left through an austere part of the city to a bridge which crosses to Corte Amai. Beyond the university buildings, on Rio dei Tolentini (left) are seen the unexpected columns of the imposing church of **San Nicola da Tolentino** (Pl.4;8). The fine Corinthian portico is by *And. Tirali* (1706–14).

The classical INTERIOR by *Vinc. Scamozzi* (1591–1602) recalls Palladian models, despite the heavy decorations added in the 17C. SOUTH SIDE, 1st chapel, paintings (right and left) by *Padovanino*; 2nd chapel, three works by *Cam. Procaccini*, including St Charles Borromeo in glory; 3rd chapel, School of *Bonifazio*, Banquet of Herod and Beheading of St John the Baptist. Over the side door in the S transept, *Ger. Forabosco*, Ecstacy of St Francis.—The tabernacle in the SANCTUARY by *Baldass. Longhena*, has sculptures by *Juste Le Court*; on the right wall, *Luca Giordano*, Annunciation. Outside the Sanctuary (left). *Johann Lys*, *St Jerome visited by an angel. On the left wall, Tomb of the patriarch Fr. Morosini (d 1678), by *Fil. Parodi* and St Laurence distributing alms by *Bernardo Strozzi*.—NORTH SIDE, 3rd chapel, *Palma Giovane*, Stories of St Cecilia and other Saints.

The bridge in front of the church crosses over to the *Giardino Papadópoli*, public gardens on the site of a church and monastery. The fondamenta (right) soon reaches the Grand Canal, almost opposite the Station; to the E lies **Piazzale Roma** (Pl.4;7) the terminal of the road from the mainland with its huge multi-story car parks (the first of which was built in 1931–33) and bus stations.

Behind the garage is the church of *Sant'Andrea della Zirada* (Pl.4;7), an early Gothic building containing a nuns' choir decorated in the 17C, and a sumptuous altar by Juste Le Court (1679).—Just to the N is the church of the *Nome di Gesù* (Pl.4;5), a neo-classical building (1815–21) by A. Selva.

The landing-stages on the Grand Canal at Piazzale Roma and the Station are served by the vaporetti for San Marco which follow the direct route along Rio Nuovo, or the prettier but longer route back along the Grand Canal.

# 11  From the Rialto to the Ca' d'Oro, the Gesuiti, and Santa Maria dei Miracoli

From Campo San Bartolomeo (Pl.6;8; comp. p 128), at the foot of the Rialto bridge, a salizzada behind the statue of Goldoni skirts the back of the huge Fóndaco dei Tedeschi (see p 106; now the central post office). There is a good view (left) of the arch of the Rialto bridge at the end of a calle. At Ponte dell'Olio this route leaves the Sestiere di San Marco and enters Cannaregio. From the bridge can be seen (left), across the Grand Canal, the corner of Palazzo dei Camerlenghi, the brick tower of San Giacomo, and the beginning of the Rialto markets. The salizzada soon reaches **San Giovanni Crisostomo** (Pl.6;6), which almost fills its small campo. The last work of *Mauro Codussi* (1497–1504), it is a masterpiece of Venetian Renaissance architecture.

The INTERIOR is on a Greek-cross plan of Byzantine inspiration. Over the high altar, (light; fee) *Seb. del Piombo*, *Seven Saints (1510–11). On the N side, St Anthony of Padua, by a follower of *Vivarini*, a classical bas-relief of the Coronation of the Virgin by *Tullio Lombardo*, and (above) a Veneto-Byzantine relief of the Madonna in prayer.—On the S side, *Giov. Bellini* (light; fee), *SS. Christopher, Jerome, and Louis of Toulouse (1513, one of his last works, recently restored).

Across the bridge begins Calle Dolfin; beyond a campiello it continues (with a view at the end of the campanile of Santi Apostoli) to a rio with a huge stone bearing a long inscription relating to the Bakers' Guild. To the left the portico of *Palazzo Falier* leads on to Ponte Santi Apostoli. The Veneto-Byzantine palace (seen from the bridge) dates from the end of the 13C and is a characteristic merchant's house of the period. It is the traditional home of doge Marin Falier, executed in 1355. In the pleasant campo is the church of **Santi Apostoli** (Pl.6;6), much rebuilt, which has a tall campanile of 1672.

*Windows of Palazzo Falier sketched by John Ruskin for 'The Stones of Venice' (1853)*

INTERIOR. The ceiling paintings are by *Fabio Canal* and *Carlo Gaspari* (1748). SOUTH SIDE. The CAPPELLA CORNER is a Lombardesque work (late 15C) attrib. to *Mauro Codussi*. Over the altar is the Communion of St Lucy, by *G.B. Tiepolo* (c 1748), and to the right and left are the tombs of Marco Corner (attrib. to *Tullio Lombardo*) and Giorgio Corner (school of the Lombardi). On the 2nd altar on this side, *Giov. Contarini*, Birth of the Virgin.—In the chapel to the right of the high altar are interesting remains of 14C frescoes (Deposition and Entombment) detached from the walls. The marble head of St Sebastian is by *Tullio Lombardo*.—In the chapel to the left of the high altar, *Fr. Maffei*, Guardian Angel, and a high relief of the Madonna and Child, a charming work by the 15C Florentine school.—The 1st altarpiece on the N side of St Jerome and Saints is by *Dom. Maggiotto*.

Here begins the wide STRADA NUOVA, opened in 1871, a busy shopping street. At the beginning is the *ex-Scuola dell'Angelo Custode* (now the Lutheran Evangelical church), with a facade by *And. Tirali* (1714). Campo Santa Sofia (left) opens out on to the Grand Canal in front of the Pescaria (and the gondola ferry over to the Rialto markets). The church of SANTA SOFIA (hidden behind the house fronts; often closed), with a squat brick campanile, is entered from the Strada Nuova. It contains four statues of Saints (on the W wall and on the high altar), by the school of Ant. Rizzo.—The next calle on the left is the inconspicuous Calle della Ca' d'Oro which leads down to the Grand Canal (with a landing-stage) and the **Ca' d'Oro** (Pl.6;5). Famous as the most beautiful Gothic palace in Venice, it was built between 1425 and c 1440 for the procurator of St Mark's, Marino Contarini, who preserved elements of the previous Veneto-Byzantine Palazzo Zeno on this site. It is the work of *Matteo Raverti* and Lombard collaborators, and of *Giov.* and *Bart. Bon*. The splendid facade is best seen from the Grand Canal (p 107). It was presented to the State by Baron Giorgio Franchetti in 1915 with his collections of paintings, antiquities, etc., which constitute the *Galleria Franchetti*. Works from the Academy and other state collections are also housed here. The Luigi Conton collection of ceramics (13C–17C) from the lagoon also belongs to the Ca' d'Oro, and will be arranged in the neighbouring Pal. Duodo. Ca' d'Oro was reopened in 1984 after it had been closed for years during which time many of the sculptures and paintings had been cleaned and restored. The collections have been beautifully rearranged. Adm, see p 65.

A small door beside the main gateway gives access to the ticket office. Beyond is the charming little entrance court and main court-yard. The fine *Well-head, by *Bart. Bon* (1427) is decorated with figures of Charity, Justice, and Fortitude. Adjoining is the Portico, through which the house was approached from the canal, now containing pieces of ancient sculpture.

A modern staircase leads up to the FIRST FLOOR, which consists of an anteroom with an alcove, and a portico, extending towards the canal, with rooms on either side. ANTEROOM (1). Veneto-Byzantine sculptural fragments; *Ant. Vivarini* (and his school), Polyptych from the convent of Corpus Domini; alabaster scenes of the life of St Catherine (English, 16C).—In the alcove (2) on the right, with a rich ceiling, is *St Sebastian, by *Mantegna*, one of the last works of the painter (1506).—In the PORTICO (3), which stretches the length of the palace from the courtyard to the facade on the Grand Canal, is exhibited a remarkable collection of Venetian sculpture: *Ant. Rizzo* (?), female statuette, called 'Rhetoric'; *Tullio Lombardo*, *Double portrait bust. There follows a series of very fine bronze reliefs: *And. Briosco*, *St Martin and the beggar, Four scenes of the Legend of the True Cross, and a door of a tabernacle, all from the church of Santa Maria dei Servi; Assumption and Coronation of the Virgin, early 16C works from the funerary monument of the doges Marco and Agostino Barbarigo in Santa Maria della Carità; *Vittore Gambello* (*Il Camelio*), Two battle scenes (also from the church of Santa Maria della Carità). On the pedestal: Bust of a boy attrib. to *Gian Crist. Romano*. Two 15C Venetian marble reliefs, one of the Death of Portia by *Gian Maria Mosca*; six statuettes of the Virtues by the Lombardo school; *Girol. Campagna*, bronze firedogs with Venus and Adonis; *Iac. Sansovino* (school of), lunette of the Madonna and Child from the Zitelle.

To the right of the Portico are three smaller rooms: ROOM 4. *Michele Giambono*, Madonna and Child; *Fr. dei Franceschi* (?), Madonna and Child; (in case) *L'Antico*, bronze statuette of *Apollo. *Alvise Vivarini* (attrib.), Madonna and Child; *Giov. Bellini*, Madonna 'dagli occhi belli'; *16C Venetian School*, Madonna and Child in a landscape, Christ between the Virgin and St John. In a case are displayed *Medals by *l'Antico*, *Gentile Bellini*, *Vittore Gambello*, *Leone Leoni*, *Pisanello*, *Matteo de' Pasti*, and *Bertoldo di Giovanni* (attrib.).—ROOM 5 has three cases of small bronzes, including Paduan and Florentine works, and paintings by *Benedetto Diana* and *Carpaccio* and his

*The Ca' d'Oro, painted in the early 19C by Samuel Prout*

bottega.—In R 6 is another case of small bronzes, and firedogs by *Roccatagliata*. A 16C Venetian tondo in bronze has a portrait of Agostino Angeli da Pesaro and his son, the scientist, Girolamo from the church of San Pietro Martire in Murano.—On the LOGGIA over-looking the Grand Canal are displayed sculptural fragments including a 13C lion. A small room to the right illustrates the history of the palace and its restoration.

Off the left side of the portico is ROOM 7 with non-Venetian paintings of the 14–16C. *Carlo Braccesco* (Milanese school), SS. Ambrose, Gregory, Augustine, and Jerome, and Martyrdom of a Saint; *And. di Bartolo*, Coronation of the Virgin. The front of a 15C Florentine dower-chest shows the Victory of Alexander, and the construction of Alexandria. *Giov. di Nic. da Pisa*, Madonna of

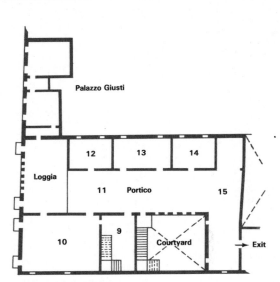

**Second Floor**

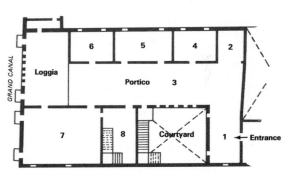

**First Floor**

**CA' D'ORO**

Humility; *Fr. Botticini*, *Madonna in Adoration of the Child; Raffaellino del Garbo*, *Madonna in Adoration of the Child and two angels; works by *Biagio d'Antonio* and *Antoniazzo Romano*; *Luca Signorelli*, *Flagellation (a tiny work).—From the next room (8) with a Madonna and Child and two angel musicians probably by *Bern. Zaganelli*, a splendid 15C carved wooden staircase (removed from a house near Santa Maria Mater Domini) leads up to the Second Floor.

SECOND FLOOR. R 9, at the top of the stairs, *Giul. Bugiardini* (attrib.), Sleeping Venus; *Girol. Macchietti* (?), Allegory of Riches; *Pontormo* (attrib.), Young girl with a dog; *Franciabigio*, Young man with a letter.—ROOM 10, a large room hung with 16C Flemish tapestries. *Iac. Tintoretto*, Portrait of the Procurator Nicolò Priuli; *Aless. Vittoria*, Busts of the Procurator Giovanni Donà, of *Benedetto Manzini, the parish priest of San Gemignano, of the Procurator Marino Grimani, of the Procurator Dom. Duodo, and of Francesco Duodo. *Titian*, Venus; *Van Dyck*, Portrait of a Gentleman; *Paris Bordone*, Sleeping Venus and cupid.—In the PORTICO (11) are detached frescoes from the cloister of Santo Stefano by *Pordenone* (c 1532: Expulsion from Paradise, Christ appearing to Mary Magdalen, and Christ and the Samaritan), and *Dom. Campagnola*.

To the right of the Portico are three smaller rooms with German, Dutch and Flemish paintings. ROOM 12. *Ant. Moor* (?), Portrait of an old lady; works by the Flemish school. *Jan van Scorel* (attrib.), Tower of Babel; *Circle of Dürer*, Deposition.—ROOM 13 has a good painted wood ceiling attrib. to *Gian Maria Falconetto* (15–16C). *Paul Brill*, Jonah and the whale; landscapes and genre scenes by the Dutch and Flemish schools. *Jan Steen*, Alchemist (1668). (In case), *Gabriel Metsu*, Sleeping woman; *Jan Steen*, Interior scene.—ROOM 14 has more Flemish works of birds, still lifes, etc., and a seascape by *Willem II Van de Velde*.—In the ANTEROOM (15) at the end of the Portico are interesting fragments of frescoes by *Giorgione* and *Titian* from the facade of the Fondaco dei Tedeschi, including a female nude by Giorgione. A case contains terracotta bozzetti by *Giac. Piazzetta, Gian Lor. Bernini* (for his fountain in Piazza Navona in Rome), and by *Stef. Maderno*. The two Venetian views of the *Piazzetta and *Molo are generally attrib. to *Fr. Guardi*. Stairs lead down from here to the exit.

The Strada Nuova continues across a bridge to SAN FELICE (Pl.6;3), a church rebuilt after 1531. Above the main door on the canal is a carved 14C angel. On the 3rd S altar is a painting of St Demetrius by Iac. Tintoretto.—From the next bridge there is a view (right) of the splendid 15C facade (with ingenious corner windows) of *Palazzo Giovanelli*.

This was given by the Republic to Francesco Maria della Rovere, duke of Urbino in 1538. It later became the property of Prince Giovanelli whose famous art collection included Giorgione's 'Tempesta' now in the Accademia galleries. —From the bridge, in the other direction, can be seen the facade of Palazzo Pésaro across the Grand Canal.—The area beyond the bridge is described in Rte 12 (see p 178).

It is now necessary to return to San Felice and follow the pretty Fondamenta di San Felice along the rio which is fronted by a portico for part of its length. From the second bridge, beyond a bridge without a parapet (one of the few to survive in the city), can be seen the lagoon in front of the island of Murano. To the left is the Scuola della Misericordia described on p 178. Across the bridge Sottoportico dei Preti leads through a courtyard into Calle della Racchetta which ends (left) on the attractive Fondamenta di Santa Caterina in a peaceful area of the city. To the left can be seen Campo dell'Abbazia (comp. p 178). The church of SANTA CATERINA (with its brick flank) is being restored; the ship's keel roof destroyed by fire in 1978 has already been rebuilt. Fondamenta Zen continues past the huge *Palazzo Zen* (Nos. 4922–4924) with its balconies (in poor repair), designed by Fr. Zen (d 1538). The family included Nicolò and Antonio, famous seafarers in the 15C. The fondamenta ends in a campo with the monumental Baroque facade (by *Fattoretto*) of the church of the **Gesuiti** (*Santa Maria Assunta*; Pl.6;4; open 10–12, 17–19).

The church was rebuilt in 1714–29 by *Dom. Rossi.* The highly elaborate Baroque INTERIOR has decorative grey and white marble intarsia in imitation of wall hangings. On the W wall is the Lezze monument attrib. to *Sansovino.* On the four piers of the dome are statues of Archangels by *Gius. Torretto.* To the N of the fantastic high altar (over the door into the Sacristy) is a monument to doge Pasquale Cicogna, with a fine effigy by *Girol. Campagna.* The SACRISTY contains paintings by *Palma Giovane.* In the N transept, Assumption, an early work by *Iac. Tintoretto.* On the 1st N altar is the *Martyrdom of St Lawrence, by *Titian* (light on night), a remarkable night scene (1548–59, recently restored).

The campo opens onto the Fondamente Nuove, looking out over the lagoon: opposite is the island of Murano, and (right) the cemetery island of San Michele. On the extreme right can be seen the campanile and dome of San Pietro di Castello and the Arsenal buildings. The landing-stages here are served by vaporetto No. 5 (comp. p 59), and the services for Murano, Burano, and Torcello.

Next to the church is the former Monastery (with a good cloister) now used as military barracks. Some of the houses here were built at the beginning of the century. Opposite, with four tall chimneys, is the little **Oratorio dei Crociferi**, restored and opened to the public in 1984 (adm see p 66). The hospital was founded in 1268 by doge Renier Zen for those returning from the Crusades, and then transformed into a hospice for old people in the 15C. The chapel, dating from 1582, with a relief of the Madonna and Child enthroned over the door, contains an interesting cycle of *Paintings by *Palma Giovane* (1583–92), illustrating the history of the hospital.

A bridge leads over Rio di Santa Caterina. In Salizzada Seriman is the fine 15C *Palazzo Contarini Seriman* (No. 4851; now a convent school). The interior (adm on request) contains a fine staircase with a fresco by the school of Tiepolo and an 'alcova' with stuccoes by Tencala.—Across the next bridge (with a view of the canal facade of Palazzo Seriman), a salizzada continues S to cross Rio terrà di Barba Fruttarol (to the left, in Campiello della Madonna, a plaque marks the house where Francesco Guardi lived and died in 1793). Rio terrà di Santi Apostoli (and 'dei Franceschi') continue into the narrow Calle Muazzo. To the left, beyond Campiello della Cason (where Agnello Participazio lived as doge in 811–827) an iron bridge is soon reached. At the end of the canal (right) stands Palazzo Falier (p 165). Beyond is the church of *San Canciano*, of ancient foundation, rebuilt in the 18C. By the brick campanile is an old house with a low portico. Adjacent is Campiello Santa Maria Nova where *Palazzo Bembo-Boldù*, with tall Gothic windows, bears a relief of a bearded figure holding a solar disc. To the left opens a larger campo bordered by a canal with the tall domed apse and tiny attached campanile of *Santa Maria dei Miracoli** (Pl.6;6), a masterpiece of the Renaissance by *Pietro Lombardo* (1481–89). Adm 9–12, 14.30–18; winter 9.30–12, 15–17; fest. 9.30–12.

The EXTERIOR has exquisite carved details and is remarkable for the position of its N flank set on a canal. The admirably proportioned facade with marble inlay and carved friezes, incorporates a Madonna by *Giorgio Lascaris* (Pyrgoteles; 16C).—The INTERIOR, with its simple clean lines and marble walls, has a raised choir and domed apse. The nuns' choir at the W end is supported by beautifully carved pillars. The nave barrel vault is adorned with 50 panels bearing heads of Prophets and Saints by *Pier Maria Pennacchi* (1528). Preceded by a pretty balustrade with fine half-length figures probably by *Tullio Lombardo* is the Choir, on which the full powers of *Pietro* and *Tullio Lombardo* were lavished; it contains exquisite *Carving. On the high altar is a charming Madonna by *Nic. di Pietro Paradisi* (1409). In the Crypt is a bas-relief of the Last Supper, a copy of Leonardo's work, attrib. to *Tullio Lombardo*.

Calle Castelli leads away from the church (past the Gothic doorway and interesting old Corte delle Muneghe). It emerges on Fondamenta Sanudo. To the left is the fine Gothic doorway of *Palazzo Soranzo-Barozzi*, with a good canal facade. Across the wide Ponte delle Erbe it is a short distance to Santi Giovanni e Paolo (see p 121). Ponte del Cristo stands at the junction of three canals. On the left is the white facade of *Palazzo Marcello-Papadópoli*, on a design attrib. to Longhena, and to the right is the 15C Gothic facade of *Palazzo Pisani*, with fine balconies. Calle del Cristo leads into Campo Santa Marina where a high archway connects the symmetrical wings of a former palace. From the end of the campo (right), Sottoportego and Calle

*S. Maria dei Miracoli, detail of the façade*

Scaletta lead to Ponte Marco Polo. Opposite the Gothic *Palazzo Bragadin Carabba* (right; on the curve of the canal with good windows and a balcony) a plaque records the home in this area of Marco Polo. Here is the side entrance to the *Teatro Malibran*, recently reopened for ballet and concerts. Handel's 'Agrippina' premiered here in 1710. A sottoportico leads into two courtyards, Corte Seconda del Milion and Corte Prima del Milion; they bear Marco Polo's nickname which is derived from the fact that his contemporaries thought he always talked in 'millions' and exaggerated in his description of his travels in the East. The *Corte Seconda del Milion* (Pl.6;6) is surrounded by ancient houses which bear 12–15C elements, and a Byzantine *Arch (possibly 12C), richly carved with animals and birds, which must have been familiar to Marco Polo.

Marco Polo (1256–1324) came from a merchant family; his father was one of three brothers who travelled regularly to the East. Marco accompanied his father and uncle in 1271 on an overland journey which took four years from Trebizond on the Black Sea, through Persia, Tibet, and the Gobi desert to Peking. He was employed at the court of the Mongol ruler, Kublai Khan, grandson of Genghis Khan for 17 years, being sent as envoy throughout the Empire from Siberia to Southern India, Japan, etc. He returned to Venice by sea along the coast of China and India. In 1298 he was taken prisoner by the Genoese in the Battle of Cursola, and during a year's imprisonment he dictated to a fellow prisoner, Rusticello di Pisa, a superb description of the world he had seen on his travels. This was the first description of Asia ever to reach the West and remained the most accurate for many centuries. His book was widely diffused in Europe in the middle ages.

Beyond Corte Prima del Milion lies San Giovanni Crisostomo (p 165); Salizzada San Giovanni returns across Ponte dell'Olio to the Rialto bridge.

# 12  Cannaregio: from the Station to the Cannaregio Canal, the Ghetto, the Madonna dell'Orto, and San Marcuola

Beside the station is the church of the **Scalzi** (Pl.4;4,6), formerly belonging to the Carmelites, a good Baroque building by *Longhena* (1670–80), with a facade by *Gius Sardi*.

The dark INTERIOR is profusely decorated with marbles and sculptures in the Baroque manner, and a huge elaborate tabernacle fills the apse. The fanciful ceiling-fresco by Tiepolo was destroyed by a bomb in 1915 and is replaced by a modern painting (Council of Ephesus) by *Ettore Tito*. The 2nd S chapel, the Manin chapel, is the burial place of Lod. Manin, the last doge of Venice. It contains *Tiepolo's* frescoes of the Life of St Teresa (1725; in poor condition); on the altar is the Saint transfixed by the Angel, attrib. to *Lazzaro Baldi* or *Enrico Meyring*. The ceiling of the 1st N chapel also has damaged frescoes by *G.B. Tiepolo*.

The garish Lista di Spagna (given over to the tourist trade) leads to Campo San Geremia. Here is the church of **San Geremia** (Pl.5;3), a clumsy building by *C. Corbellini* (1753–60). The interior is more successful, and the fine campanile is among the oldest in Venice.

The body of St Lucy (martyred in Syracuse in 304), stolen from Constantinople in 1204 by Venetian crusaders was placed in this church when in 1863 Santa Lucia was demolished to make way for the railway station (with architectural fragments from the 16C church designed by Palladio). A painting of her by *Palma Giovane* is preserved with a few relics and church vestments in a room to the right of her chapel in the N transept (unlocked on request). The painting of St Magnus crowning Venice (2nd S altar) is by the same artist.

PALAZZO LABIA has a facade in the campo by *Aless.* (or *Paolo*) *Tremignon* (completed c 1750). The main facade on the Cannaregio canal is by *And. Cominelli* (late 17C).

The INTERIOR (now the regional headquarters of the R.A.I., Italian radio and television) is shown on request when not in use (usually Tues and Thurs 14.30–16.30). In the Ballroom the trompe l'oeil frescoes by *Gerolamo Mengozzi-Colonna* provide a setting for *G.B. Tiepolo*'s *Frescoes of Antony and Cleopatra. A famous ball was held here in the 1950s by Charles de Besteigui. Concerts (which are recorded) are held in the ballroom on Mon & Fri (open free to the public; tickets have to booked by telephone in advance).

The salizzada leads onto the CANNAREGIO CANAL (Pl.5;3 and Pl.4;2), a busy waterway with two broad fondamenta, which traverses a distinctive part of the city. The stone *Ponte delle Guglie* (1580; restored 1776) has a pretty balustrade. The fondamenta leads along the canal past the huge 18C *Palazzo Savorgnan* (No. 349), a wing of which is being restored, and the 15C *Palazzo Testa* (No. 468). Farther on, at *Ponte dei Tre Archi* (of the Three Arches; by A. Tirali, 1688; restored in 1980) the secluded Campo di San Giobbe is reached on the left. The church of **San Giobbe** (Pl.4;2; if closed it can usually be entered through the courtyard on the right) was built after 1450 by *Ant. Gambello* and enlarged by *Pietro Lombardo* who is responsible (with assistants) for the fine *DOORWAY. The Gothic campanile can be seen from the courtyard.

The INTERIOR is one of the earliest examples of a Franciscan Observant church plan. It is in need of repair. A carved triumphal arch flanked by two smaller semi-circular chapels precedes the domed *SANCTUARY (c 1471), a masterpiece of Renaissance architecture and carving by *Pietro Lombardo* and assistants. In the centre of the pavement (sometimes covered) is the beautifully carved tomb slab of the founder of the church, doge Crist. Moro (d 1471) and his wife Cristina Sanudo. Behind the altar extends the long choir with 16C wood stalls. SOUTH SIDE. 2nd altar, *L. Querena*, Vision of God to Job, in a beautiful marble frame, which belonged to Giov. Bellini's famous altarpiece which was removed from here in the early 19C and which is now in the Accademia gallery (comp. p 136). Beyond the conspicuous monument by Claude Perrault, 1651, 4th altar, Three Saints by *Paris Bordone.*—The two chapels at the beginning of the NORTH SIDE are beautifully decorated: in the 1st is a statue of St Luke by *Lor. Bregno*; the second (CAPPELLA MARTINI) was built for a family of silk-workers from Lucca by 15C Tuscan artists. The vault is lined with majolica tiles and contains five pretty roundels by the *della Robbia* workshop. The marble altar with statuettes of St John the Baptist and other Saints is by a follower of *Ant. Rossellino.*—The Stations of the Cross in the 3rd chapel are attrib. to *Ant. Zucchi.*—From the S side is the entrance to the Ante-Sacristy, part of a late 14C oratory, with a Nativity by *Girol. Savoldo* (removed for restoration in 1985). The Sacristy has a 16C wooden ceiling, a small painting in a fine frame of the Marriage of St Catherine by *And. Previtali*, and a portrait of doge Crist. Moro. At the other end is the Cappella Da Mula with an Annunciation between SS. Michael and Anthony, a triptych by *Ant. Vivarini* and *Giov. d'Alemagna* (1440–50), and a terracotta bust of St Bernardino da Siena attrib. to *Bart. Bellano* which was left to the church by Cristoforo Moro.

Across Ponte dei Tre Archi (with a view out to the lagoon) a fondamenta leads back down the other side of the Cannaregio. It passes (No. 967) *Palazzo Surian*, attrib. to Gius. Sardi. This was once the French Embassy and Jean Jacques Rousseau was Secretary here in 1743–44.—Just before Ponte delle Guglie, Sottoportico del Ghetto diverges left into the **Ghetto** (Pl.5;3,1).

The word 'ghetto' is derived from 'getto', to 'cast' metals; there was an iron foundry here for making cannons until 1390 when it was transferred to the Arsenal. In 1516 the Maggior Consiglio gave Jews permission to inhabit this part of the city. The name 'Ghetto' was subsequently used for isolated Jewish communities in other cities. The first settlement was on the island of Ghetto Nuovo (see below); in 1541 it expanded to Ghetto Vecchio, and in 1633 to Ghetto Nuovissimo. It is estimated that there were c 5000 Jewish inhabitants here in the 16–17C. Not until 1797 were Jews allowed to leave the Ghetto and live in other parts of the city. The five main synagogues remain here. The Jewish cemetery is on the Lido (comp. p 197).

At the beginning of the sottoportico are signs of the gate which closed the entrance at night. The dark calle leads past a stone (left) with a long list of the rules for the inhabitants of the Ghetto inscribed in 1541. Beyond several carpenters' shops is CAMPIELLO DELLE SCUOLE with two synagogues and a tall house with numerous windows, typical of this area. To the left, with an inconspicuous exterior, is the *Scola Spagnola*, founded in 1555 or 1584, with an interior attrib. to Longhena (1635, being restored). Opposite, the *Scola Levantina* (1538) has a fine exterior by Longhena, and, inside, elaborate wood carving by And. Brustolon (adm to both synagogues on request at the Museum, see below).—Ponte di Ghetto Vecchio leads over to the island of GHETTO NUOVO, the oldest area of the Ghetto.

The campo, with its three wells and clump of trees, is surrounded by tall 17C houses, with numerous windows and some with as many as seven floors. Here are three more synagogues. Above a portico of four columns is the *Scola Italiana* (1575); it has five windows on the top floor and a cupola. In the corner of the campo is the *Scola Canton* (1531), with its tiny wood cupola just visible. The *Scola Grande Tedesca*, the oldest in Venice (1528), is now open as part of the MUSEUM (adm see p 65; if closed, ask locally or at No. 1189 Ghetto Vecchio, for the custodian). The two rooms have an interesting display of Jewish treasures. The custodian will usually accompany visitors to the synagogues in the Ghetto Vecchio (see above); the other synagogues in this campo are closed for restoration.—A calle leads out of the right side of the campo into the Ghetto Nuovissimo, added in 1633, with more tall houses.

The Ghetto is left by a bridge with wrought-iron railings (1865–66). Fondamenta degli Ormesini continues right along a wide and busy canal; opposite the end of the next bridge Calle della Malvasia leads N to cross the pretty Rio della Sensa, one of several parallel canals in this area with views (left) out to the lagoon. Calle del Capitello continues N. Across the next rio is Campo Sant'Alvise in a remote part of the city. The church of **Sant'Alvise** (Pl.5;2) dates from the late 14C.

The Gothic brick facade bears an early-15C Tuscan statue of the titular Saint. The paintings have all been removed from the interior while the church is undergoing a lengthy restoration. They include a Crown of Thorns and Flagellation (S wall of the nave), and, in the choir, a *Calvary (1743), all by G.B. Tiepolo, and eight little 15C tempera paintings (beneath the nuns' choir).

It is now necessary to recross the bridge (view left of the campanile of the Madonna dell'Orto, with its onion-shaped cupola) and return to Rio della Sensa which is now followed left. On the opposite side of the canal is a house with a double facade on either side of a calle connected by two arches, and, on this side, (No. 3291) a palace with a relief of St George and the Dragon. From Ponte Rosso there is a view out to the lagoon, and from Ponte Braso can be seen the facade of the Madonna dell'Orto which is reached by the next turning left, Campo dei Mori. On the fondamenta, just beyond the campo, a plaque at No. 3399 marks the charming residence of Tintoretto from 1574 to his death in 1594. A quaint figure in a turban in a niche and standing on an ancient Roman altar is incorporated into its facade (with several other ancient sculptural fragments), similar to the three statues of Moors in the Campo dei Mori. These are popularly supposed to be the Levantine merchants of the Mastelli family whose palace stands on the canal to the N (comp. below). The cupola seen in the distance, at the end of Rio della Sensa, belongs to San Giovanni e Paolo. At the upper end of the campo a bridge crosses a canal (where funeral barges are usually moored) to reach the *Madonna dell'Orto (Pl.6;1; open 9–12, 15–17 or 19). The church contains important works by *Tintoretto* who is buried here in his parish church. The building and paintings were well restored in 1968–69. The campo is paved in stone and brick.

The first church on this site, dedicated to St Christopher, was founded c 1350 by Fra Tiberio da Parma, General of the Umiliati. After 1377 it became known as the Madonna dell'Orto from a miraculous statue of the Madonna and Child by Giov. de'Santi which had been abandoned in a nearby orchard.

The *FACADE is a fine example of Venetian Gothic, with good early-15C tracery in the windows. The statues of the Apostles in the niches are attrib. to the *Dalle Masegne* brothers. The Madonna and Annunciatory angel flanking the doorway are considered to be early works by *Ant. Rizzo*. The statue of St Christopher, above, is traditionally attributed (as a late work) to *Bart. Bon*. This was restored in 1969, the first of many Istrian stone statues in the city to be cleaned successfully.—The CAMPANILE (1503), with its onion-shaped cupola is conspicuous from the lagoon towards Murano.

INTERIOR. The nave and aisles are divided by columns of Turkish marble; the semi-circular apse is vaulted. (Coin-operated lights to right of the apse). SOUTH AISLE. 1st altar (a good Renaissance work), *Cima da Conegliano's* masterpiece of *St John the Baptist and four other Saints (c 1493). Beyond the 4th altar, on the wall, is the *Presentation of the Virgin in the Temple, by *Tintoretto*. In the CAPPELLA DI SAN MAURO is a colossal stone statue (radically restored) of the Madonna and Child by *Giov. de'Sancti*, which gave the church its name (comp. above). A modest slab in the chapel on the right of the choir marks *Tintoretto's* resting-place; the CHOIR is adorned by two huge paintings by him, the *Last Judgement and the *Making of the Golden Calf. In the apse, flanking an Annunciation by *Palma Giovane*, is the Vision of the Cross to St Peter, and the Beheading of St Paul, also by *Tintoretto*. In the vault, five Virtues, also by *Tintoretto*, except for the central one, Faith, which is by an unknown 17C painter.—NORTH AISLE. The 4th chapel (CAPPELLA CON-TARINI) contains family busts (one by *Danese Cattaneo*, and the two in the centre by *Vittoria*), and, over the altar, St Agnes raising Licinius, another notable work by *Tintoretto*. The elegant Renaissance CAPPELLA VALIER (1st chapel) was completed in 1526 by *And.* and *Ant. Buora*; it has a cupola and a semi-circular apse (restored in 1969). Over the altar (light; fee), the *Madonna by *Giov. Bellini* (c 1478), in a charming sculpted tabernacle, has been returned here after its restoration (and damage in a theft).—In the campo is the Scuola dei Mercanti (begun in 1570) with a 16C relief.

Fondamenta Gasparo Contarini leads along the canal; on the opposite side the fine *Palazzo Mastelli* (or *del Cammello*) bears a charming relief of a man leading a camel (familiar to Venetian merchants who brought merchandise from the E by caravan), and ancient sculptural fragments. Beyond is the double facade of a simple low house with symmetrical chimneys and water-gates. On this side is *Palazzo*

*Minelli Spada* with two obelisks, and the long *Palazzo Contarini Dal Zaffo* (16C; No. 3539), with a garden. At the end, in this remote part of the town, the Sacca della Misericordia opens on to the lagoon (with a view of the islands of San Michele with its dark cypresses and church facade, and of Murano with its lighthouse and bell towers). Across the bridge, Rio della Sensa is soon reached. A short

*St. Christopher, attrib. to Bart. Bon, on the facade of the Madonna dell'Orto, the first Istrian stone statue in Venice to be cleaned (in 1969)*

way to the right the wooden Ponte dei Muti crosses above an old 'squero', still in use for the repair of boats; in the other direction Fondamenta dell'Abbazia passes Corte Nuovo. Entered by a fine Gothic doorway with reliefs of the Madonna of the Misericordia and Saints, these were the almshouses (1506) of the Scuola della Misericordia.—The early 16C portico continues beneath the *Scuola Vecchia della Misericordia* (founded 1308; restored in the 15C) into the Campo dell'Abbazia, with its old pavement, and well-head. Here is the worn Gothic facade of the Scuola Vecchia, and the church (facade of 1659, deconsecrated) next to a 14C relief of the Madonna, Byzantine in style. The abbey buildings are used as a restoration centre.

A wooden bridge crosses the rio and a fondamenta skirts the massive flank of the SCUOLA GRANDE DELLA MISERICORDIA, begun in 1532 by Sansovino, but still unfinished at his death because of lack of funds. It was finally opened in 1589 and contains a splendid lower hall. The huge brick facade remains unfinished. At present used as a gymnasium there are plans to convert it into a Museum of Venetian sculpture, and decorative stonework.—Fondamenta della Misericordia continues past the large *Palazzo Lezze* (by Longhena, 1654); the first bridge leads over the canal to the church of **San Marciliano** (*San Marziale;* Pl.6;3).

In the vault, in pretty frames, are *Paintings by *Seb. Ricci,* among his best works. On the 2nd S altar, *Iac. Tintoretto,* St Martial and two Saints (over-restored), and on the 2nd N altar, 15C wood statue of the Madonna and Child. On either side of the chancel, *Dom. Tintoretto,* Annunciation.—In the SACRISTY is a damaged work by *Titian* (Tobias and the Archangel, c 1540).

Calle Zancani leads down to Rio Diedo. On the right, beyond the 17C *Palazzo Diedo* (attrib. to And. Tirali), across another canal, are the remains of the convent and church of *Santa Maria dei Servi,* destroyed in 1812. A Gothic doorway survives. To the left, on Fondamenta Vendramin, is the noble Renaissance facade of *Palazzo Vendramin* (No. 2400). Campo Santa Fosca has a monument to Fra' Paolo Sarpi (by Emilio Marsili, 1892). Here is the fine long 15C facade of *Palazzo Correr.* The facade of SANTA FOSCA (Pl.6;3; often closed) dates from 1741. This contains (at the end of the N aisle) a Byzantine Pietà and Saints, and, above, a darkened Holy Family with donor, by Dom. Tintoretto. The domed brick campanile dates from the 15C.

The busy Strada Nuova (comp. p 166) continues right across Ponte Sant'Antonio (good view right of Pal. Diedo, comp. above) to Campo della Maddalena, with a fine well-head (being restored), surrounded by quaint old houses with tall chimney-pots. *Palazzo Magno* has a doorway with a Gothic lunette. The small round domed church of the **Maddalena** (Pl.5;4) is attractively sited on its canal. It is a neo-classical building by *Tommaso Temanza* (c 1760). It contains a Last Supper, thought to be a copy from Gian Dom. Tiepolo, and, above the W door a fine painting of the Sacrifice of Isaac. In the calle behind a grille protects a 15C relief of the Madonna and Child.

Rio terrà della Maddalena, a crowded shopping street, dates from 1398. It continues the Strada Nuova past (right) *Palazzo Donà delle Rose* (No. 2343) of the 17C, and the 15C *Palazzo Contin* (No. 2347). Calle Larga Vendramin soon diverges left; the Rio terrà continues to Rio terrà San Leonardo with its market (comp. Pl.5;3,4). At the end of Calle Larga Vendramin is the land entrance to *Palazzo Vendramin* (the winter home of the Casino; the facade is described on p 107). In the courtyard is a fine Byzantine (11C) well-head. A plaque records Wagner's death here in 1883 while a guest of the Duke of Chambord. Ponte Storto (with a view over the Grand Canal of the end of the Fóndaco dei Turchi) leads into Rio di San Marcuola. Behind the church can be seen the facade of the *Scuola del Cristo*, founded in 1644. The church of **San Marcuola** (Pl.5;4; *Santi Ermagora e Fortunato*) by *Giorgio Massari* (1728–36), has an unfinished facade towards the Grand Canal.

The INTERIOR contains statues by *G.M. Morleiter* and assistants. Around the two facing pulpits are some unusual paintings including: the Christ Child blessing between SS. Catherine and Andrew, and the Head of Christ between two male portraits, thought to be by pupils of *Titian* (Fr. *Vecellio*?). On the left wall of the chancel, Last Supper, a good early work (1547) by *Iac. Tintoretto*; on the right wall is a copy of The Washing of the Feet also by *Tintoretto* now in Newcastle-upon-Tyne (and almost identical with another painting by him in the Prado, Madrid). The original painting was substituted by this copy in the 17C. The church also contains paintings (on the ceiling, in the presbytery, on the high altar and in the 18C Sacristy) by *Fr. Migliori* a little-known 18C Venetian.

From the campo in front of the church can be seen (right) the dome of San Geremia, and, in the distance, the facade of the Scalzi by the Station; opposite stands the Fóndaco dei Turchi and (left) the Granaries of the Republic and Palazzo Belloni-Bettagià with its two obelisks. The landing-stage here is served by vaporetto No. 1 which can be taken back towards the centre of the city.

# 13  Castello: Via Garibaldi, San Pietro di Castello, Sant'Elena, and the Public Gardens

Since the distances in this route are considerable, a vaporetto is recommended from the public gardens ('Giardini') to Sant'Elena.

Beyond the end of Riva degli Schiavoni, across the Arsenal canal (pp 115–116), is the naval church of *San Biagio* (rebuilt in the 18C). Adjacent is the former Granary of the Republic which now houses the **Museo Storico Navale** (Pl.12;3; adm see p 66).

The exhibits are well arranged on four floors. TOP FLOOR. R 20, *Models of Far Eastern Junks (left to the museum in 1964).—R 21 is mostly filled by the 'Lusoria', an 18C boat. The walls are hung with ex-votoes. The Turkish caique was used until 1920 by the Italian ambassador in Istanbul to cross the Bosphorus.—RR 22, 23. Fishing vessels, etc.—R 24 is devoted to gondolas (the wooden shelter, or *Felze*, which used to protect passengers in bad weather is now no longer used).—R 26 has models of ocean-going liners.—SECOND FLOOR. RR 14–18, naval history; warships, torpedoes, etc.—FIRST FLOOR. Wood sculpture of two Turks in chains from the galley sailed by Morosini in 1684.—R 6. Nautical instruments, and 17C charts.—R 7. Models of the Roman ships found in Lake Nemi near Rome.—R 8. Models, including a trireme. Elaborate 17C carvings from a Venetian galley.—R 9. Wood statue of Venice as Justice and a *Model of the last Bucintoro (1728), the gala ship used for the ceremonial marriage of Venice with the sea.—R 10. 18C and 19C models, including a vessel built in the Arsenal by order of Napoleon which carried 80 cannon.—GROUND FLOOR. Monument by Canova to Angelo Emo (1731–92), last admiral of the Venetian Republic. Torpedo invented in 1935 which destroyed 16 ships in the Second World War. In the room behind are cannon, one cast by Cosimo Cenni in 1643. The rest of the ground floor is still being arranged.

Across the bridge the long broad **Via Garibaldi** (Pl.12;3,4) leads away from the water-front. This was laid out by Napoleon in 1808 by filling in a canal (as the pavement shows); it is a lively street with shops. The house at the beginning (right; plaque) was the residence of John and Sebastian Cabot in 1581. Farther on, Corte Nuova opens on the left with two well-heads and the Arsenal buildings in the distance. Just before the public gardens (right), a house (No. 1310) has a doorway with a good relief. Opposite stands the church of **San Francesco di Paola** (Pl.12;4).

INTERIOR. The paintings on the ceiling are by *Giov. Contarini* (1603); those around the top of the walls are by 18C artists incl. *Gian Dom. Tiepolo* (Liberation of a possessed).—Left side, 1st chapel, *Marieschi*, Martyrdom of St Bartholomew; right side (on either side of the last altar), paintings by *Palma Giovane*.

The calle beside the church leads down to Rio della Tana which skirts the Arsenal wall (comp. p 115); behind it is the Corderia, where the ropes were made for the Arsenal. Characteristic courtyards open off the fondamenta.

The *Giardini Garibaldi* (public gardens), laid out in 1808–12 by G.A. Selva, extend to the water-front and adjoin the 'Biennale' gardens (comp. p 182). The statue of Garibaldi is by A. Benvenuti (1885). Beyond a street market is the end of Rio di Sant'Anna (No. 1132 is a Gothic house with Byzantine roundels); the fondamenta on the left leads over a bridge (with a view left down Rio di San Daniele of the Arsenal wall and tower) to Calle San Gioachino which diverges left at the end of the next bridge. It passes a lunette of the Madonna and Child with SS. Peter and Paul (mid-15C) and continues to the pretty Rio Riello lined with small houses, typical of this area. Across the bridge a fondamenta leads beneath a portico down the right side of the canal and, at the end, diverges right through Campiello del Figaretto (with a view of the campanile of San Pietro di Castello). From Campo Ruga, Salizzada Stretta continues towards the Arsenal wall. Just before the canal, Calle Larga di Castello leads right to an iron bridge over the wide Canale di San Pietro with its busy boat-yards and the Arsenal conspicuous to the left. On the solitary ISOLA DI SAN PIETRO (Pl.13;1,3), near the E limit of the city, the grass-grown Campo di San Pietro with its grove of trees, opens out before the church and isolated campanile of **San Pietro di Castello** (Pl.13;1; open 8–12, 15–18; summer 8–12, 16.30–19). This was the cathedral of Venice from the 11C until 1807 when St Mark's was designated cathedral (comp. p72). The first church on this site probably dates from the 7C. The present church was built on a Palladian design of 1557.

In the light INTERIOR, on the West wall, above the left doorway, sarcophagus of Filippo Correr (d 1417). In the S aisle a venerable marble throne from Antioch has a Muslim funerary stele and is decorated with verses from the Koran. The sumptuous high altar was designed by *Longhena*; behind it is the organ by *Nacchini* (1754). On the right wall of the Sanctuary, doge Nicolò Contarini before Beato Lorenzo Giustiniani during the plague of 1630, a large painting executed by *Ant. Bellucci* shortly after the canonisation of the saint in 1690. In the chapel to the left of the high altar, dark wood Crucifix with terminals in beaten copper (14C).—NORTH AISLE. The Baroque CAPPELLA VENDRAMIN was designed by *Longhena*; it contains an altarpiece by *Luca Giordano*. On the aisle wall, *Veronese*, SS. John the Evangelist, Peter, and Paul. The CAPPELLA LANDO (usually locked, but partly visible through an iron grille) contains a 6C pluteus as an altar-front, and, in the pavement in front, an interesting mosaic fragment, thought to date from the 5C and showing the influence of Roman mosaic design. Also here, columns from the Baptistery with Veneto-Byzantine capitals, and a bust of San Lorenzo Giustiniani (attrib. to a follower of *Ant. Rizzo*), who became the first Patriarch of Venice in 1451.—The isolated CAMPANILE, in Istrian stone, by *Mauro Codussi*, dates from 1482–88, with a cupola of 1670. On the house behind the campanile are 15C statues and reliefs. The cloister is now used as part of a boat-building yard.

The calle behind the campanile soon rejoins Canale di San Pietro beside a good Renaissance relief of the Madonna and Child with St Peter. The fondamenta continues to a long wooden bridge which recrosses the canal near several busy boat repair yards. At the foot of the bridge is the former church of *Sant'Anna*, now part of a naval hospital. Opposite, the canal is lined by a quaint row of old houses with chimney-pots. Calle Correra diverges left from Rio Sant'Anna (comp. p 180) to traverse an area regularly laid out with stark 19C houses. Beyond the more colourful Secco Marina, Corte del Soldà continues across a bridge to the campo in front of the church of **San Giuseppe di Castello** (Pl.13;5).

The facade bears a relief of the Adoration of the Magi by *Giulio Del Moro*. The perspective ceiling is attrib. to *Giov. Ant. Torriglia*. SOUTH SIDE. 1st altar, St Michael and the senator Michele Bon, attrib. to the workshop of *Tintoretto*. On the wall of the SANCTUARY is a monument to the procurator G. Grimani (d 1570), with a portrait bust by *Aless. Vittoria*. On the NORTH SIDE, the 2nd altar bears a curious relief of the Battle of Lépanto. The huge monument to doge Marino Grimani (d 1605) was designed by *Vinc. Scamozzi*, with two bronze reliefs by *Gerol. Campagna*.

From here it is a short way along the rio out to the water-front and the landing-stage of 'Giardini'. It is one stop on vaporetto No. 1 from here to Sant'Elena, which can otherwise be reached on foot by the route described below (a long walk through a lonely uninteresting part of the city). From Campo San Giuseppe (with a doorway leading in to the public gardens on the water-front), Rio terrà San Giuseppe leads left. Ramo Primo di Sant'Antonio skirts the outer wall of the Italian pavilion in the 'Biennale' gardens (comp. below). A bridge leads over the canal with a view of the gardens, and Viale XXIV Maggio continues through a residential quarter spaciously laid out in this century, with handsome buildings. Viale Piave skirts a large harbour, and beyond extends the lagoon with its islands. The viale leads S along the Canale Sant'Elena. At the end of the sports stadium an avenue across the canal leads up to the church of **Sant'Elena** (Pl.13;8). Dedicated to St Helena, mother of Constantine, it was founded in the early 13C and rebuilt in 1435. It was abandoned in 1807, but reopened in 1928. Over the doorway is a sculptured *Group attrib. to *Ant. Rizzo* (c 1467) representing admiral Vitt. Cappello kneeling before St Helena. The cloister and bare Gothic interior have recently been restored.

The canal ends on the water-front near the landing-stage ('Sant'Elena') of vaporetto No. 1 which returns to San Marco. The view embraces many of the lagoon islands: to the left, close at hand, is the Lido with the island of San Lazzaro degli Armeni (marked by its campanile); in front, opposite the landing-stage is the island of San Servolo, and, in the distance, Santo Spirito. To the right, San Clemente (with Sacca Sessola behind, and Poveglia in the far distance), then La Grazia. In the distance, above the green trees of the island of San Giorgio, can be seen the cupolas of the churches of the Zitelle and Redentore on the island of the Giudecca; next come the domes of the Salute, the campanile of San Giorgio, and, on the extreme right, the campanile of San Marco and the Palazzo Ducale.

It is a long but pleasant walk back towards San Marco along the water-front via the public gardens and the entrance to the 'BIENNALE' exhibition grounds (the *International Exhibition of Modern Art*), known as the 'Biennale' since it is held every two years (comp. p 63). The first exhibition was held in 1895, and during this century various nations have built permanent pavilions within the gardens.—Beyond the gardens, Riva dei Setti Martiri, and Riva Ca' di Dio continue to Riva degli Schiavoni (comp. p 112) and San Marco.

# 14   The Island of San Giorgio Maggiore and the Giudecca

The island of SAN GIORGIO MAGGIORE (Pl.11;6) can be reached by vaporetto from San Marco (No. 5; 'circolare destra') or from the Zattere and the Giudecca (No. 5; 'circolare sinistra'). This lovely small island was for long occupied by a Benedictine convent, which was the most important in the lagoon. In 1951 the Giorgio Cini Foundation was established here and the buildings beautifully restored. It stands at the entrance to the city across the basin of St Mark's, separated from the island of the Giudecca by a narrow canal.

The church of *San Giorgio Maggiore* (Pl.11;6; open 9–12.30, 14–19; winter, 9–12, 15–17) is one of the most conspicuous churches in Venice, in a magnificent position on a separate islet facing St Mark's. The white facade, tall campanile, and brick building reflect the changing light of the lagoon, and are especially beautiful at sunset. The original church dedicated to St George was probably founded in the 10C. The present building was begun in 1566 by *Palladio* and finished in 1610 by *Sim. Sorella*.

The FACADE was designed by *Palladio* in 1565 and built in 1607–10 after his death. It is modelled on a temple portico with four giant columns, and is particularly effective when seen from a distance across the water. The CAMPANILE was rebuilt in 1791 by *Bened. Buratti* on the lines of that of St Mark's.

The white INTERIOR is remarkable for its clean architectural lines and the absence of decoration; it is enhanced by the proximity of water. The cruciform design has a central dome (being restored) and a long choir separated from the chancel. On the W wall, Monument to doge Leonardo Donà (d 1612), the friend of Galileo, by *Aless. Vittoria*.—SOUTH AISLE, 1st altar. *Jac. Bassano*, Adoration of the Shepherds; 2nd altar, wood Crucifix, formerly attrib. to Nic. Lamberti, but now considered to be the work of a Venetian master (c 1470; restored in 1984); 3rd altar, *School of Iac. Tintoretto*, Martyrdom of SS. Cosmas and Damian, a well composed painting.—SOUTH TRANSEPT. On the altar, *Iac. Tintoretto* (attrib.), Coronation of the Virgin. Altar to the right of the high altar, *Seb. Ricci*, Madonna and Saints.—The CHANCEL is entered between two candelabra by *Nic. Roccatagliata* (1598). The High Altar, designed by *Aliense*, has a fine bronze group of the Saviour on a globe borne by the Evangelists by *Gerol. Campagna*, and two bronze angels by *Pietro Boselli* (1644). On the walls are two good late works by *Tintoretto*: *The Last Supper (1594), and *The Shower of Manna. In the CHOIR behind, the Baroque *Stalls and lectern are by *A. van der Brulle* and *Gasp. Gatti* (1594–98). The two small bronzes on the balustrade of St George and St Stephen are by *Nic. Roccatagliata* (1593).—The SACRISTY

*San Giorgio Maggiore, with the Punta della Dogana, by Canaletto*

contains handsome dossals. In the corridor to the right of the Choir (door usually unlocked) are a Monument to doge Dom. Michiel, from a design attrib. to *Baldass. Longhena*, and, set in to the wall, the tomb slab of Bonincontro de' Boateri by the *Dalle Masegne*.—THE CHAPEL OF THE DEAD (1592). *Iac. Tintoretto* painted the *Deposition (light; fee) for this chapel in 1594. It is a very late work and he possibly had the help of his son *Domenico*. Here has been placed a photograph of *Carpaccio*'s St George and the Dragon which is housed in an upper chapel (now closed) where the Conclave met in 1799–1800 (comp. below). The tempera painting is in very poor condition. It is another version (painted about eight years later) of the more famous work in the Scuola di San Giorgio degli Schiavone (comp. p 113).—On the altar to the left of the high altar, *Iac. Tintoretto* (finished by his son *Domenico*), Resurrection (with portraits of the Morosini family).—NORTH TRANSEPT. *School of Tintoretto*, Martyrdom of St Stephen. As the inscription states, the body of St Stephen was brought to the church in 1110 from Constantinople.

The CAMPANILE may be ascended (lift; adm as for church; see p 65). It provides one of the best views in Venice: beyond the city extend the lagoon, the Adriatic, the Euganean Hills, and the distant Alps.

From outside the church there is a good view of St Mark's, the mouth of the Grand Canal, and the Punta della Dogana with its golden ball. The adjoining Benedictine *Monastery is now part of the Giorgio Cini Foundation. It may be visited when exhibitions are being held, or by request when the rooms are not in use (preferably by previous appointment). The Library is open to students.

In 982 Giovanni Morosini gave the island to the Benedictines. It was rebuilt in 1223, and again in 1433 when Cosimo de'Medici was exiled here for a brief period. At this time his architect, Michelozzo built the first library (later destroyed). The monastery was the scene in 1799–1800 of the Conclave that elected pope Pius VII. After many years' use as barracks, it was in 1951–56 restored the GIORGIO CINI FOUNDATION, set up as a memorial to Count Vittorio Cini's son, killed in an air crash in 1949. It includes a Centre of Culture and Civilisation, an Arts and Crafts Centre, and a Naval Training School (which incorporates two State boarding schools). In the large park are an open-air theatre, a swimming-pool, and a gymnasium. Outstanding art exhibitions are held here.

The FIRST CLOISTER (entered to the right of the church) was designed by *Palladio* (1579). It is separated from the second cloister by the LIBRARY wing designed by *Longhena*, which contains 17C woodwork by *Fr. Pauc*, and ceiling paintings by *Fil. Gherardi* and *Giov. Coli*. The SECOND CLOISTER is by *And. Buora* (1516–40). Off it, and preceded by an anteroom with elaborate lavabi, is the handsome *REFECTORY, a splendid work by *Palladio* (1560; now used as a conference hall). The Marriage of the Virgin by the *School of Tintoretto* hangs here in the place of Paolo Veronese's Marriage at Cana (now in the Louvre). From the first cloister a monumental double staircase by *Baldass. Longhena* (1643–45) leads up to the Institute offices and exhibition rooms.—The DORMITORY was begun when *Michelozzo* was staying in the convent (comp. above) and completed by *Giov. Buora* (1494–1533). It closes the far wing of the second cloister and runs for 128 metres behind the church. It has a pretty gabled facade (with a relief of St George by *Lor. Bregno*) overlooking the little PORT. The two Istrian-stone lighthouses were designed by *Gius. Mezzani* in 1813. In 1829 the island became a free port. Here the 'Giorgio Cini' training ship is usually moored (it replaces a schooner built in 1894).—By the landing-stage is the water-gate of the boat house.

From the island of San Giorgio Maggiore the vaporetto (No. 5; 'circolare destra') crosses to **La Giudecca** (Pl.11;5), occupying eight islands, and also connected directly by a ferry with the Zattere (comp. p 59). Originally called *Spinalunga* from its elongated shape, it is thought to owe its present name from the fact that Jews established a colony here at the end of the 13C. Later on it was the site of aristocratic villas and pleasure-gardens. Michelangelo stayed here in 1529. It is one of the most characteristic parts of the city, rarely visited by tourists. Its long fondamenta lining the Giudecca canal (comp. p 148) commands magnificent views.

The boat from San Giorgio calls first at the landing-stage in front of the church of LE ZITELLE (Pl.11;5; open Sun only 10–11.30). This was planned c 1570 by Palladio but built after his death in 1582–86. It is flanked by two wings of a hospice for young girls who were here taught the art of lace-making. To the left the deserted fondamenta continues up to the entrance of the headquarters of the customs police (from here there is a fine view of San Marco). The Corte di Ca' Mosto has an overgrown garden. To the right of the Zitelle is the neo-Gothic 'Casa di Maria' with an elaborate brick facade and three large windows. It was built as a painter's studio in 1910–13.

Calle Michelangelo leads away from the water-front through a stark modern quarter to the other side of the island (one of the few points where this bank is accessible from land). From the end of the calle there is a view of the Lido. To the left, beyond the school, is the garden of the famous Cipriani hotel.

Fondamenta della Croce continues past ship-building warehouses and the Venice Youth Hostel. Just before Rio della Croce is a mooring for tug-boats. On the left can be seen the huge church of *Santa Croce* (now part of an Institution). Across the canal Ramo della Croce leads inland to Rio della Croce. Here the fondamenta is lined with quaint old houses with boats moored alongside. A small iron bridge leads over to the 'Garden of Eden' (no adm) one of the largest and finest private gardens in Venice. On the return to the Giudecca canal there is a view (in the distance) of the dome of Santa Maria della Salute, and (left) the dome of the Redentore (comp. below), and, at the end, the golden ball of the Dogana and the campanile and domes of San Marco can be glimpsed. On the Giudecca canal, a short way farther on (left) stands the Franciscan church of the **'Redentore** (Pl.10;7; open 7–12, 15.30–19.30), the most complete and perhaps the most successful of *Palladio's* churches (1577–92), with a good facade. It was built in thanksgiving for the deliverance of Venice from the plague in 1575–77 which left some 46,000 dead (25–30 per cent of the population), and the doge vowed to visit the church annually across a bridge of boats which united the Zattere with the Giudecca. The feast of the Redentore (3rd Sun in July) remains one of the most popular festivals (comp. p 64), and the bridge of boats is still usually constructed for the occasion.

The splendid INTERIOR has elements derived from Roman classical buildings. The design of the chancel is particularly fine. SOUTH SIDE. 1st chapel, *Fr. Bassano*, Nativity; 2nd chapel, *School of Veronese*, Baptism of Christ; 3rd chapel, *School of Tintoretto*, Flagellation of Christ.—NORTH SIDE. 3rd chapel, *Palma Giovane*, Deposition; 2nd chapel, *Fr. Bassano*, Resurrection; 1st chapel, *Workshop of Tintoretto*, Ascension. On the Baroque high altar (by *Gius. Mazza*) are fine bronzes by *Campagna* of the Crucifixion, St Francis, and St Mark. In the small SACRISTY (on the S side of the church, opened on request) is a fine collection of paintings: *Alvise Vivarini*, in an elaborate frame, Madonna in Adoration of the Child and two Angels; *Veronese* (attrib.), Baptism of Christ; *Lazzaro Bastiani*, Madonna in Adoration of the Child; *Carlo Saraceni*, Ecstasy of St Francis. The wax heads of Franciscan monks date from the 18C.

The fondamenta continues to a wide rio crossed by the Ponte Lungo, a long iron bridge. The canal is filled with fishing boats. A brief detour inland may be made here (via Calle delle Erbe, Rio della Palada, and Corte Ferrando; comp. Pl.9;8) through an area inhabited by fishermen. The fondamenta ends at the church of SANT' EUFEMIA (Pl.9;5; open for services only), founded in the 9C. It is preceded by a 16C Doric portico. The rococo interior incorporates Veneto-Byzantine capitals. The 1st altar on the right has St Roch and the angel (with a Madonna and Child in the lunette above) signed by *Bart. Vivarini* (1480; recently restored).

At the W extremity of the island rises the huge brick *Mulino Stucky*, a neo-Gothic flour-mill, built by Ernst Wullekopf in 1895. It dominates the view of the Giudecca from the Zattere. Abandoned for years, its future is uncertain. A long bridge connects the Giudecca to the island of Sacca Fisola (Pl.8;5), a modern residential area.

From the landing-stage in front of Sant'Eufemia, vaporetto No. 5 ('circolare sinistra') runs to San Marco, or, a short way E, is the landing-stage for the ferry ('traghetto') across the Giudecca canal to the Zattere (landing-stage near Santa Maria della Visitazione, comp. Atlas 14–15).

# THE VENETIAN LAGOON

The **Venetian Lagoon** (*Laguna Véneta*), separated from the Adriatic by the low and narrow sand-bars of the Lido and Pellestrina which are pierced by three channels, the Porto di Lido, the Porto di Malamocco, and the Porto di Chioggia, is a shallow expanse of water, 544sq. km in area. Rather more than half of this (298sq. km) is the *Laguna Morta*, under water only at high spring tides; the remainder is the *Laguna Viva*, perennially flooded. On some of the islands townships and monasteries were established in the Middle Ages, most of which are now decayed. The future of many of the smaller islands, abandoned in the 1960s and 1970s is uncertain. The hauntingly beautiful but desolate lagoon today supports a few small fishing communities and market gardens, apart from the famous Lido and the glass manufactories of Murano. Motor-launches provide an excellent service between the main islands.

# 15 The Islands of San Michele and Murano

VAPORETTO No. 5, 'circolare destra' and 'circolare sinistra' (the 'right circular' and the 'left circular') operates every 15 minutes; it calls at the island of San Michele and then Murano (landing-stages at *Colonna, Fondamenta Venier, Museo, Navagero*, and *Faro*. The 'circolare destra' runs via the Station, the Cannaregio canal, and the Fondamente Nuove, while the 'circolare sinistra' takes the more interesting (and shorter) route from San Marco (*San Zaccaria* landing-stage) via the Arsenal (comp. p 115) and the Fondamente Nuove.—On Murano the landing-stages of *Fondamenta Venier* and *Serenella* are served by a half-hourly service.

The walled **ISLAND OF SAN MICHELE** (Pl.7;1,2) is the Cemetery of Venice. By the landing-stage is **San Michele in Isola** by *Mauro Codussi* (1469–78), the earliest Renaissance church in the city.

The elegant and well-sited *FACADE was the first church facade in Istrian Stone in Venice. It has a good Doorway with a 15C statue of the Madonna and Child. The dome to the left belongs to the Cappella Emiliana (comp. below). A gateway surrounded by a Gothic carving of St Michael and the dragon, leads into the 15C cloister, from which the church is entered if the main door is closed.

INTERIOR. The Vestibule is separated from the rest of the church by the Monks' choir, prettily decorated. In front of the W door a marble lozenge in the floor marks the burial place of Fra Paolo Sarpi (d 1623). The Monument to Card. Giovanni Dolfin (d 1622) around the W door is by *Pietro Bernini*, with a bust of the cardinal by *Gian Lorenzo Bernini* (1622). On the right wall are wood sculptures of Christ between the Madonna and St John (16C) and, beneath the Monks' choir, is a stone statue of St Jerome by *Juste Le Court*.—In the main body of the church, the left apse chapel contains St Mary of Cortona before the Crucifix, by *Gian Dom. Tiepolo*. The SACRISTY has an unusual perspective ceiling. On the N wall of the church is an exquisitely carved Renaissance tablet (1501). At the beginning of the N side is the entrance, through a domed

*San Michele in Isola*

vestibule, to the charming little Renaissance CAPPELLA EMILIANA, by *Gugl. dei Grigi Bergamasco* (c 1530). Hexagonal in form, it is beautifully designed with fine marble inlay and reliefs by *Giov. Ant. da Carona* (16C).—The CAMPANILE was completed in 1460.

A Camaldolensian monastery, famous as a centre of learning, occupied the island from 1212 to 1810. Fra Mauro (1433–1459), the cartographer, was a monk here, and in 1450–59 drew his map of the world (now in the Library of St Mark's, comp. p 100), forty years before the discovery of America. Silvio Pellico (1789–1854), the patriot author, was imprisoned here by Austrians before being sent to the Spielberg.—In the CEMETERY, planted with magnificent cypresses, G.P.R. James (1801–60), who died as British consul in Venice, the composer Wolf-Ferrari, the writer Baron Corvo (Frederick Rolfe), and the poet Ezra Pound, are buried (in the Protestant enclosure). Serge Diaghilev (1872–1929) lies in the Orthodox cemetery, and near him his composer protégé Igor Stravinsky (1882–1971; died in New York).

The boat continues to the **ISLAND OF MURANO** (Plan on p 188), about 1.5km from Venice. It occupies five islets and contains 7500 inhabitants. Since 1292 it has been the centre of the Venetian glass industry, which under protective laws reached its zenith in the early 16C.

The island was first settled by refugees from Altino fleeing the Barbarian invasions. It had a considerable degree of independence from Venice as early as 1000, with its own governor, laws, and mint. The glass industry, established in Venice as early as the 10C, was moved here in the 13C from the city because of the danger of fire. The art of making crystal glass was rediscovered by the

Venetians who retained the monopoly throughout the 16C. The special characteristics of Venetian glass are its elaborate design, lightness, and bright colour. After a period of decline the industry was revived at the end of the 19C under the impulse of Ant. Salviati and others, and the production of artistic glass is still thriving.—In 1441–50 Murano was the seat of a famous school of painters, headed by Ant. Vivarini and Giov. d'Alemagna. At the beginning of the 16C it is estimated that there were as many as 50,000 inhabitants, and it was a favourite retreat of Venetian noblemen, many of whom built villas here.

For the vaporetto services and landing-stages on the island, see p 59.

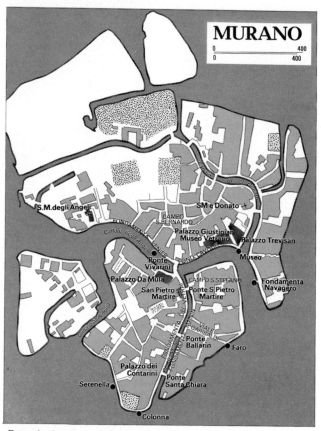

From the landing-stage of Colonna the fondamenta follows Rio dei Vetrai past numerous glass factories (all of which welcome visitors). *Palazzo dei Contarini* (No. 27) is a Renaissance building (which has suffered neglect and alterations). The name of Ponte Santa Chiara recalls the church and convent which once stood here. No. 37 is a simple Gothic house. On the other side of the canal, beyond a modern building, is a pretty small 14C house with an overhanging upper story above a portico. Ponte Ballarin marks the centre of the island; proclamations were read by the column with the symbolic lion. On the last stretch of the canal, as it bends left, the houses diminish in size. To the right of Ponte San Pietro Martire opens Campo Santo Stefano with a bell tower on the site of a church demolished in the 19C. A trattoria here occupies an ancient house. **San Pietro Martire** is a Dominican Gothic church partly rebuilt in 1511 and restored in 1928.

The fine INTERIOR (open 9.30–12, 14.30–19.30; summer 9.30–12, 13.30–19.30) is hung with chandeliers made on the island at the beginning of this century. Above the nave arches are quaint 16C frescoes of Dominican Saints. SOUTH SIDE (light; 100 l.), *Madonna with angels and Saints, and doge Agostino Barbarigo signed and dated 1488 by *Giov. Bellini* (recently restored). The Immaculate Conception (1510–13), also by *Giov. Bellini*, has been removed for restoration.—In the SANCTUARY are large paintings (1721–23) by *Bart. Letterini*.—In the Gothic chapel to the left of the Sanctuary (light; fee) is a good collection of paintings, some of which are being restored in situ: (right wall): *School of Pordenone* (Bern. Licinio?), Madonna and Child with SS. Lawrence and Ursula and senator Pasqualigo; (left wall) *Agost. da Lodi*, Madonna and Child with four Saints: *Fr. di Simone da Santacroce*, Madonna and Child with SS. Jeremiah and Jerome and an angel playing a musical instrument. The four angels are by *Nic. Rondinelli*. The Renaissance altar has a good relief of the Pietà dated 1495, and to the left is a painting of a miracle of St Mark attrib. to *Dom. Tintoretto.*—On the NORTH SIDE, above the Sacristy door, is a St Jerome by *Veronese*. In the SACRISTY the elaborately carved panelling (1652–56) is the work of *Pietro Morando*. On the N wall of the church is a huge painting of the Deposition by *Il Salviati*.

Fondamenta dei Vetrai continues past a Pharmacy with a ceiling painting by Fr. Fontebasso (1750–60). Ponte Vivarini crosses the main Canale degli Angeli near the restored *Palazzo Da Mula*, one of the few traces of Murano's ancient splendour. Across the bridge Fondamenta Venier leads left to SANTA MARIA DEGLI ANGELI (usually closed; open for a service on Sun), in a remote part of the island. Over the churchyard door is an Annunciation attrib. to *Ant. Rizzo*. The interior has a ceiling with panels painted by *P.M. Pennacchi* (c 1520; recently restored), and a high altarpiece of the Annunciation by *Pordenone*.—From Ponte Vivarini, Fondamenta Cavour leads in the other direction to *Palazzo Giustinian*. This has been the seat of the *Museo Vetrario*, or *Museum of Glass*, since 1861. It has recently been reopened after restoration and the collection of glass from the oldest Roman period to the 18C is beautifully displayed (adm see p 66).

The COURTYARD and pretty loggia contain four well-heads and sculptural fragments. On the GROUND FLOOR, a room has archaeological material including objects from Yugoslavia, and examples of Roman glass (1–3C AD; note the rare bottle showing the Argonauts).—On the FIRST FLOOR the SALONE is hung with three huge chandeliers. This is reserved for conferences and exhibitions. On the left ROOM I contains the earliest Murano glass which survives (15C). Here is displayed the famous dark blue *Barovier Marriage Cup (1470–80); a 'Tiepolo' lamp (a type which often appears in Venetian paintings of the late 15C); and Renaissance enamelled and decorated glass.—RR II & III (right) display 16C glass including crystal ware and filigree glass.—ROOM IV, 18C works; examples from the Piratti workshops (showing the influence of Bohemian masters).—ROOM V is arranged as an 18C interior. In 1985 the sections which display 19C glass, and, in the Salone on the upper floor, contemporary glass, were opened.

Opposite the Museum stands *Palazzo Trevisan*, attrib. to Palladio. It contains traces of frescoes by Veronese and reliefs (in poor repair) by Vittoria. A little farther on is the splendid Venetian Byzantine

*The apse of S. Maria e Donato (Murano)*

basilica of *Santa Maria e Donato. It stands on the former main square (the war memorial is on the site of the town hall) with its magnificent *Apse facing the canal, once the entrance to Murano from the lagoon. The apse is beautifully decorated in an unusual and intricate design with two tiers of arches on twin marble columns, the upper arcade forming a balcony, and the lower arcade blind. It bears fine dog-tooth mouldings and carved and inlaid zig-zag friezes.

The church was founded in the 7C by several wealthy families from Altino. Restored in the 9C, the present church was rebuilt in the 12C. In 1125 the body of St Donato, Bishop of Eurorea in the 4C, was brought here from Cephalonia, together with bones supposed to be those of the dragon he killed. In the early 18C the wealthy Marco Giustinian became Bishop and damaged the ancient church and destroyed many of its most beautiful possessions. A very thorough and admirable restoration of the church was carried out in 1973–79, when the foundations were also strengthened.

The simple FACADE was formerly preceded by the Baptistery (destroyed in 1719). It bears a late-14C marble relief of St Donato and a devotee, and two worn carved pilasters, good 2C Veneto-Roman works.—In the beautifully proportioned INTERIOR (open 8–12, 16–19), with an early 15C ship's keel roof, the columns of the nave with Corinthian capitals (dating from the late Roman period to the 6C) support stilted arches. The splendid *PAVEMENT in mosaic bears an inscription in the centre of the nave with the date of 1141. It was taken up in 1977, restored, and relaid on a concrete base. The Byzantine style pulpit dates from the 6C, and the stoup is placed on a carved pillar (7–8C). In the apse is a fine 12C *Mosaic of the Virgin with her hands raised in prayer on a gold ground. Beneath are 15C frescoes of the Evangelists. Behind the Baroque altar have been hung four bones said to be those of the dragon killed by St Donato. A finely carved 9C sarcophagus in Greek marble, discovered in the 1979 restoration, has been set up as an altar in the chancel.—NORTH AISLE. Large Ancona of St Donato in low relief, dated 1310 and commissioned by the

Podestà of Murano, Donato Memo who is shown with his wife, kneeling. The lunette of the Madonna and Child with Saints and donor (the canon of the church, Giovanni degli Angeli) is by Lazzaro Bastiani (1484). The polyptych with the Dormition of the Virgin (mid-14C) formerly covered a large silver gilt pala on the high altar.—In the chapel off this aisle (the present entrance to the church) are Roman and medieval sarcophaghi. The unusual square Roman sarcophagus from Altino (2C) was used as the baptismal font.

The nearest landing-stage for vaporetto No. 5 which returns to Venice is outside the Museum ('Museo'). The boats which continue to Burano and Torcello (comp. Rte 16) leave roughly every hour from the 'Faro' landing-stage, reached from Rio dei Vetrai (comp. p 188) via Viale Garibaldi.

# 16  The Islands of Torcello and Burano

STEAMER or VAPORETTO SERVICE (No. 12) from Fondamente Nuove (Pl.6;4; reached by vaporetto No. 5; comp. Rte 15), stopping at *Murano* (*Faro*), *Mazzorbo*, *Torcello*, *Burano*, and *Treporti*, c every 1–1½ hrs. To Torcello and Burano in 40–50 min.; to Treporti in 1 hr 10 min. Some boats call first at Torcello, while others call first at Burano (the journey between the two islands takes less than 10 min.).

Excursion steamer (much more expensive) in summer from the Riva degli Schiavoni, making the round trip in 4 hrs (and including Murano, Burano, and Torcello), but allowing only a very brief stay at Torcello.—The Cipriani motor-launch operates a direct service from San Marco to Torcello.

Burano has a number of good trattorie. Torcello now has several restaurants; it is a beautiful place to picnic (since it has no shops, food must be brought from Venice).

From the Fondamente Nuove to *Murano*, see Rte 15. After leaving the Faro landing-stage the boat skirts the E side of Murano and then steers out into the lagoon along a channel marked by piles. The sandbanks to the right are part of *Sant'Erasmo*. Ahead, the green island of San Francesco del Deserto and the leaning campanile of Burano soon come into view, and, in the far distance, to the left of Burano, the cathedral and campanile of Torcello. The boat passes to the left of *San Giacomo in Palude* (with a relief of the Madonna), an island abandoned in 1964. In the distance to the left can be seen Marco Polo airport. The cypresses of San Francesco del Deserto are now prominent to the right, rising out of the flat marshlands. The boat passes close to the island of the *Madonna del Monte* (right), and its dependent islet, with an ammunition factory abandoned after the war. Beyond, the canal forks left (the right branch goes on towards the conspicuous church of Santa Caterina (comp. below), and the boat soon enters the pretty canal of **Mazzorbo**, lined with a few villas and a boat-yard. Near the landing-stage is a campanile (covered with scaffolding in 1985), which belonged to the destroyed convent of Santa Maria Valverde, behind a churchyard wall and next to a lone cypress. The church of *Santa Caterina* dates from 1283–9. Above the door is a 14C bas-relief of the Marriage of St Catherine. It has an interesting interior. The little settlement, where new houses are being built and others restored, is connected by a long bridge with Burano which is now left to the right (if the boat calls first at Torcello, comp. above). On the approach to Torcello there is a good view of the campanile and cathedral.

**TORCELLO**, though now a small group of houses in a lonely part of the lagoon, still preserves some lovely relics of its days of splendour, when, from the 7C to the 13C, it was the island stronghold of the people of Altinum, who were driven from the mainland by the Lombard invaders. They had already taken temporary shelter here in the 5C and 6C. Bishop Paolo moved the bishopric of Altinum to Torcello in 639 bringing with him the relics of St Heliodorus (still preserved in the cathedral, see below); the foundation stone of the cathedral he dedicated in the same year survives. At one time Torcello is said to have had 20,000 inhabitants and it was a thriving centre of wool manufacturing, but by the 15C the rivalry of Venice and the malaria due to the marshes formed by the silting up of the Sile had brought about its downfall. In the 17C the population had already dwindled to a few hundred, and it now has only 75 inhabitants.

A pleasant walk (c 10 min.) leads along a canal from the landing-stage past an old stone bridge without a parapet to the Cipriani restaurant. Just beyond is the group of monuments: to the left is Palazzo del Consiglio (now the Museum), ahead, the loggia of Palazzo dell'Archivio, and to the right the cathedral and the church of Santa Fosca.

The *Cathedral (Santa Maria dell'Assunta*; open 10–12.30, 14–17; summer 10–12.30, 14–18), founded in 639, is a Veneto-Byzantine building, derived from the Ravenna-type basilicas. Altered in 864, it was rebuilt in 1008 by Bp Otto Orseolo (later Doge). At the W end, in front of the facade, are remains of the 7C circular Baptistery (the foundations of the perimeter wall and bases of the columns, often water-logged). The 11C shutters of the windows on the S side are formed of hinged stone slabs.

The dignified and cool aisled INTERIOR has 18 slender marble columns with good capitals, a superb pavement of 'opus Alexandrinum', and wooden tie-beams. An elaborate Byzantine *Mosaic (11–12C; and later restored) of the Last Judgement covers the W wall. The marble pulpit and ambo on the N side are made up from fragments from the earliest church. The iconostasis consists of four large marble *Plutei (11C), elaborately carved with late Byzantine designs, and, above columns (also with good capitals) are 15C local paintings of the Virgin and Apostles. Higher up is a Gothic Crucifix in wood. Behind it is the Choir, with a marble Synthronon (7C) in the apse, in which steps rise to the bishop's throne in the centre. Beneath the lovely marble panels, fragments of frescoed decoration and figures have been revealed. Below the high altar is a pagan sarcophagus (3C) which contains the relics of St Heliodorus, first bishop of Altinum. On the left, set in to the wall, is the foundation stone of the church (639). In the semi-dome of the central apse, on a stark gold ground, is a mosaic of the *Madonna, one of the most striking figures ever produced in Byzantine art. Beneath are the Apostles (mid-11C), and on the outer arch, the Annunciation, added in the second half of the 12C. In the S apse are more ancient mosaics (covered for restoration), Christ in benediction with Saints and angels, and a delightful vault decoration of four angels with the mystic lamb (11C, possibly replacing an 8C or even 7C mosaic). In front of the N apse is the pavement tomb of Nicola Morosini, Bp of Torcello (d 1305). The Crypt, thought to date from the 9C, is water-logged at its lowest point. In the nave are two altars with gilded and painted wood tabernacles. Near the W door is a stoup with strange carved animals.—The tall square detached CAMPANILE (11–12C; no adm) is a striking landmark in the lagoon.

The church of *Santa Fosca, nearby, was built to house the body of St Fosca brought to the island before 1011. The remarkable design, on a Greek-cross plan, probably survives from the 11C building, although it has been drastically restored. It is surrounded by an octagonal portico (probably added in the 12C) on three sides. In the

*Apse mosaics of Torcello Cathedral*

bare interior the beautiful marble columns have Byzantine capitals and support a circular drum and conical wooden roof.

On the grass outside is a primitive stone seat known as 'Attila's chair'. *Palazzo dell'Archivio* is being restored in 1985 as an archaeological museum. Here will be displayed fine Roman sculptural fragments (altars, funerary cippae), and statues dating from the Late Empire, from Torcello and Altinum, as well as other local archaeological material. *Palazzo del Consiglio* houses the MUSEO DI TORCELLO which contains an interesting collection of objects from the demolished churches of Torcello (which numbered at least 10), and archaeological material.

The collection is well displayed and labelled. Admission see p 66. GROUND FLOOR. Mosaic fragments including two 7C heads of angels, and original 12C fragments from the cathedral; in the cathedral; 6C stoup with a Greek inscription; Medieval lance with a runic inscription. Among the architectural fragments are several plutei, and a 10C well-head. Part of the early-13C Pala d'Oro formerly over the high altar of the cathedral, is also displayed here.—UPPER FLOOR. The 15C Venetian wood sculptures include the beautifully carved tomb of Santa Fosca. Also here: 11C Latin cross in marble; St Christopher, an early-15C Venetian painting; 10 small wooden panels (from a ceiling decoration) with Biblical scenes, attrib. to Bonifacio Bembo da Cremona (15C); 16C paintings from the organ of Sant'Antonio; historical documents, illuminated antiphonals, etc.

**BURANO** is a cheerful little fishing village (5300 inhab.) of great charm, with brightly painted houses and miniature canals. From the landing-stage it is a short walk along a canal (left) to Via Baldassare Galuppi, the wide main street of the island. Baldassare Galuppi (1706–85), 'il Buranello', the operatic composer celebrated in verse by Browning, was born here. The street ends in the piazza with the parish church of *San Martino* containing a painting by Girol. da Santacroce behind the altar, a Crucifixion by G.B. Tiepolo in the N aisle, and three charming small paintings by Giov. Mansueti in the Sacristy. Opposite the church is the SCUOLA DEI MERLETTI (lacemaking school; open 9–18 exc. Tues). Burano has for long been celebrated as the centre of the Venetian lace industry and the school was founded in 1872 to revive the industry which had decayed in the 18C. The school, which still takes students, has a beautifully displayed *Museum of Lace*. Many of the inhabitants still practise the art of lace-making and their products are sold in numerous shops on the island.

**San Francesco del Deserto**, 20 min. S by sándolo (on hire in Burano), an island in the most deserted part of the lagoon, is identified by its clump of cypresses. It is said to have been a retreat of St Francis in 1220 and now contains a little church, two charming cloisters, and beautiful gardens. Eleven friars live on the island. Visitors are welcome every day 9–11, 15–17.30.

Some of the regular steamers go on to **Treporti** (connected by bus with Cavallino and Lido di Jesolo, comp. p 59).

# 17   The Islands of the Lido and Pellestrina

The island of the Lido is reached from Venice by water-buses (comp. p 59): No. 1 from Piazzale Roma and the Station (via the Grand Canal, San Marco, etc.), and No. 2 from Piazzale Roma and the Station (via Rio Nuovo); and by steamer (No. 6) direct from Riva degli Schiavoni.—In summer it is also served by vaporetto No. 4; and Nos 18 & 21 (for the bathing beaches).—For the direct summer service to the Casinò, see p 63.—For the car ferry, see p 59.
   The best way of seeing the S part of the Lido island and Pellestrina is by Bus No. 11 (from Piazzale S.M. Elisabetta on the Lido) which continues from Alberoni (by ferry) to the island of Pellestrina (and connects with the Chioggia boat, comp. p 198).

*The steamer landing-stage at the Lido, and the horse-drawn trams in 1897*

For bus services on the Lido, see p 60. A selection of HOTELS on the Lido is listed on p 52.

The **LIDO** (18,800 inhab.), is the largest of the islands between the Lagoon and the Adriatic. The first bathing establishments were opened here in 1857 and by the beginning of this century it had become the most fashionable seaside resort in Italy. It has bequeathed its name to numerous bathing resorts all over the world. The Adriatic sea-front consists of a group of luxurious hotels and villas bordering the fine sandy beach, which is divided up into sections, each belonging (except at the extreme ends) to a particular hotel or bathing establishment. The rest of the N part of the island has become a residential quarter of Venice, with fine trees and gardens, and traversed by several canals. The atmosphere on the Lido is very different from that in the city of Venice itself, not least because of the presence of cars.

The landing-stage of *Santa Maria Elisabetta*, where the water-bus services from Venice terminate, is named after the church here of 1627. Buses to all destinations on the Lido (see p 60) pass through the Piazzale, and there is a taxi stand. The GRAN VIALE SANTA MARIA ELISABETTA, the main street traversing the widest part of the island, leads from the Piazzale (and the Lagoon) past the tourist office, the post office, and numerous hotels and shops, to (1km) PIAZZALE BUCINTORO on the sea-front. To the left Lungomare d'Annunzio leads to the Hospital and the public bathing beaches of San Nicolò, while to the right Lungomare Marconi leads along the front (with its

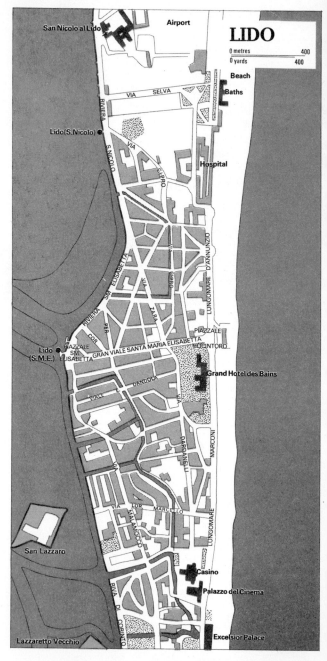

numerous beach-huts and private beaches) past the *Grand Hotel des Bains*, which provided the setting for Thomas Mann's 'Death in Venice'. Farther on (c 1km) is the CASINÒ (comp. p 63) and Palazzo del Cinema where an international film festival is usually held in summer. Both these conspicuous buildings were built in 1936–38 by Miozzi and Quagliata. Just beyond is the famous *Excelsior Palace Hotel* (an elaborate building by Giov. Sardi, 1898–1908), with its landing-stage on a canal (used by the hotel motor-launches, and the Casinò motor-boat).

The N end of the island is reached by Bus A (from Lungomare Marconi, or Piazzale Santa Maria Elisabetta). The road skirts the lagoon past the conspicuous war memorial to reach **San Nicolò al Lido**, now in a remote part of the island.

The monastery and church were founded in 1044 and the present convent built in the 16C. Because of its strategic position near the main entrance to the lagoon, the monastery was used by the Doge as the official place to receive visitors. Here the emperor Barbarossa stayed before his meeting with pope Alexander III in San Marco in 1177, and elaborate celebrations were held in honour of Henry III, king of France in 1574. Domenico Selvo was elected doge here in 1071 while the basilica of San Marco was being completed. The Doge attended mass every year in San Nicolò after the ceremonial marriage with the sea at the Porto di Lido (comp. p 64).

Above the door of the church is a monument to doge Dom. Contarini, the founder. In the interior, at the end of the left side is a 14C wood Crucifix. The choir is finely carved by Giov. da Crema (1635).

Outside the church there is a view across the lagoon to the campanile of San Marco, and the dome and campanile of San Pietro di Castello. Near at hand is the green island of La Certosa. Next to the church stands the *Palazzetto del Consiglio dei Dieci* (1520), probably on the site of a 14C building. The road continues past the airport (private planes) and 16C military buildings.

The English Protestant Cemetery (1684–1810) was obliterated in the 1930s when the airport was extended. The tomb-stones have been moved to a corner of the Catholic cemetery farther S. Among the graves were those of consul Joseph Smith (1682–1770; tomb slab now in the English church, comp. p 65) and his wife Catherine Tofts (d 1756), the singer.—The Jewish community were granted land nearby in 1386 for their burial ground.

The N tip of the island overlooks the **Porto di Lido**, the main entrance to the lagoon and always strongly defended (at one time it was closed by huge chains to prevent the entrance of enemy ships). Facing the Lido, on the island of Le Vignole, is the *Fortezza di Sant'Andrea*, the masterpiece of Sanmicheli (1543), the architect and engineer who had been appointed in 1534 to examine the defences of the lagoon. It is being restored, after years of neglect. In the channel here the Doge performed the annual ceremony of the marriage with the sea, when he threw his ring into the sea from the Bucintoro and it was retrieved by a young fisherman. The custom commemorated the Conquest of Dalmatia in AD 1000, and acquired its later more magnificent trappings after the visit of Alexander III and Frederick I in 1177.

Across the channel is *Punta Sabbioni* on the mainland, connected by road with (18km) **Lido di Jesolo**, a popular bathing resort 15km long, between the old and new mouths of the Piave. It has over 450 hotels and pensions, numerous camping sites, sports facilities, etc. The old village of *Jesolo*, formerly Cavazuccherina, 2km N of the E end, perpetuates the name of an early medieval centre, known also as *Equilium* (since horses were bred on the marshes here), the rival of Heraclea in the affairs of the lagoon. Here some remains of the Romanesque church survived until the Austrian offensive of June 1918. The coast was formerly thickly wooded with pines; a grove survives near Cortellazzo on the Piave.—Lido di Jesolo is reached from Venice by steamer No. 14 (from Riva degli Schiavoni via the Lido to Punta Sabbioni, where a bus continues to Jesolo), and in summer by steamer No. 15 (direct from Riva degli Schiavoni to Punta Sabbioni). The steamer service for Murano and Torcello (No. 12; comp. p 59) terminates at Treporti (15km from Jesolo) where buses run to Cavallino.

The Southern part of the Lido island is traversed by Bus C (and No. 11; comp. p60). From Piazzale Santa Maria Elisabetta Via Malamocco runs S, a little inland from the lagoon, through a residential area with numerous gardens. The buildings become fewer as the island narrows.—5.5km **Malamocco**, a quiet fishing village overlooking the lagoon. The ancient *Metamauco*, one of the first places to be inhabited in the lagoon, was the seat of the lagoon government in the 8C. It was the scene of the famous defeat of king Pepin who had laid siege to the city in 810. Submerged by a tidal wave c 1107, the settlement was moved to this side of the island. It now consists of a small group of pretty houses, with a 15C Palazzo del Podestà in a little campo. The church contains a large painting by Girol. Forabosco, and a carved polyptych of the Dormition of the Virgin (early 15C). The campanile is modelled on that of San Marco. There is a view across the lagoon to Venice (on the extreme right), and, in front, the port of Marghera is conspicuous. Just offshore lies the island of *Poveglia* (its hospital was abandoned in 1968).

Via Alberoni continues, now skirting the edge of the lagoon.—12km **Alberoni**, a little bathing resort, with the Lido golf course (18 holes) and an extensive public bathing beach.—The road continues to the end of the promontory where a car ferry (in connection with Bus No. 11) crosses (in 5 min.) the **Porto di Malamocco**, the narrow channel separating the islands of the Lido and Pellestrina.

The thin **Island of Pellestrina** (10km long) is traversed by a road separated from the sea by a stone dike. The first settlement is **San Pietro in Volta**, a colourful fishing village with a long row of houses facing the lagoon.—Pellestrina is strung out for nearly 3km along its narrow sand-bar. It is a fishing village with a lace industry. The octagonal church of San Vito is by And. Tirali (1723).

To the S stretch the remarkable MURAZZI, a great sea wall undertaken in 1744–82 by Temanza in two sections on either side of the **Porto di Chioggia**, the third and last entrance to the lagoon. The wall is built of irregular blocks of Istrian stone and extends for over 3km. It is best seen from the boat (which connects with bus No. 11) which continues from the end of Pellestrina to (25 min.) Chioggia via Caroman. For **Chioggia**, see Rte 18.

# 18   Chioggia

The most pleasant way of reaching Chioggia from Venice is by boat. A direct A.C.T.V. service operates in July and August from Riva degli Schiavoni through the Southern part of the lagoon (the journey takes c 2 hrs). At other times of the year Bus 11 (every ½–1 hr) operates from the Lido (Santa Maria Elisabetta) via Malamocco and Alberoni (comp. p 194). From Alberoni (Santa Maria del

Mare) the bus boards a connecting car ferry (5 min.) for San Pietro in Volta and Pellestrina. At Pellestrina (Cimitero) it connects with a steamer which continues (in 25 min.) via Caroman to Chioggia. The whole journey takes c 1½ hours.—Chioggia and Sottomarina can also be reached by bus from Piazzale Roma (SIAMIC services) via Mestre in c 1 hr.

**CHIOGGIA** (49,800 inhab.), one of the main fishing ports on the Adriatic, is situated at the Southern extremity of the Venetian lagoon, connected to the mainland by a bridge. The most important town

*Lace-makers in a Chioggia street c 1918*

after Venice in the lagoon, its unusual urban structure survives. It is visited also for its bathing beach at Sottomarina (see below).

The history of Chioggia has been intimately involved with that of Venice since it was first settled by inhabitants of Este, Monselice, and Padua, in the 5–7C. Always loyal to Venice, Chioggia suffered destruction at the hands of the Genoese in 1379; but the Venetians under Vettor Pisani succeeded immediately afterwards in shutting up the Genoese fleet in the harbour, and its subsequent surrender marked the end of the struggle between the two rival maritime powers. The saltworks of Chioggia, first developed in the 12C, were the most important in the lagoon and survived up until this century.

Famous natives include Cristoforo Sabbadino (1489–1560), the hydraulic engineer of the Republic, John Cabot (1425–c 1500), the navigator, Giuseppe Zerlino (1517–1590), the musical theorist, Rosalba Carriera (1675–1757), the painter, and Eleonora Duse (1859–1924), the actress.

The boats from the Lido (and Venice) dock on the quay by Piazzetta Vigo, with its Greek marble column bearing the Lion of St Mark. To the left Canale della Vena, used by the fishing fleet, is crossed by Ponte Vigo (1685) to reach the church of **San Domenico**.

INTERIOR. On either side of the W door, large historical canvases by *Pietro Damini* (1617–19). SOUTH SIDE. 1st altar, Three Saints, signed by *And. Vicentino*; beyond the 2nd altar, St Paul, the last known work by *Carpaccio* (signed and dated 1520; removed for restoration). On the right and left of the choir arch, *Leandro Bassano*, Deposition and Saints; and *Iac. Tintoretto* (attrib.), Christ crucified and Saints. On the high altar is an imposing wood Crucifix (15C?). On the 1st N altar, *And. Vicentino*, Martyrdom of St Peter.

In Piazzetta Vigo (comp. above) begins *CORSO DEL POPOLO, the lively main street, with porticoes and cafés, which traverses the town parallel to the picturesque Canale della Vena. On the left stands the church of **Sant'Andrea**, with its Veneto-Byzantine campanile (13C).

INTERIOR. 2nd S altar, St Nicholas, a polychrome wood statue of the 16C. In the apse, St Andrew, by *Il Chioggiotto* (Ant. Marinetti). The SACRISTY contains a Crucifix and Saints by an unknown 16C artist, and ivory reliefs in Baroque frames. In the 1st N chapel is a 16C marble tabernacle.

The Corso opens out in front of the **Granaio** (1322; restored 1864), with a Madonna and Child on the facade by Jac. Sansovino. It now serves as a market hall. On the canal behind is the FISH MARKET (open every morning); the fish are displayed on specially designed marble slabs. The *Town Hall* was built in the 19C. In the Piazzetta, behind the Post Office is the church of the **Santissima Trinità**, rebuilt by And. Tirali (1703).

The well designed INTERIOR has an Oratory behind the high altar. The two organs bear paintings by *G.B. Mariotti*. On the N altar, behind a sculptured group of the Flight into Egypt, is the Presentation in the Temple, by *Matteo Ponzone*. The ORATORY (in restoration) has a fine ceiling with paintings by the *School of Tintoretto*.

Across the canal is the church of the FILIPPINI. It contains (2nd S chapel) a Visitation, by Fr. Fontebasso, and (2nd N chapel), Madonna and Child with Saints, by Carlo Bevilacqua (1794).—On the Corso is the church of SAN GIACOMO. The ceiling bears a fresco of St James by Il Chioggiotto. On the 3rd S altar, a painting of St Roch and St Sebastian by the school of Bellini, incorporating a 15C fresco fragment, has been removed for restoration. On the high altar, a Pietà by the 15C Venetian school is much venerated as the 'Madonna della Navicella'.—Farther on, facing the little church of San Francesco (right) is the family mansion of Rosalba Carriera, later occupied by Goldoni. The early Gothic church of *San Martino* has an interesting exterior (1392); it is now disused. In the piazza stands the **Duomo** with its detached campanile (1347–50).

The INTERIOR was reconstructed by *Longhena* in 1624. Beyond the 3rd S altar, small Madonna and Child by the school of Bellini. The sacristy contains paintings (1593–98) of episodes in the history of Chioggia by *And. Vicentino, Alvise dal Friso, Pietro Malombra,* and *Bened. Caliari.* On the right of the Sanctuary is a chapel decorated with marbles and stucco work which contains two oval paintings and a vault fresco by Il Chioggiotto. The chapel to the left of the Sanctuary contains six good paintings by *G.B. Cignaroli* (attrib.), *Gaspare Diziani, G.B. Tiepolo* (Torture of two Martyrs), *G.B. Piazzetta* (attrib.), *Pietro Liberi,* and *Gian Mattei.* On the 2nd N altar is a statue of St Agnes signed by *Ant. Bonazza.* The marble baptistery contains three statues of Virtues by *Alvise Tagliapietra.*

The tree-planted piazza beyond has a marble balustrade overlooking the canal and adorned with 18C statues, one of which, a Madonna, is held in great reverence. At the end of the Corso is Porta Garibaldi, some distance beyond which, to the right, is the railway station (on the Ferrara line).

From San Giacomo the Calle San Giacomo leads across a long bridge (bus from the Corso) to **Sottomarina**, once a village of fishermen and market-gardeners with narrow houses closely wedged together. It has now developed into a seaside resort with innumerable small hotels lining the sandy beach on the Adriatic.—To the N is the southern section of the Murazzi (see p 198).

# 19   The Minor Islands of the Lagoon

The islands in the Northern part of the lagoon are described in Rtes 15 and 16.—Poveglia is described on p 198.

## A. San Lazzaro degli Armeni

Vaporetto No. 20 from Riva degli Schiavoni five times daily in 15 min. Visitors are admitted to the island on Sun & Thurs, 15–17 (in connection with the boats).

The boat passes close to the island of *San Servolo*, the site of one of the oldest and most important Benedictine convents in the lagoon founded in the 9C and dedicated to a Roman soldier martyred at the time of Diocletian. It became an important religious centre, and the buildings were transformed in the 18C by Temanza. Later used as a hospital, since 1980 it has been occupied by the workshops for the Council of Europe's School of Craftsmanship which offers courses in restoration.

The island of **San Lazzaro degli Armeni**, just off the Lido, is distinguished by its tall campanile crowned by an oriental cupola. It was used from 1182 as a leper colony, and after a period of abandon it became the seat in 1717 of a Roman Catholic Armenian monastery, founded by Peter of Manug, called Mechitar (the 'Consoler'). The present community consists of 15 fathers and c 25 novices. It is celebrated for its polyglot printing press. Visitors are shown the monastery by a father.

The fine collection of illuminated manuscripts includes an Evangelistery by Sarkis Pizak (1331). In the library hall is a fresco of Peace and Justice by G.B. Tiepolo. There is also a small museum and a picture gallery of 16–18C works by Armenian and Venetian artists. Some incunabula printed on the island and vestments were destroyed by fire in 1975. Byron was a frequent visitor, and studied Armenian as a means of conquering his boredom. He helped publish an Armenian-English dictionary and grammar. His room is shown. In 1980 some of his books, etc., formerly belonging to the Casa Magni at Lérici, were donated to the monastery.

To the S., also close to the Lido, is thé island of *Lazzaretto Vecchio*. A hospice for pilgrims was founded here in the 12C. The island was occupied by the Agostinian monastery of Santa Maria di Nazareth when in 1423 a hospital was set up here by order of the Republic for plague victims. It was the first-known permanent isolation hospital in Europe, and the name 'Lazzaretto' (a corruption of 'Nazareth') was later adopted for all leper hospitals. After a period of use as a military deposit it was abandoned in 1965. It is now a home for stray dogs. There are plans to open a sports centre here.

# B. La Grazia, San Servolo, San Clemente, and Santo Spirito

The vaporetto service (No. 10) known as 'Ospedali' runs from Monumento Vitt. Emanuele calling at La Grazia, San Servolo, and San Clemente.

*La Grazia* is occupied by an isolation hospital.—San Servolo is described in Rte 19A.—The hospital of *San Clemente* is to be closed. The 15C church has a fine series of Baroque monuments of the Morosini family.—To the S is the island of *Santo Spirito*, the site of a famous monastery destroyed in 1656. It was later used as an ammunition factory and was abandoned in 1965. It is destined to become a sports centre. *Sacca Sessola*, a large island to the W, was occupied by a hospital until it was abandoned in 1980.

# C. Le Vignole and Sant'Erasmo

Vaporetto No. 13 (c every hour) from Fondamente Nuove via Murano (Faro) to Vignole and Sant'Erasmo (calling at Capannone, Chiesa, and Punta Vela) in c 1 hr.

*Le Vignole* and *Sant'Erasmo* are both mainly occupied by market gardens. On the extreme S tip of Vignole is the Forte di Sant'Andrea guarding the Porto di Lido (comp. p 197).—The island of *La Certosa*, between Vignole and Sant'Elena used to be occupied by an explosives factory; it was abandoned in 1968, and may become a public park.—The island of *Lazzaretto Nuovo*, just to the N of Sant'Erasmo, became a quarantine hospital for plague victims in 1468. In the 19C and early 20C it was occupied by the armed forces, and it was finally abandoned in 1975.

# 20  The Mainland: the Brenta Canal

The best way of seeing the Brenta Canal is from the 'Burchiello' motor-launch, see p 60.—Malcontenta can be reached easily by Bus from Piazzale Roma.—For other buses, see p 60.—The shortest route to Padua is by the motorway (20km).

Venice is connected to the mainland by a road bridge (over 3.5km long), Ponte della Libertà, built in 1931–32, and a (parallel) railway bridge which dates from 1841–45. They cross the lagoon with views to the right of the end of Venice with the tall campanile of the church of the Madonna dell'Orto, and the islands of San Michele and Murano. In the distance (on clear days) can be seen the cathedral and campanile of Torcello and the airport of Venice at Tessera. On the left the industrial port of Marghera is conspicuous.

8km. Motorway junction and fly-over for **MESTRE** (184,000 inhab.), a dull modern town. Of Roman origin, it became part of the Venetian Republic in 1337. Since 1926 it has been incorporated in the municipality of Venice which it has outgrown. Many Venetians now live in Mestre. The two cities voted in 1979 to remain united as one municipality. The station of Venezia-Mestre is an important rail junction.—From the fly-over a road (SS. 11) continues left to **Marghera**, the commercial port of Venice. It was built in 1919–28 and has an oil depot.—12.5km. Turning for **Malcontenta**, with the famous *Villa Fóscari (adm 1 May–30 Oct, Tues, Sat, and 1st Sun of month, 9–12). One of the most beautiful and typical of the Venetian villas it was built in 1555–60 by Palladio (and has recently been well restored). Its temple-like plan was extremely influential in European architecture. The interior contains damaged frescoes by Battista Franco and G.B. Zelotti. Here is the last stretch of the Brenta canal which reaches the lagoon at *Fusina* (4km), connected to Venice in summer by a vaporetto service (from the car park; comp. p 59).

The road (SS. 11) now follows the **BRENTA CANAL**, lined by numerous beautiful villas built by the Venetian aristocracy, and typified in English literature by Portia's villa of Belmont. In these country houses, often surrounded by orchards, the Venetians would spend the early summer. Many of them have now fallen into disrepair, and only a few are open to the public.

16km. **Oriago**. Just beyond the town is the *Villa Costanzo (Widmann-Foscari)* dating from 1719, but transformed in the 18C in the French Baroque style (adm daily exc. Mon 9–12, 15–18). It contains frescoes attrib. to Jac. Guarana.—The long village of (20km) **Mira** is one of the most attractive places on the Brenta. Here the post office occupies the *Palazzo Foscarini*, where Byron between 1817 and 1819, wrote the fourth canto of 'Childe Harold' and was visited by Thomas Moore. Here, too, he first met Margherita Cogni, whom he called 'la bella Fornarina'. Beyond *Dolo* is (30km) **Strà**, famous for the **Villa Nazionale** (or *Pisani*), the largest of the 18C Venetian villas (adm 9–13.30 exc. Mon; the park is open 9–dusk).

The interior contains a remarkable *Fresco of the Apotheosis of the Pisani family (1761–2) in the Ballroom by G.B. Tiepolo. Other rooms are decorated in the Empire style by Carlo Bevilacqua and others. The villa was built by Girolamo Frigimelica and Francesco Preti in 1736–56. It was brought from Francesco and Alvise Pisani by Napoleon, who presented it to Eugène Beauharnais. It was the scene of the first meeting of Hitler and Mussolini in 1934.—The fine park is open.

Beyond Stra the road crosses the Brenta river and leaves the canal. Just before (36km) Ponte di Brenta is *Noventa Padovana*, with the Villa Valmarana (now a deaf and dumb institution) and other villas.—The road passes under the motorway and soon joins the Padua ringroad.—42km. **Padua**, a town of great interest (see 'Blue Guide Northern Italy').

Other places (all described in 'Blue Guide Northern Italy') on the mainland within easy reach of Venice include (25km) *Treviso*, reached by the Terraglio road lined with more Venetian villas; (13km) *Altino*, a Roman town near the lagoon (excavations in progress, and archaeological museum); and (57km) *Vicenza*, famous for its Palladian buildings.

# INDEX OF THE PRINCIPAL ITALIAN ARTISTS

whose works are referred to in the text, with their birthplaces or the schools to which they belonged. — Abbreviations: A. = architect, engr. = engraver, G. = goldsmith, illum. = illuminator, min. = miniaturist, mos. = mosaicist, P. = painter, S. = sculptor, stuc. = stuccoist, W = woodworker.

ABBREVIATIONS OF CHRISTIAN NAMES

| | | | |
|---|---|---|---|
| Agost. | = Agostino | Gaud. | = Gaudenzio |
| Aless. | = Alessandro | Giac. | = Giacomo |
| Alf. | = Alfonso | Giov. | = Giovanni |
| Ambr. | = Ambrogio | Girol. | = Girolamo |
| And. | = Andrea | Giul. | = Giuliano |
| Ang. | = Angelo | Gius. | = Giuseppe |
| Ann. | = Annibale | Greg. | = Gregorio |
| Ant. | = Antonio | Gugl. | = Guglielmo |
| Baldas. | = Baldassare | Iac. | = Iacopo |
| Bart. | = Bartolomeo | Inn. | = Innocenzo |
| Batt. | = Battista | Ipp. | = Ippolito |
| Bened. | = Benedetto | Laz. | = Lazzaro |
| Benv. | = Benvenuto | Leon. | = Leonardo |
| Bern. | = Bernardino | Lod. | = Lodovico |
| Cam. | = Camillo | Lor. | = Lorenzo |
| Ces. | = Cesare | Mart. | = Martino |
| Crist. | = Cristoforo | Matt. | = Matteo |
| Dan. | = Daniele | Mich. | = Michele |
| Dav. | = Davide | Nic. | = Nicola |
| Def. | = Defendente | Pell. | = Pellegrino |
| Des. | = Desiderio | Raff. | = Raffaele |
| Dom. | = Domenico | Rid. | = Ridolfo |
| Elis. | = Elisabetta | Seb. | = Sebastiano |
| Fed. | = Federigo | Sim. | = Simone |
| Fel. | = Felice | Stef. | = Stefano |
| Ferd. | = Ferdinando | Tim. | = Timoteo |
| Fil. | = Filippo | Tom. | = Tomaso |
| Fr. | = Francesco | Vinc. | = Vincenzo |
| G. B. | = Giambattista | Vitt. | = Vittorio |
| Gasp. | = Gaspare | | |

ABBREVIATIONS OF THE NAMES OF TOWNS AND PROVINCES

| | | | |
|---|---|---|---|
| Anc. | = Ancona | Orv. | = Orvieto |
| Are. | = Arezzo | Pad. | = Padua |
| Ass. | = Assisi | Parm. | = Parma |
| Berg. | = Bergamo | Pav. | = Pavia |
| Bol. | = Bologna | Per. | = Perugia |
| Bres. | = Brescia | Piac. | = Piacenza |
| Crem. | = Cremona | Pied. | = Piedmont |
| Emil. | = Emilia | Pist. | = Pistoia |
| Faen. | = Faenza | Rav. | = Ravenna |
| Ferr. | = Ferrara | Rom. | = Romagna |
| Fies. | = Fiesole | Sett. | = Settignano |
| Flor. | = Florence | Trev. | = Treviso |
| Gen. | = Genoa | Tur. | = Turin |
| Lig. | = Liguria | Tusc. | = Tuscany |
| Lomb. | = Lombardy | Umbr. | = Umbria |
| Mant. | = Mantua | Urb. | = Urbino |
| Mil. | = Milan | Ven. | = Venice |
| Mod. | = Modena | Ver. | = Verona |
| Nap. | = Naples | Vic. | = Vicenza |

Abbondi, *see* Scarpagnino

Agostino (Giovanni) da Lodi (pseudo Boccaccino; c 1500), P at Ven.—139, 189

Albaregno, Jac. (d c 1379), P at Ven.—134

Alberghetti, Alfonso (16C), S, Ferr.—93

Alberti, Camillo (fl. 1520), A at Ven—83

Alemagna, *see* Giovanni d'

Aliense (Ant. Vassilacchi; c 1556–1629), P, Ven. sch., born on the island of Milos—28, 80, 81, 88, 96, 98, 122, 147, 182

Amigoni, Jacopo (1675–1752), P & engr., Naples—143, 153

Andrea del Castagno (1423–57), P, Flor.—19, 84, 113

Andrea da Murano (fl. 1462–1502), P, Murano—139

Angeli, Gius. (c 1710–98), P, Ven.—117, 129, 153, 162, 163, 164

Antelami, Benedetto (12C), S, Parma—74, 82, 83

Antico, L' (Pier Iac. Alari Bonacolsi; 1460–1528), S & Medallist, Mant.—167

Antonello da Messina (c 1430–79), P, Messina—20, 88, 99

Antonello de Saliba (c 1466–1535), P, Messina—139

Antonio da Negroponte (15C), P, Negroponte (Greece)—20, 114

Aspetti, Tiziano (c 1559–1606), S, Pad.—94, 100, 109, 114, 115

Baccio da Montelupo (1469–1535), A & S, Flor. sch.—159

Bachiacca, Il (Ant. Ubertini; 1490–1557), P, Flor.—147

Baldi, Lazzaro (17C), S at Ven.—173

Balestra, Ant. (1666–1740), P, Ver.—32, 112, 153

Ballini, Cam. (16–17C), P at Ven.—107

Bambini, Nicolò (1651–1736), P, Ven.—29, 131, 140, 153

Bandini, Giov. (dell'Opera; 1540–99), S, Flor.—93, 97–8

Barbari, *see* De' Barbari

Barthel, Melchiorre (1625–72), S, Dresden—27, 160

Bartolomeo di Fr. da Bergamo (fl. 1520–35), S, Berg.—21, 123

Basaiti, Marco (fl. 1496–1530), P, Friuli—23, 89, 136, 139, 146, 160

Bassano (Fr. Giambattista da Ponte, the Younger; 1549–92), P, Bassano—24, 96, 98, 138, 155, 185

Bassano (Jac. da Ponte or dal Ponte; c 1510–92), P, Bassano—24, 94, 182

Bassano (Leandro da Ponte; 1557–1622), P, Bassano—24, 81, 96, 98, 99, 121, 124, 138, 152, 200

Bastiani, Lazzaro (?1425–1512), P, Ven.—88, 89, 114, 121, 138, 139, 185, 191

Beccafumi, Dom. (1485–1551), P, Siena—147

Beccaruzzi, Fr. (c 1492–1561), P, Conegliano—140

Bella, Gabriel (1730–99), P at Ven.—32, 118

Bellano, Bart. (1434–96), S & A, Pad.—100, 174

Bellini, Gentile (son of Jac.; c 1429–1507), P, Ven.—20, 88, 118, 138, 139, 146, 167

Bellini, Giov. (son of Jac.; c 1435–1516), P, Ven.—20, 88, 99, 112, 114, 118, 122, 124, 128, 136, 137, 138, 159, 165, 167, 176, 189, 200, 201

Bellini, Jacopo (c 1400–70/71), P, Ven.—20, 84, 88, 136

Bello, Fr. (late 16C), W, Ven.—94

Bellotti, Pietro (1627–1700), P, Brescia—98

Bellucci, Ant. (1654–1727), P, Soligo (Treviso)—29, 180

Benato, Iac. di Marco (14C), G at Ven.—83

Benoni, Gius. (1618–84), A, Trieste & Ven.—111, 148

Benvenuti, Augusto (1838–99), S, Ven.—180

Bergamasco, Gian Giacomo (dei Grigi; son of Gugl.; d 1572), S, Bergamo—21, 103

Bergamasco, Gugl. (dei Grigi; fl. 1515–30), A & S, Bergamo—21, 86, 88, 109, 126, 187

Bernini, Gian Lorenzo (1598–1680), A, P & S, Naples—147, 170, 186

Bernini, Pietro (father of Gian Lor.; 1562–1629), S, Flor.—186

Bertoldo, Giovanni di (1410–91), S, Flor.—167

Bertuccio (14C), G, Ven.—14, 74

Bevilacqua, Carlo (1775–1849), P, Ven.—33, 88, 200, 203

Biagio da Faenza (fl. 1503–26), W, Ven.—94, 126

Bianchini, Vincenzo (fl. 1517–63), Mosaicist at Ven.—81

Bissolo, Fr. (fl. 1492–d 1554), P, Trev.—23, 117, 122, 153

Boccaccino (pseudo), *see* Agostino da Lodi

Boccaccino, Boccaccio (c 1467–1524), P, Crem.?—89, 127, 139

Boldrini, Leonardo (fl. 1452–98), P, Ven.—88

# INDEX

Topographical entries are in **bold** type, names of eminent people in *italics*, other entries in Roman type.

Typeset by MCL Dataset Ltd, Ruislip, England, using a Prefis Book Machine.
Printed in Great Britain by Richard Clay (The Chaucer Press) Ltd,
Bungay, Suffolk

# ATLAS

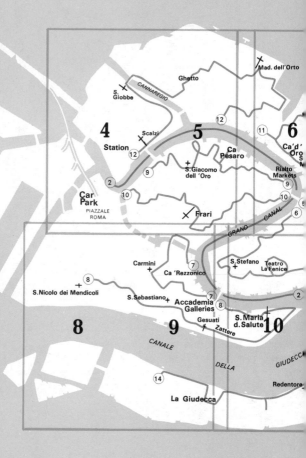

## key map

(10)━━(10) main routes in text

scale

| 0 | | 500 metres |
| 0 | | 500 yards |

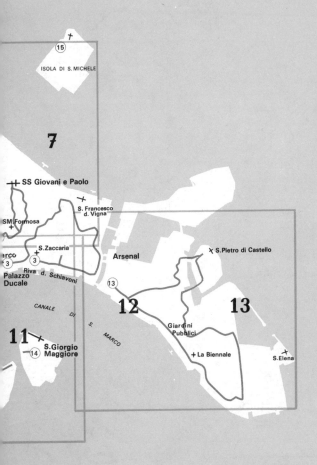

(15)

ISOLA DI S. MICHELE

**7**

✠ SS Giovani e Paolo

✠ S. Francesco
d. Vigna

SM.Formosa

S.Zaccaria

arco

(3)

(3)

Riva d. Schiavoni

Palazzo
Ducale

Arsenal

✗ S.Pietro di Castello

(13)

**12**

**13**

CANALE  DI

S.

MARCO

Giardini
Pubblici

**11** ✠ S.Giorgio
Maggiore

(14)

✠ La Biennale

✠ S.Elena

# Key Map to Atlas Pages

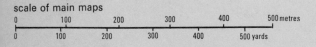

scale of main maps

| 0 | 100 | 200 | 300 | 400 | 500 metres |

| 0 | 100 | 200 | 300 | 400 | 500 yards |

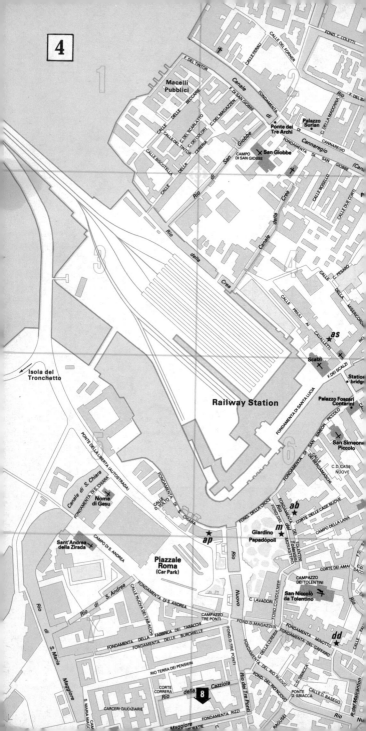

**4**

Macelli Pubblici

F. DEL TINTOR

CALLE DEL FORNER

FOND. C. COLETTI

Canale

CALLE FERMI

CALLE DELLE BECCARIE

C. DI SAN GIOBBE

FONDAMENTA

Rio DEL BA

RIO DELLA MADONNA

Palazzo Surian

CALLE DEL SCALZATO

C. DEL MAGAZEN

C. DEI COLORI

CALLE DEL TINTOR

CEREBIA

C. DER MAGAZEN

di

San

Giobbe

Ponte dei Tre Archi

CANNAREGIO

FONDAMENTA

DI

SAN

GIOBBE

CALLE BISCOTELLA

CALLE

DELLA

CAMPO DI SAN GIOBBE

✕ San Giobbe

Cannaregio

(Canal

Rio

di

Rio

della

Crea

Canale

della

Crea

CALLE BOSELLO

CALLE DUE CORTI

CALLE C. PESARO

CALLE DELLA MISERICORDIA

CALLE PRIULI AI CAVALLETTI

**as**

Scalzi

F. DEI SCALZI

Station bridge

Palazzo Foscari Contarini

**Railway Station**

FONDAMENTA DI SANTA LUCIA

CALLE

Isola del Tronchetto →

FONDAMENTA DI S. SIMEON PICCOLO

✕ San Simeone Piccolo

C. D. CASE NUOVE

PONTE DELLA LIBERTA (AUTOSTRADA)

Canale di S. Chiara

FONDAMENTA DI S. CHIARA

Nome di Gesù

CALLE O. D. POLO

FONDAMENTA DI S. CHIARA

FOND. DELLA CROCE

RIO PARA

FOND. DEI TOLENTINI

CORTE DELLE CASE NUOVE

CAMPO DELLA LANA

**ab**

Giardino Papadópoli

**m**

CALLE DEI TOLENTINI

FONDAMENTA TOLENTINO

CAMPAZZO DEI TOLENTINI

**ap**

Sant'Andrea della Zirada ✕

CAMPO DI S. ANDREA

**Piazzale Roma**
(Car Park)

Rio Nuovo

C. LAVADORI

FOND. CONDULMER

San Niccolò da Tolentino

CORTE DEI AMAI

C. D. SACCO

**dd**

FONDAMENTA MINOTTO

CALLE NUOVA DEI TABACCHI

FONDAMENTA DI S. ANDREA

Rio di S. Andrea

Rio di S. Maria Maggiore

FONDAMENTA DELLA FABBRICA DEI TABACCHI

FONDAMENTA DELLE BURCHIELLE

CAMPAZZO TRE PONTI

FOND. D. TRE PONTI

FOND. D. MAGAZZEN

FOND. CA. DELLA CEREBIA

FONDAMENTA DEL GAFFARO

FOND. A DEL RIO NUOVO

PONTE CALLE D. BASEGO

CALLE D. BASEGO

S. Maria Maggiore

RIO TERRA DEI PENSIERI

CORTE CORRERA

Rio della Cazziola

**8**

FONDAMENTA RIZZI

FOND. DEL RIO NUOVO

RIO del RIO NUOVO

C. SBIACCA

RAGUSEI

FOND. CA. MADALANA

CARCERI GIUDIZIARIE

S. MARIA MAGG

Maggiore

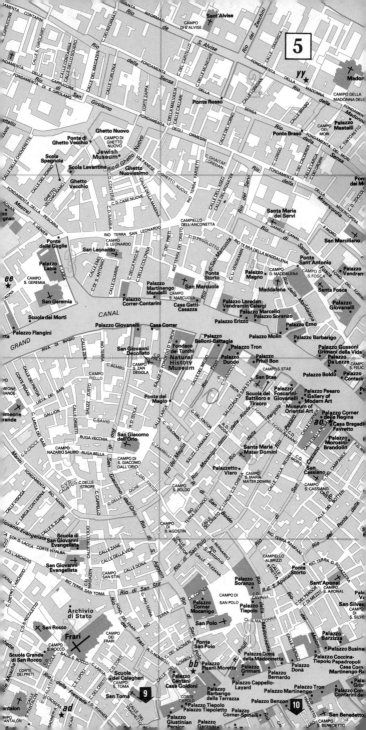

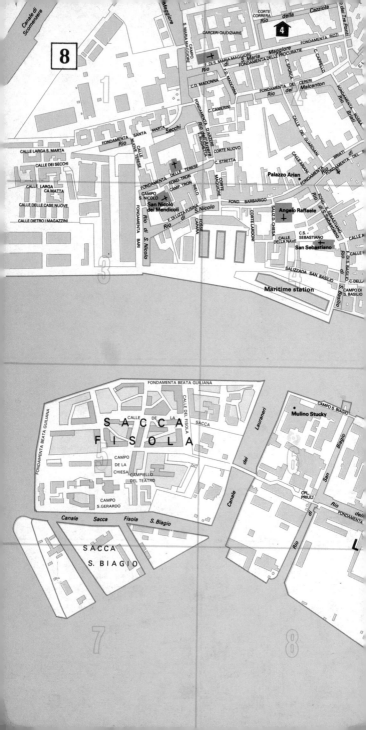

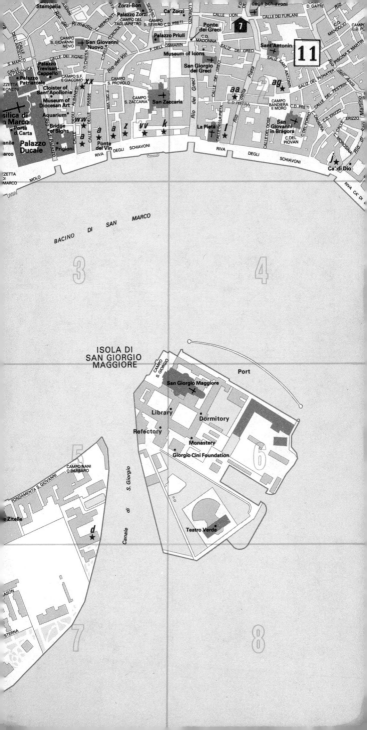

**12**

ARSENAL

CAMPO
D. GATTE

CAMPO
DD. POZZI

CALLE MAGNO

CAMPO
DELLE GORNE

Arsenal
Gateway

CAMPO S. MARTINO
San Martino

CAMPO
DELL'
ARSENALE

FOND. DELLA MADONNA

Rio di San

Rio di San Daniele

Ca' di Dio

Forni
Pubblici

RIVA CA' DI DIO

Corderia

CAMPO DELLA TANA

Rio della Tana

Museo
Navale

CAMPO
S. BIAGIO

FONDAMENTA

RIO DELLA TANA

FBD. TANA

San Biagio

CALLE NUOVA

CALLE DEI PRETI

CORTE
COLTRERA

San Francesco
di Paola

VIA GARIBALDI

RIVA DEI

CALLE COPPO

CALLE VECCHIA

CALLE SCHIAVONA

CALLE VECCHIA

CORTE
COLONNE

VIA GARIBALDI

CALLE DI SAN DOMENICO

Giardini
Garibaldi

VIALE GARIBALDI

CALLE SARESINA

CORTE SARESINA

C. SECCO MARINA

CALLE DELLE ANCORE

CAMPO NICOLI

FD. FORNER

SETTE MARTIRI

Rio

Giardi
Pubbli

VIALE

5

6

7

8

**13**

ISOLA DI SAN PIETRO

CAMPO DI SAN PIETRO

San Pietro di Castello

C. LARGA PIETRO

CANALE DI SAN PIETRO

FOND. QUINTAVALLE

C. LUNGA QUINTAVALLE

LAMON

C.S. ANNA

CAMPIELLO DEI POMERI

E. CASTEL OLIVOLLO

Rio di S. Elena

Sant'Anna

MARINA

CO. CRISTO

C.LA. DI GIUSEPPE

Giuseppe

San Giuseppe di Castello

RIO TERRA DI SAN GIUSEPPE

PALLIDO DI SANT'ANTONIO

Port

VIALE 24 MAGGIO

ISOLA DI SANT'ELENA

Giardini

CALLE DEL MONTELLO

CALLE DEL CENGIO

C.D. CONGREGAZIONE

CALLE DEL PASUBIO

CAMPO DEL GRAPPA

CALLE OSLAVIA

La Biennale
International Exhibition
of Modern Art

Rio dei Giardini

Sports Stadium

VIALE PIAVE

Canale di S. Elena

CALLE DEL CARSO

CALLE DEL SABOTINO

CALLE GEN. CHINOTTO

CAMPO DELL'INDIP.

CALLE POLVERIO

ZUGNA

Sant'Elena

CALLE D.CO D'AOSTA

CALLE

CALLE DEL

CARNARO

VIALE QUATTRO

NOVEMBRE

CALLE BUCCARI

VIALE VITTORIO VENETO

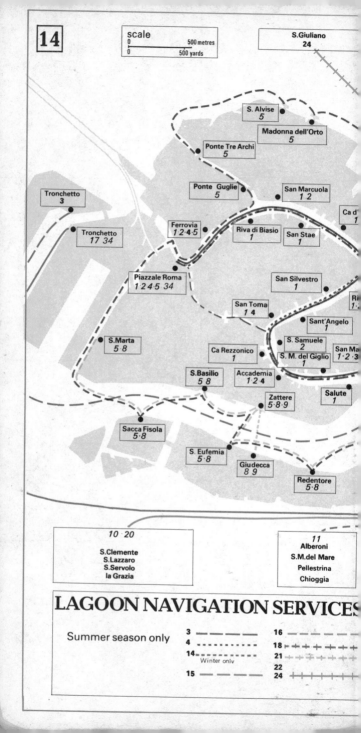

**14**

scale
0 — 500 metres
0 — 500 yards

S.Giuliano
24

S. Alvise
5

Madonna dell'Orto
5

Ponte Tre Archi
5

Ponte Guglie
5

San Marcuola
1 2

Ca d'
1

Tronchetto
3

Tronchetto
17 34

Ferrovia
1 2·4·5

Riva di Biasio
1

San Stae
1

Piazzale Roma
1 2 4 5 34

San Silvestro
1

Ri
1·

San Toma
1 4

Sant'Angelo

S.Marta
5·8

Ca Rezzonico
1

S. Samuele
2

San Ma
1·2·3

S. M. del Giglio
1

S.Basilio
5·8

Accademia
1·2 4

Zattere
5·8·9

Salute
1

Sacca Fisola
5·8

S. Eufemia
5·8

Giudecca
8 9

Redentore
5·8

10 · 20

S.Clemente
S.Lazzaro
S.Servolo
la Grazia

11
Alberoni
S.M.del Mare
Pellestrina
Chioggia

# LAGOON NAVIGATION SERVICES

Summer season only

3 ——
4 ········
14 —·—·—
Winter only
15 ——

16 ——
18 ·+·+·+
21 ·+·+·+
22
24 ++++++

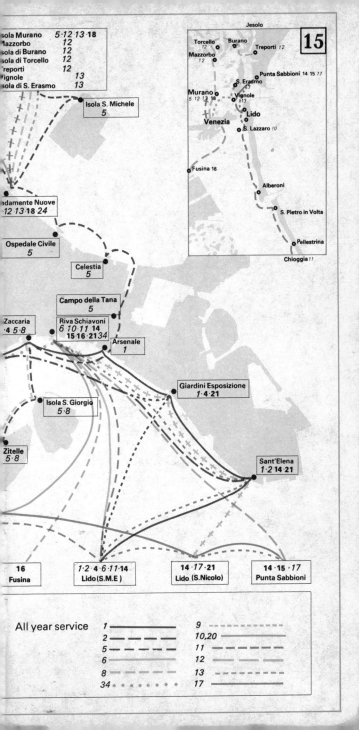

**15**

Isola Murano 5·12·13·18
Mazzorbo 12
Isola di Burano 12
Isola di Torcello 12
Treporti 12
Vignole 13
Isola di S. Erasmo 13

Jesolo

Torcello 12
Burano
Mazzorbo 12
Treporti 12
Punta Sabbioni 14 15 17
S. Erasmo
Murano 5·12·13 18
Vignole 13
Lido
Venezia
S. Lazzaro 10
Fusina 16
Alberoni
S. Pietro in Volta
Pellestrina
Chioggia 11

Isola S. Michele 5

Fondamente Nuove 12·13·18·24

Ospedale Civile 5

Celestia 5

Campo della Tana 5

Zaccaria 4·5·8

Riva Schiavoni 6·10·11·14 15·16·21·34

Arsenale 1

Giardini Esposizione 1·4·21

Isola S. Giorgio 5·8

Zitelle 5·8

Sant'Elena 1·2·14·21

16 Fusina

1·2·4·6·11·14 Lido (S.M.E)

14·17·21 Lido (S.Nicolo)

14·15·17 Punta Sabbioni

**All year service**

| | | |
|---|---|---|
| 1 | — | 9 |
| 2 | – – – | 10,20 |
| 5 | – – – | 11 |
| 6 | | 12 |
| 8 | | 13 |
| 34 | • • • • • | 17 |

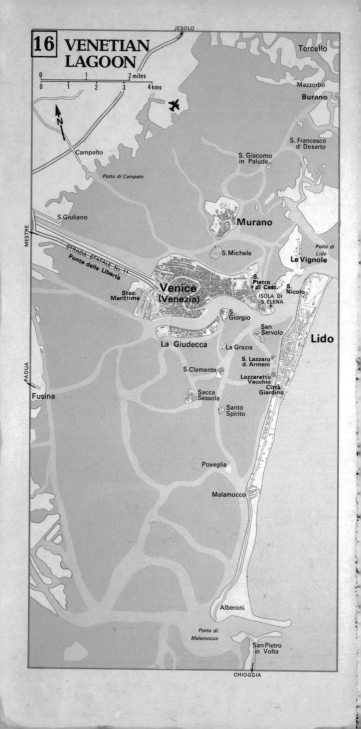